Writing Clearly
An Editing Guide

SECOND EDITION

JANET LANE AND ELLEN LANGE
University of California, Davis

Heinle & Heinle Publishers

Boston • Albany • Bonn • Cincinnati • Detroit • London
Madrid • Melbourne • Mexico City • New York • Pacific Grove • Paris
San Francisco • Tokyo • Toronto • Washington

The Publication of *Writing Clearly: An Editing Guide,* Second Edition, was directed by the members of the Newbury House Publishing Team at Heinle & Heinle:

Erik Gundersen, *Editorial Director*

Charlotte Sturdy, *Market Development Director*

Maryellen E. Killeen, *Production Services Coordinator*

Stanley J. Galek, *Vice President and Publisher*

Also participating in the publication of this program were:

Evelyn Nelson, *Director of Global ELT Training and Development*

Amy Mabley, *International Marketing Manager*

Tom Dare, *Market Development Director*

Amy Lawler, *Managing Developmental Director*

Jonathan Stark, *Image Resource Director*

Elise Kaiser, *Director, Production and Manufacturing*

Marianne Bartow, *Associate Market Development Director*

Jill Kinkade, *Assistant Editor*

Rachel Youngman, Hockett Editorial Service, *Project Manager*

Mary Beth Hennebury, *Senior Manufacturing Coordinator*

Carol H. Rose, *Interior Text Designer*

Jeff Cosloy, *Cover Artist and Designer*

Accu-color, *Composition*

CNN is a registered trademark of Cable News Network

Library of Congress Cataloging-in-Publication Data

Lane, Janet.
    Writing clearly: an editing guide / Janet Lane and Ellen Lange. -
- 2nd ed.
        p.   cm.
    ISBN 0-8384-0949-0
    1. English language—Textbooks for foreign speakers.   2. English
language—Rhetoric—Problems, exercises, etc.   3. Report writing—
Problems, exercises, etc.   4. Editing—Problems, exercises, etc.
I. Lange, Ellen.   II. Title.
PE1128.L3375   1999
808'.042—dc21   98-46403
                                                                    CIP

Manufactured in the United States of America.

10   9   8   7   6   5

ISBN 0-8384-09490

To our students,
whose desire to write clearly
was our inspiration for this book
and
To Emil,
whose unfailing support
made this book possible

Contents

SECTION **1**

Global Errors 1

SECTION 2

Local Errors 181

SECTION 3

Beyond Grammar: Other Ways to Make Writing Clear 265

APPENDIX A

APPENDIX B

Acknowledgments

We are indebted to our students at the University of California, Davis, whose interest in achieving language control in their writing prompted us to write this textbook.

During the process of writing this textbook, we have been fortunate to have had the encouragement and guidance of the staff of Heinle & Heinle, including Erik Gundersen, editor, and Jill E. Kinkade, associate editor, whose unfailing support helped us visualize and execute a second edition. We are also indebted to Maryellen Eschmann-Killeen, production editor, for skillfully overseeing the project. Our deepest appreciation goes to our project manager, Rachel Youngman of Hockett Editorial Service, whose excellent suggestions strengthened the text and whose enthusiasm for exactness motivated us as writers. For her help with the initial drafting of the videotape lessons, we would like to thank Sharon Peters. We are also indebted to those students who so generously contributed their sentences, paragraphs, and essays as examples for this textbook and to our colleagues whose positive feedback and helpful suggestions have contributed to making this second edition a richer text.

A Special Thanks

The authors and publisher would like to thank the following individuals who reviewed *Writing Clearly: An Editing Guide*, Second Edition, at various stages during the revision of the text and who offered helpful feedback and suggestions:

- Dorrie Brass—University of Maryland, Baltimore City
- Glenda Bro—Mt. San Antonio College, CA
- Kara Dworak—San Jose State University, CA
- Cynthia Fenimore—Delaware County Community College, PA
- Jan Frodesen—University of California, Santa Barbara
- Susan E. Hoehing—University of Toledo, OH
- Vicki L. Holmes—University of Nevada, Las Vegas
- Nancy Mayer Schwarz—Washington University, St. Louis, MO
- John O'Neill—San Jose State University, CA
- Diana Pascoe-Chavez—Webster University, St. Louis, MO
- Sharon Person—St. Louis Community College, MO
- Meredith Pike-Baky—University of California, Berkeley
- Linda Robinson Fellag—Community College of Philadelphia, PA

Preface to the Teacher

Writing Clearly: An Editing Guide, Second Edition, is an ESL composition text-book designed to help high-intermediate and advanced ESL students become aware of common ESL language problems in their writing. It offers ESL writers effective strategies for reducing their errors and prepares them to become self-editors of their own writing. Students are systematically guided through fifteen common ESL errors. First, students learn to recognize the errors; then they learn to correct these errors in controlled exercises and, finally, in their own writing by planning, writing, and revising a response to one or more writing topics.

The Scope of the Text

The focus of *Writing Clearly: An Editing Guide,* Second Edition, is error analysis rather than a comprehensive study of grammar. Through using this textbook, students will learn not only to analyze their specific sentence-level weaknesses but also to develop strategies for improving their sentence-level control when they write. The ultimate goal is for ESL writers to be able to rely on themselves when they write in English, rather than on the instructor, a tutor, a peer, or a native speaker.

Each unit in the text includes grammar guidelines and self-help strategies for students to study. In addition, students are encouraged to consult supplementary references such as an advanced ESL grammar text or an ESL dictionary if they wish to do a more comprehensive study of a particular grammatical point. Students are also encouraged throughout the book to read as much as possible as a means of increasing their knowledge of English structure and vocabulary and to look for and correct errors in writing assignments in other courses they are taking.

Finally, to help students go beyond error analysis, Section 3 of the text, "Beyond Grammar: Other Ways to Make Writing Clear," encourages ESL students to work on other important aspects of their writing.

New Features in the Second Edition

New Features in Each Unit

➤ **Goals at the Beginning of Each Unit** give students four clearly defined objectives to work towards while going through the unit.

➤ **Test Your Understanding of the Error** utilizes two short-answer questions to test students' grasp of essential information necessary to understand the error.

➤ **A Grammar Journal Entry** asks students to respond in journal form to two thought-provoking questions related to the error treated in the unit.

➤ A **Pretest** gives students the opportunity to discover what they already know about the error. It allows students to decide what aspects of the error they need to work on and helps teachers decide which parts of the unit to emphasize based on the students' self-assessment.

➤ **Self-Help Strategies** offer brief, user-friendly pointers to help students continue working on the error by themselves.

➤ **Improve Your Writing Style** moves students beyond grammatical correctness and empowers them to make stylistic choices about the grammatical point they have just studied.

➤ A **Photo Writing Topic** visually stimulates students by connecting a writing topic to a human-interest photograph.

➤ A **CNN Video Activity and Writing Topic** generates meaningful discussion about a timely, high-interest CNN feature story and leads to a writing activity.

New Units, Sections, and Appendices

➤ **Two New Units** give students in-depth work on relative, adverbial, and noun clauses (Unit 6) and prepositions (Unit 15).

➤ A new section, **Beyond Grammar: Other Ways to Make Writing Clear,** treats nonidiomatic and unclear writing, vocabulary expansion, academic style, flow of ideas, and revision strategies.

➤ **Additional Exercises for Practice: Editing for a Variety of Errors** integrates several grammatical errors into short essay exercises, providing extensive, realistic editing practice.

➤ **A Glossary of Grammatical Terminology** gives concise definitions and examples for grammatical terms used in the book.

Options for Using the Text

Writing Clearly: An Editing Guide, Second Edition, can be used in different teaching situations. It can be used **as the sole text for a course** on improving language control in the context of writing.

Alternatively, the text can be used **as a component of a writing course** in which students are doing writing assignments other than those in this textbook. In this case, it can be used effectively as a companion to a separate composition book/reader.

Finally, the text works effectively **as supplementary material** for ESL writers enrolled in a composition course geared toward native speakers of English, such as a college writing course for undergraduates, a technical writing course for engineers, or a writing course for science majors. In this situation, the instructor can use the symbols in the text when marking an ESL student's paper. The instructor can have the student purchase the text and can then meet with the student to set priorities for working on errors. The student can then work independently using the explanations and exercises in the units.

Options for Ordering the Fifteen Units

The fifteen units in this book have been designed for use in either consecutive or nonconsecutive order. **Instructors who plan to use the entire book** may choose to go straight through the units in the order they appear, beginning with the first nine units, which cover more serious (global) errors, and proceeding to the final six units, which cover less serious (local) errors. Alternatively, an instructor may choose the units according to the needs of the class. In this case, the instructor should still focus on global errors first, since these are the errors that most affect meaning. However, this does not mean that an instructor should not teach a local error, such as subject-verb agreement or singular and plural of nouns, early in the course if the students particularly need work on it.

Instructors who plan to use the book selectively can make their choice of units to be taught based on the needs of the class. Again, it is recommended that global errors be covered first.

Instructors who have students working independently with the book can have a student writer work straight through the book or do selected units based on the student's needs. Note that the five parts of Section 3, "Beyond Grammar," can be incorporated into the course as the instructor wishes or can be assigned for students to read on their own.

Time Required to Cover the Fifteen Units and Section Three

The fifteen units in this book can be covered in fifteen weeks with five hours per week of class time. Alternatively, the book can be covered in less time if some material is either omitted or assigned for students to do outside of class. To determine which parts of each unit students need most, instructors can use the unit pretest. Another effective way to reduce the class time spent on each unit is to focus on doing the exercises in Part III of a unit during class and to spend less class time on the grammatical explanations in Part II.

Each unit can be covered in approximately four to six class hours. Generally speaking, units that treat one major grammatical point, such as conditional or subject-verb agreement, can be covered more quickly than units that include several grammatical points grouped into one major category, such as dependent clauses or verb forms. Because they are shorter, the five parts of Section 3, "Beyond Grammar," can be covered more quickly than each of the fifteen units; alternatively, they can be assigned for students to read on their own outside of class. The exercises in Appendix B, "Editing for a Variety of Errors," can be used in class, assigned as homework, or given as quizzes.

The Grading Symbols in the Text

The ESL grading symbols cover fifteen common ESL errors, which are divided into two parts: global errors and local errors. Each error corresponds to one of the fifteen units in *Writing Clearly: An Editing Guide,* Second Edition. Also included are symbols for twelve additional errors, which are commonly made by native speakers of English; some ESL writers, particularly those who have spent a number of years in an English-speaking country, also will have problems with these errors. Although these additional errors are not covered in individual units of their own, several of them—coherence, comma splices, fragments, run-ons, unclear language, and nonidiomatic usage—are addressed within this textbook.

The Global/Local Error Distinction

Some grammatical errors are much more serious than others and can seriously affect the reader's ability to understand a piece of writing. You will want to have students work on these serious errors first.

The list of ESL grading symbols in this book is divided into two parts to distinguish more serious from less serious errors. The nine errors listed in the top box of the list, called **global errors,** are usually the most serious because they generally affect more than just a small part of a sentence and impede the reader's understanding of the writer's ideas. In contrast, the six errors in the middle box, called **local errors,** are less serious because they usually affect a smaller part of a sentence and, while they are distracting, generally do not affect the reader's understanding.*

It is important to keep in mind that, in some cases, the global/local distinction may not always be clear. That is, an error that is usually local, such as word choice, could become global if it affects a large portion of a text. Some types of global errors, such as omitting the *-ed* ending of a past participle, might be considered less serious than other verb-form errors by some instructors. Although this global/local error distinction is designed to help you make decisions about how serious an error is, you will sometimes need, or want, to decide yourself how serious a certain error is in a given piece of writing.

---

*The terms *global* and *local* come from M.K. Burt and C. Kiparsky's *The Gooficon: A Repair Manual for English.* Rowley, Mass., Newbury House, 1972.

Options for Using the Grading Symbols

In responding to students' writing, the instructor may choose to mark on students' papers several types of errors starting at the beginning of the course, keeping in mind the importance of choosing the most serious errors to mark and of giving high priority to those errors that occur frequently. In contrast, some instructors may choose to mark only the error covered in the unit being studied when responding to students' writing or to mark errors covered in previous units in addition to the error currently being covered in class.

The Error Awareness Sheet

In addition to the grading symbols, you may want to use the Error Awareness Sheet (p. xx) to help your students see in chart form what their errors are and to help them decide which errors to work on first.* You can mark this sheet yourself or have the students record their errors after you have returned a paper to them. At the top of the Error Awareness Sheet are complete instructions on how to use it.

The Writing Topics in Each Unit

Part IV of each unit contains two traditional writing topics as well as one topic based on a photograph. Part V, the CNN video activity in each unit, offers another topic based on a short, high-interest CNN feature story. No length is suggested for the writing topics so that the instructor may elect to have students write a paragraph or several paragraphs in response to a topic. Instructors can make this decision depending on the level of the class, the amount of time allotted to each unit and the function of the text (main text or a supplementary text) in the course.

As much as possible, the writing topics have been chosen to elicit the error covered in the unit. However, instructors will want to encourage students to respond to the topics naturally rather than putting the focus on incorporating the grammar point taught in the unit. Such an approach to the topics will help students see that the primary focus in writing is on content and that the topics are geared to prepare them for future writing tasks in the academic and professional worlds, where writing tasks are not focused on a particular grammar point.

---

*The term *Error Awareness Sheet* was used by J.F. Lalande in "Reducing Composition Errors: An Experiment." *Modern Language Journal*, 66, 140-149.

Other Important Resources for the Instructor

The **Instructors' Manual** that accompanies this text includes additional information on how to use the units in the text. It also includes (1) a complete answer key to all the exercises in the textbook, (2) a complete transcript of the fifteen CNN videotape segments, and (3) ways to effectively and efficiently respond to ESL writing in terms of both content and sentences.

The **teacher resource book** *Writing Clearly: Responding to ESL Compositions* (Bates, Lane, Lange, and Heinle & Heinle, 1993) offers instructors more detailed information than the Instructors' Manual on responding to ESL writing. It provides an overall system for responding to content and sentences in ESL students' writing. With a number of sample graded papers as illustrations, this resource book also includes information on how to assign grades to an ESL paper and suggests ways to help ESL students benefit from the instructor's feedback on content and sentences.

Preface to the Student

For all writers in the academic and professional worlds, native and nonnative speakers alike, both content and language control are important. For ESL writers, however, achieving sentence-level accuracy is doubly challenging because English is not their native language.

As an ESL writer, you will make language errors when you write. While making errors is a natural part of learning a second language, you will need to work on eliminating these errors, particularly in formal writing. When you are doing academic writing or any kind of formal writing, you must keep in mind that the readers' demands and expectations are very high. Readers of formal written English are aware not only of content but also of sentence-level accuracy, and they expect sentences to be correct. Also, when your writing contains ESL errors, you risk either not getting your meaning across to the reader or causing the reader to be distracted from the content of what you have written. Therefore, as an ESL writer, you cannot ignore the need for sentence-level accuracy in your work.

Although getting back a paper covered with marks indicating there are problems can be discouraging, you must keep in mind that your instructor's feedback can be extremely valuable. When you read your instructor's comments on your drafts or final drafts, you can become aware of strengths in your writing as well as problems to focus on while writing your next paper. Receiving feedback on your writing will be easier if you view your instructor positively, remembering that he or she is not merely a judge or a hunter of errors but an interested reader of your work who wants to give you feedback to help you learn to write effectively.

Introduction

Part I: Ways to Use Your Instructor's Feedback Effectively

Understanding Your Instructor's Symbols

In order to improve your sentence-level accuracy, you will first need to know what kinds of errors you are making. One way to find out what your errors are is to look at the symbols your instructor has written on your paper. These symbols are often abbreviations (such as **ss** for sentence structure). In Part III in this introduction, you will find a list of ESL grading symbols and an explanation of each one. If your instructor is not using the symbols in this book or if he or she is using additional symbols, you will need to find out exactly what your instructor's symbols mean.

Deciding Which Errors to Work on First

Once you know what your errors are, you must prioritize them and not try to work on all of them at once. Some errors are much more serious than others because they can interfere with the reader's ability to understand the content of your writing. The ESL grading symbols in Part III of this introduction will help you learn which errors are more serious and which are less serious. The nine errors listed in the top box are the most serious. They are called **global** errors because they usually affect more than just a small part of a sentence as well as impede the reader's understanding of your ideas. The six errors in the middle box of the list are usually less serious. They are called **local** errors because they affect a smaller part of a sentence and, while they are distracting, generally do not interfere with the reader's understanding. The twelve errors in the bottom box are additional errors, many of which are commonly made by native speakers. If you are having problems with these errors, you will also need to work on them.

In some cases, the global/local error distinction may not be clear. That is, an error that is usually local, such as word choice, could become global if it affects a large portion of a text. Some types of global errors (such as leaving off the *-ed* ending of a past participle) might be considered less serious than other errors within the same category (in this case, verb form).

In order to make the most progress in improving your sentence-level accuracy, you will want to prioritize your errors according to their seriousness. If you find that your instructor has marked most of your errors **vt** (verb tense), **vf** (verb form), **art** (article), and **num** (number), you will want to work on the two global errors, *verb tense* and *verb form,* first. You will also need to consider the frequency of your errors. If you are making many global errors, it would be best for you to start working on the ones you are making most often; likewise, if there is a certain local error that you are making quite frequently, you would be wise to work on this error also, especially if you are not making many global errors.

Your instructor may assist you in deciding which errors to work on first by helping you prioritize your errors. For example, your instructor might write at the end of your paper that you need to work on sentence structure and verb-tense errors first. Or your instructor might fill out a checklist for you such as the Error Awareness Sheet in Part III of this introduction. He or she will tally your errors for you in the middle column so that you can see how frequent they are. In the right column, your instructor will indicate which of these errors you should begin working on first. Alternatively, your instructor may have you fill out the Error Awareness Sheet yourself.

Part II: Strategies for Working on Your Errors

Using the Fifteen Units in This Book

Once you know what your errors are, you can use the fifteen units in this book to find out more about each error and how to correct it. Each unit treats one sentence-level error that ESL writers commonly make. In each unit, a short introduction to the error defines the error, explains why it is important to avoid the error, and suggests ways to master it. Following the introduction are problems that ESL writers commonly have with that error along with incorrect sentences to show you the error with its appropriate correction. The pretest in each unit will direct you to those problems that you need to concentrate on. In addition, selected rules of grammar and self-help strategies will help you learn how to master the error. These rules and strategies, however, are not meant to be comprehensive, so you may sometimes choose to increase your knowledge of a particular grammatical point by studying it in depth in an ESL grammar text. In each unit, you will also find exercises to help you test your ability to identify and correct the error and produce grammatically correct sentences of your own. You will also find writing topics in each unit.

In using the units, you should always read all of Parts I and II in order to discover exactly what your individual problems are. For example, if you are making sentence-structure errors, ask yourself whether your problem is omitting the verb *to be* as in *I happy* or doubling the subject as in *My friends and I we like ice cream.* If you use the units in this way to discover just what aspects of the error you need to work on, you will increase your chances of avoiding the error in writing. The selected grammar guidelines and self-help strategies in each unit will also help give you the background you need to avoid making errors.

Setting Realistic Goals

As you work on your errors, remember to set realistic goals for yourself. Do not try to work on all your errors at once. Even if you can eliminate only two or three of your most serious and frequent errors, your writing should improve significantly.

Revising Your Writing by Yourself or with a Tutor

Once you have decided which errors to work on and have read about them in this textbook, a good strategy for improving your sentence control is to revise each sentence containing these errors. Do not write out the incorrect sentence; instead, write out only the new, correct sentence. By writing out the entire sentence and not just part of it, you will more likely remember the correct pattern. If you are working with a tutor, you can share your corrected sentence with the tutor. You can also ask the tutor to check the essays you are working on for errors of the type you frequently make. In working with a tutor, you can also do extra exercises on the errors you are making, using exercises from an ESL grammar text or those provided by the tutor.

Becoming an Independent Self-Editor

Once you are aware of and know how to correct your most serious and frequent sentence-level problems, you must monitor for them when you write. *Monitoring* means consciously trying to avoid making these errors while you are writing or going back and correcting them after writing. In other words, you begin to know which errors you are likely to make in English.

You should decide whether you find it easier to monitor while you are writing or to go back and check for certain errors after you have completed a piece of writing. Of course, the final goal is to write without making these errors. But remember that reaching this goal will take time. Thus, until you are able to avoid making these errors, you need to be aware of and monitor for them during your writing process. It will probably not be possible for you to monitor for all of your errors at once, especially if you are writing under time pressure. You might, for example, choose to monitor only for sentence-structure and verb-tense errors in a piece of writing if you know that these are your most serious errors.

By learning to monitor in this way, you will become an editor of your own writing, and you will find that you have to rely far less on your instructor, a tutor, or a native speaker for help.

Looking Ahead

Applying What You Have Learned about Sentence-Level Errors to Current and Future Writing

As part of the process of becoming an independent self-editor of your own writing, you should try to apply what you have learned in each unit to past and future assignments. Follow the suggestions below:

➤ If you are in a composition class, take one of the papers that has recently been returned to you and check to see whether the instructor has marked any cases of the error you have been studying in a specific unit of this text. If so, try to correct them using the rules and guidelines given in the unit.

➤ Take a paper you have written for any other class and check it yourself for correct use of the grammatical points covered in a specific unit of this text. If you are not sure whether your sentences are correct, ask a classmate, a tutor, or your instructor.

➤ When you do writing assignments for any class in the future, be sure to check for correct use of the grammatical points you have covered in each unit of this text.

Part III: Grading Symbols, Error Awareness Sheet, and Sample Paper

ESL Grading Symbols

GLOBAL ERRORS—more serious errors

(These errors usually impede understanding.)

SYMBOL	EXPLANATION	PAGE*
vt	incorrect verb tense	4
vf	verb incorrectly formed	29
modal	incorrect use or formation of a modal	50
cond	incorrect use or formation of conditional sentence	69
pass	incorrect use or formation of passive voice	88
cl	incorrect use or formation of a dependent clause	104
ss	incorrect sentence structure	131
wo	incorrect or awkward word order	148
conn	incorrect or missing connecting word(s)	165

LOCAL ERRORS—less serious errors

(These errors, while distracting, most often do not impede understanding.)

SYMBOL	EXPLANATION	PAGE*
sv	incorrect subject-verb agreement	184
art	incorrect or missing article	198
s/pl	problem with the singular or plural of a noun	213
wc	incorrect word choice	226
wf	incorrect word form	238
prep	incorrect use of a preposition	253

*Note: The pages listed in the right-hand column refer to pages in *Writing Clearly: An Editing Guide*, Second Edition, where a full explanation of each error is given.

ESL Grading Symbols

OTHER ERRORS

SYMBOL	EXPLANATION
cap	capitalization—capital letter needed
coh	coherence—one idea does not lead to the next
cs	comma splice—two independent clauses joined by a comma
dm	dangling modifier—phrase or clause with no word(s) to modify in a sentence
frag	fragment—incomplete sentence
lc	lower case—word(s) incorrectly capitalized
nonidiom	nonidiomatic—not expressed this way in English
p	punctuation—punctuation incorrect or missing
pro ref **pro agree**	pronoun reference/agreement—pronoun reference unclear or agreement incorrect
ro	run-on—two independent clauses joined with no punctuation
sp	spelling error—word incorrectly spelled
unclear	unclear—message not clear

Error Awareness Sheet

Directions: This Error Awareness Sheet will help you discover what your sentence-level errors are and prioritize them. Put a check in the second column for each error marked on your returned paper. Then, from the most frequent errors in the second column, select two or three that you can begin working on first and put a check next to them in the third column. Always remember that you need to work on frequent global errors first.

TYPE OF ERROR	TOTAL NUMBER OF ERRORS	TOP-PRIORITY ERRORS TO WORK ON
GLOBAL ERRORS (more serious)		
vt		
vf		
modal		
cond		
pass		
cl		
ss		
wo		
conn		
LOCAL ERRORS (less serious)		
sv		
art		
s/pl		
wc		
wf		
prep		
OTHER ERRORS		
cap		
coh		
cs		
dm		
frag		
lc		
nonidiom		
p		
pro ref/agree		
ro		
sp		
unclear		

Sample Paper

Writing Topic: Discuss the progress you have made so far on your English 25 term-paper assignment. In addition to explaining what you have already done and what you are currently working on, comment on the aspect of writing a term paper that has been most challenging for you.

After five weeks of studies at this university, I learned many skills from English 25 course. One of the most important is writing term paper. I would like to write something about my term paper right now.

I scheduled my term-paper writing progress into ten parts: (1) deciding topics, (2) collecting reference papers/books, (3) briefly reading those papers/books, (4) writing down the outline, (5) reading the papers/books carefully and taking notes, (6) write first draft, (7) revising the draft, (8) asking my tutor to comment on my paper, (9) typing it, and (10) finally checking the paper. So far, I finished the first four steps and is proceeding to the fifth step. I hope I can speed up; otherwise it will be very busy on the end of November because [it dues] on December 4.

In order to type my term paper, I must learn how to operate Macintosh or IBM compatible computers because I never use them before, especially two kinds of word processing packages (Word for Macintosh and WordPerfect for Windows). As a result, I attended several lab classes offered by computer center. It is really interesting and I enjoyed it very much. It is useful for my future career too, and I think it is most challenging to me in writing my term paper.

In this response, you have done a careful job of addressing both parts of the question and have illustrated your points with good specifics, including the names of word-processing programs. Good organization, too!

Because your organization is strong, I have marked most of your sentence-level errors as you requested. I would suggest, however, that you first work on verb tense and articles. Also, you will want to work on avoiding unclear references when you use the pronoun it.

Error Awareness Sheet: Filled Out for Sample Paper

TYPE OF ERROR	TOTAL NUMBER OF ERRORS	TOP-PRIORITY ERRORS TO WORK ON
GLOBAL ERRORS (more serious)		
vt	✔✔✔✔✔	✔
vf	✔	
modal		
cond		
pass		
cl		
ss	✔	
wo		
conn		
LOCAL ERRORS (less serious)		
sv	✔	
art	✔✔✔	✔
s/pl	✔	
wc	✔✔	
wf		
prep		

TYPE OF ERROR	TOTAL NUMBER OF ERRORS	TOP-PRIORITY ERRORS TO WORK ON
OTHER ERRORS		
cap		
coh		
cs		
dm		
frag		
lc		
nonidiom		
p		
pro ref/agree	✔✔✔	✔
ro		
sp		
unclear		

Global Errors

This section contains nine units, each one addressing a global error that ESL writers commonly have difficulty with. Each unit has an introduction to the error, examples of the kinds of problems writers frequently have with the error, self-help strategies and grammar guidelines, exercises for practice, writing topics, and a videotape activity with an additional writing topic.

Global errors are more serious errors because they can significantly affect the reader's ability to comprehend what you have written. Just as we have chosen to put them first in this text, we believe that if you are making these errors, you need to address them first in order to make significant improvement in your writing.

Goals

- To learn the importance of mastering verb tenses in writing
- To review two problems ESL writers commonly encounter with verb tenses
- To learn to form and use verb tenses correctly
- To develop confidence in using correct verb tenses through practice with exercises and writing assignments

Verb Tenses

A student helps a fellow classmate on orientation day at the University of Nevada, Las Vegas.
Photo courtesy of Publications Reprographics.

Think about and discuss the following question:
What are three ways that attending your campus's
orientation can make you a better
college student?

PART I

WHAT YOU NEED TO KNOW ABOUT VERB-TENSE ERRORS

In Part I, you will learn

- The definition of a verb-tense error
- The importance of using verb tenses correctly in writing
- Suggestions for mastering verb tenses in writing

Definition of the Error (vt*)

Verb tense refers to the time that a verb expresses. The form of the verb *ride* in the sentence *We rode our bicycles to campus* indicates that the time of the action of riding our bicycles was in the past, not in the present or the future. A verb-tense error **(vt)** may be one of two types: incorrect choice of a verb tense within a sentence or inappropriate shifting of verb tenses within a paragraph or group of paragraphs.

Errors marked verb tense **(vt)** may also relate to **aspect.** Aspect refers to some characteristic of an event or action beyond its time. For example, both of the following sentences describe actions that take place in the present. The difference is one of aspect: *Matt studies in the library in the evening* and *Matt is studying in the library this evening.* The verb in the first sentence shows a habitual action, whereas the verb in the second sentence shows a temporary action that is in progress right now.

There are also different aspects in past time as illustrated by the following sentences: *I was working on my essay yesterday* and *I worked on my essay yesterday.* While both sentences describe actions in past time, only the first sentence emphasizes the duration of the action.

The present perfect tense (and present perfect progressive) also shows aspect. In the sentence *Alicia has moved to a new apartment*, the act of moving has already occurred, but the use of the present perfect indicates that the action occurred close to the present time. In the sentence *Alicia moved to a new apartment*, the use of the past tense indicates that the moving occurred at a definite time in the past. Thus, both verbs (*has moved* and *moved*) show a completed past action, but only the first verb shows a close link to present time.

Importance of Mastering Verb Tenses in Writing

Verb-tense errors are global (more serious) errors and can make a piece of writing difficult for the reader to understand. Because time is an important message

*****vt** = grading symbol for an error in verb tense.

expressed by the verb in English, a writer must be able to control verb tenses in order for the reader to understand when actions and events take place. In addition, as explained above, you will need to control verb tenses in order to communicate other information such as duration (as opposed to the completion of an event in the past), as in *The phone was ringing when I arrived home* versus *The phone rang at 10 PM.* In sum, if you do not control verb tenses, your readers will have great difficulty following the sequence of events in your writing.

Suggestions for Mastering Verb Tenses in Writing

- Review the verb-tense chart in Part II of this unit to make sure you understand the uses of the 12 verb tenses in English. Make sure you carefully study the six most commonly used verb tenses in English. One of these is the present perfect tense, one of the most difficult tenses for ESL students to master. Other commonly used verb tenses are the simple present, present progressive, simple past, past progressive, and future.

- Remember that in English, even when you have a time word or phrase (such as *last week, tomorrow,* or *yesterday*) stated in a clause or sentence, the verb must also express time, as in the sentence *We went to the movies yesterday.*

- Be highly aware of how you move from one verb tense to another in a piece of writing (the sequencing of verbs). Avoid unnecessary shifts in tense, yet also be aware that you will often need to use several different verb tenses. The sample paragraphs in Parts II and III of this unit will guide you in using different verb tenses in a passage.

- Become aware of the variety of verb tenses that can occur in a piece of writing by examining the verb tenses in your academic, professional, and leisure-time reading material. Note that when a writer shifts to a different verb tense, this shift is often signaled by a time-reference word or phrase, such as *when I was in high school, yesterday,* or *tomorrow.* These words alert the reader to a shift from one time frame to another.

Test Your Understanding of Verb Tenses

Write answers to the following questions. Share your answers with another student.

1. Why are verb-tense errors such serious errors?
2. Aside from time, what other kinds of information do some verb tenses convey?

Grammar Journal Entry 1: Verb Tenses

Write a short entry in your grammar journal in response to the following questions.

1. Describe your week so far. What have you done? Overall, has this week been hectic, busy, routine, or slow?

2. Underline all of the verbs in this journal entry and notice what different verb tenses you have used. Do you think they are correct? If you are not sure, check with a classmate or your instructor.

PART II

COMMON PROBLEMS, SELF-HELP STRATEGIES, AND GRAMMAR GUIDELINES

In Part II, you will study

- Two problems ESL writers commonly encounter with verb tenses
- Grammar guidelines for verb tenses
- Self-help strategies for controlling verb tenses in your writing

This section presents two problems that ESL writers commonly encounter with verb tenses. First, take the pretest to see what you already know about verb tenses. In checking your answers, note that the pretest questions cover the same types of errors in the same order as the problems in this section. Then carefully study each problem and the examples that illustrate it, giving particular attention to those problems that correspond to the pretest questions you had difficulty with. Using the boxes to the left of each problem, check [✓] *yes, no,* or *don't know* to indicate to yourself which problems you should focus the most attention on in this unit and also when you write in English. Remember that becoming aware of the types of errors you most often make with verb tenses will increase your chances of avoiding these errors in your writing.

Pretest: What Do You Already Know About Verb Tenses?

Test your ability to recognize errors in verb tenses by finding and correcting the one verb-tense error in each of the following sentences.

Answers on p. 291

1. Since I moved to my new house 15 days ago, I was very busy.

2. Human beings make mistakes. Sometimes we did things we regretted.

Two Problems ESL Writers Commonly Encounter with Verb Tenses

yes	no	don't know	**PROBLEM 1**
☐	☐	☐	An incorrect verb tense has been used in a sentence or clause.

vt

Incorrect: Alex <u>has sent out</u> several job applications last month.

Correct: Alex <u>sent out</u> several job applications last month.

Explanation: The action of sending out the applications has been completed. Thus, the simple past tense is needed.

vt

Incorrect: I <u>was</u> in the United States since 1985.

Correct: I <u>have been</u> in the United States since 1985.

Explanation: The action of being in the United States started in the past and is continuing into the present. Thus, the present perfect tense is needed.

vt

Incorrect: At the moment I live in the dormitory, but I <u>decided</u> to move into an apartment next year.

Correct: At the moment I live in the dormitory, but I <u>have decided</u> to move into an apartment next year.

Explanation: In some contexts, the simple past tense would be correct; however, since no definite time has been given and since the decision to move into an apartment has probably been recently made, the present perfect tense is needed.

vt

Incorrect: Students <u>pay</u> less tuition last year than this year.

Correct: Students <u>paid</u> less tuition last year than this year.

Explanation: Less tuition was paid by students last year. Thus, a past-tense verb is needed to agree with the time expression *last year*.

vt

Incorrect: Yosemite Park <u>was</u> one of the most popular of all the national parks.

Correct: Yosemite Park <u>is</u> one of the most popular of all the national parks.

Explanation: The comment about Yosemite Park is a general statement that is true in the present. Thus, the present tense is needed.

vt

Incorrect: Many students <u>participate</u> in the commencement ceremony next month.

Correct: Many students <u>will participate</u> (or <u>are participating</u>) in the commencement ceremony next month.

Explanation: The commencement will take place next month. Thus, a verb that shows future time is needed to agree with the time expression *next month*.

Self-Help Strategy: Make sure that the verb tense you use fits the time you want to express. For example, if you are writing about something that will happen in the future, the verb should express future time. Also, remember that even when the time is indicated with a time word, such as *yesterday, today,* or *tomorrow,* the verb must still show the time of the action. When the time is not explicitly stated, think carefully about the time you are trying to express. In the following sentence, the time is not stated in words, yet the writer is remembering a past action **now.** Thus, the verb *remember* is in the present tense even though the verb *had* and *went* are in the past tense.

[right now]   [past]   [past]

Example: I remember the fun we had when we all went to Disneyland.

yes   no   don't know   **PROBLEM 2**

☐   ☐   ☐   The verb tenses within a piece of writing (the sequence of verb tenses) shift inappropriately from one time frame to another.

Incorrect: Although this is my first year in college, I have already found that
   vt
   there <u>were</u> some differences between high school and college. One of the things I
   vt
   <u>learned</u> in college is that a person has to be independent.

Explanation: Since the writer is in his or her first year of college, he or she appropriately started out in the present time frame *(is, have found).* However, the writer then inappropriately shifts to the past *(were, learned)* instead of staying in the present.

Correct: Although this is my first year in college, I have already found that there <u>are</u> some differences between high school and college. One of the things I <u>have learned</u> in college is that a person has to be independent.

Incorrect: Most students have many expectations and ideas about college before they actually enter. Some of these expectations are similar to reality, yet some are quite dif-
   vt
   ferent. Before I started college, I <u>have imagined</u> how the classes and teachers
   vt
   would be and came to the conclusion that they <u>will</u> not be any different from those in high school.

Explanation: The writer appropriately begins in the present with two general statements. However, the writer needs to shift to the past when writing about an experience that took place before she started college.

Correct: Most students have many different expectations and ideas about college before they actually enter. Some of these expectations are similar to reality, yet some are quite different. Before I started college, I <u>imagined</u> how the classes and teachers would be and came to the conclusion that they <u>would</u> not be any different from those in high school.

Self-Help Strategy: Remember that although you want to avoid unnecessary shifts in verb tense, it is often appropriate to shift tenses in a piece of writing. See the Grammar Guidelines in this unit for suggestions on how to master verb-tense sequencing.

Grammar Guidelines for Verb Tenses

Forms and Uses of Verb Tenses in English

The following charts provide an explanation of the forms and uses of verb tenses in English. You may want to begin by reviewing all of the tenses. Then study more carefully those tenses that you find difficult.

SIMPLE PRESENT

Use	Examples
To express a habitual or repeated action in the present or to express a condition that is true at any time.	• Thuy <u>rides</u> her bicycle to school every day. • I <u>am</u> not a morning person. In fact, I usually <u>do not get up</u> until 10:00 AM.
To express general truths that are timeless (well-known laws or principles or even generally accepted truths about people, places, and customs).	• Water <u>boils</u> at 100 degrees Celsius. • Generally speaking, Spaniards <u>eat</u> dinner much later than Americans <u>do</u>. • University students often <u>do not get</u> enough sleep.
To report what appears in print. This use is common in academic writing when the writer is referring to texts and quotations. In the example, even though Norman Cousins wrote his article in the past, the writer has put the underlined verb in the present tense.	• In his article "The Communication Collapse," Norman Cousins <u>asserts</u> that schools encourage poor writing habits by forcing students to write under time pressure. **(Note:** The writer could also use the past tense, *asserted*.)
To describe past events as if they were happening now. This use is called the **historical present.** In the example, taken from a longer account of a visit to Nepal, the writer has chosen to narrate his adventures using the present tense, even though the trip is over and he is back in the United States.	• My friend and I <u>arrive</u> at Kathmandu Airport on February 25. Jim <u>meets</u> us with a taxi, and we <u>drive</u> to what is to be our apartment for nearly three weeks. The drive <u>is</u> culture shock number one.

SIMPLE PRESENT, cont.

Formation

Base form of the verb (infinitive without *to*) or, for third-person singular, add *-s* or *-es*.

Examples: I write, you write, we write, he/she/the student writes, they/the students write

PRESENT PROGRESSIVE

Use*	Examples
To express an action or activity that is happening right now (at this moment, today, this year); the action has begun and is still happening.	• Tammy <u>is working</u> on the first draft of her essay. • Monica <u>is majoring</u> in aeronautical engineering.
To express that an action or activity is happening at the present time and is temporary.	• Mark <u>is working</u> for his uncle. (allows for the possibility that although Mark is working for his uncle now, he may not work for him permanently)
To express an action that is already in progress at a specified point of time in the present.	• When my roommate gets home after class, I <u>am</u> usually <u>cooking</u>. At 8:00 PM, Teresa <u>is</u> usually <u>studying</u> in the library.

Formation

am/is/are + present participle *(-ing)*

Examples: I am reading, you are reading, he/she/the student is reading, we are reading, they/the students are reading

*When a verb expresses a state of being (a stative verb), it cannot be used in the progressive tense. Instead, such verbs take the simple present tense to express a state of being in the present. In the sentence, *She <u>seems</u> tired,* although the time expressed is right now, the present progressive cannot be used. Many verbs, however, can have both a stative or an active use. Such verbs can be used in the progressive only when they are expressing an active meaning, for example, *The food <u>smells</u> good* (stative meaning; time = right now) versus *Mark <u>is smelling</u> the roses in the garden* (active meaning; time = right now). For a list of common stative verbs, consult an ESL grammar book.

SIMPLE PAST

Use	Examples
To indicate that an action or event took place at a specific time in the past.	• I <u>visited</u> Japan last year. • Last night we <u>saw</u> a movie about India.
To indicate that an action or event occurred over a period of time in the past with the implication that it is no longer true in the present.	• I <u>lived</u> in Los Angeles for 15 years. • Barbara <u>was</u> on the volleyball team in college.

Formation

Regular verbs: base form + *-ed*

Examples: I walked, you walked, he/she/the student walked, we walked, they/the students walked

Note: Many verbs have irregular past-tense forms. Some common irregular past-tense forms include *took, ate,* and *came.* Consult an ESL grammar book for list of common verbs that have irregular past-tense forms. You can also find irregular past-tense forms in the dictionary under the base form of the verb.

PAST PROGRESSIVE

Use	Examples
To express that an activity was in progress at a specific point of time in the past.	• At 8:00 PM last night, I <u>was studying</u> in the library. • I <u>was cooking</u> when the phone rang.
To show that an activity lasted for a period of time in the past (emphasis on the duration).	• I <u>was working</u> when the phone rang. • I <u>was cooking</u> while you <u>were sleeping</u>.

Formation

was/were + present participle *(-ing)*

Examples: I was reading, you were reading, he/she/the student was reading, we were reading, they/the students were reading

PRESENT PERFECT

Use	Examples
To express an action or state that began in the past and continues in the present.	• Hiroaki <u>has lived</u> in California for two years. • I <u>have known</u> Hiroaki since he came to California.
To indicate that an action or event occurred some time in the past, although the exact time is not specified or important.	• Veronique <u>has moved</u> back to France. • I <u>have</u> already <u>filed</u> my income taxes.
Note: This tense can also indicate that an event has very recently happened. The adverb *just* is often used in this case.	• I <u>have</u> just <u>completed</u> the math problem set.
To indicate that an action or event has occurred more than once in the past (specific times are not given or important).	• Susan <u>has seen</u> the doctor several times about her allergy problem.

Formation

has/have + past participle

Examples: I have walked, you have walked, he/she/the student has walked, we have walked, they/the students have walked

Note: Many past-participle forms are irregular (for example, *known, seen, written, met*). Check an ESL grammar book for lists of common verbs that have irregular past-participle forms. You will also find irregular past participles of individual verbs in the dictionary, under the base form of the verb.

PRESENT PERFECT PROGRESSIVE

Use	Examples
To emphasize the duration of an activity that started in the past and has continued into the present.	• I <u>have been waiting</u> for you for an hour. • Abdulaziz <u>has been living</u> in California for two years.
To indicate that an activity has been in progress recently (the activity started in the past and is still going on).	• Ramon <u>has been reading</u> the book *War and Peace.* • I <u>have been thinking</u> about moving out of the dormitory.

PRESENT PERFECT PROGRESSIVE, cont.

Formation

has/have + been + present participle *(-ing)*

Examples: I have been waiting, you have been waiting, he/she/the student has been waiting, we have been waiting, they/the students have been waiting

PAST PERFECT

Use	Examples
To indicate an action that was completed by a definite time or before another action was completed in the past.	• In English class I suddenly realized that I <u>had forgotten</u> to bring my textbook. • I <u>had</u> never <u>read</u> anything by Jane Austen until last month.
Note: If the word *before* or *after* is in the sentence, the simple past may be used instead of the past perfect.	• After all my friends <u>left</u> (or <u>had left</u>), I cleaned up the apartment.

Formation

had + past participle

Examples: I had called, you had called, he/she/the student had called, we had called, they/the students had called

Note: Many past-participle forms are irregular (for example, *written, met, known*). Check an ESL grammar book for lists of common verbs that have irregular past-participle forms. You can also look up irregular past participles of individual verbs in the dictionary under the base form of the verb.

PAST PERFECT PROGRESSIVE

Use	Examples
To emphasize the duration of an activity that was completed before another action or time in the past.	• I <u>had been waiting</u> for him for an hour when he finally arrived.

PAST PERFECT PROGRESSIVE, cont.

Formation

had + been + present participle *(-ing)*

Examples: I had been waiting, you had been waiting, he/she/the student had been waiting, we had been waiting, they/the students had been waiting

FUTURE

Use	**Examples**
To express an action, event, or state that will occur in the future.	• I <u>will drive</u> you to the airport tomorrow. • Terry <u>will graduate</u> next June.

Formation

will + base form

Examples: I will attend, you will attend, he/she/the student will attend, we will attend, they/the students will attend

Note: Do not use an *–s* on the base form of the verb in the third-person singular.

Other important information about expressing future time

Future time can also be expressed in the following ways:

• am/is/are going to + base form

Examples:

We <u>are going to take</u> the midterm on Friday.
The city <u>is going to have</u> a parade on July 4.

• simple present or present progressive (especially with verbs of arriving and departing)

Examples:

The plane <u>leaves</u> at 8:00 PM this evening.
The plane <u>is leaving</u> at 8:00 PM this evening.

When the future is expressed in a sentence that is in past time, *will* becomes *would*.

Examples:

1. **Present/future time:** The instructor <u>says</u> that the exam <u>will cover</u> the first five units of the textbook.

   Past time: The instructor <u>said</u> that the exam <u>would cover</u> the first five units of the textbook.

2. **Present/future time:** Even though I plan to go to college next year, I <u>do not know</u> how demanding college classes <u>will be</u>.

   Past time: When I <u>was</u> in high school, I <u>did not know</u> how demanding college classes <u>would be</u>.

FUTURE PROGRESSIVE

Use	Examples
To express an action that will be happening over a period of time at some specific point in the future.	• Even though <u>I will be studying</u> when you call, I do not mind being interrupted.
To emphasize the duration of an action in the future.	• Lin <u>will be working</u> on this essay for the next week.

Formation

will + be + present participle *(-ing)*

Examples: I will be leaving, you will be leaving, he/she/the student will be leaving, we will be leaving, they/the students will be leaving

FUTURE PERFECT

Formation

Use	Examples
To indicate that an activity will be completed before another event or

time in the future. | • Maria <u>will have finished</u> her Ph.D. by the time she leaves for a two-year stay in France.
• We <u>will have finished</u> five essays by the end of the semester. |

Formation

will + have + past participle

Examples: I will have gone, you will have gone, he/she/the student will have gone, we will have gone, they/the students will have gone

FUTURE PERFECT PROGRESSIVE

Use	Examples
To indicate that an action has been in progress for a period of time before another event or time in the future.	• Carlos <u>will have been working</u> on his dissertation for three years before he gets his Ph.D. degree.
• By this time next year, I <u>will have been living</u> here for two years.

FUTURE PERFECT PROGRESSIVE, cont.

Formation

will + have + been + present participle

Examples: I will have been practicing, you will have been practicing,
he/she/the student will have been practicing, they/the students
will have been practicing

Guidelines for Correct Verb-Tense Sequencing

Verb-tense sequencing refers to the way a writer can move from one verb tense to another in a piece of writing. Being able to move appropriately from one verb tense to another in a piece of writing is crucial for writers and is one of the most important keys to using verb tenses correctly.

Sometimes a shift in verb tenses is appropriate and sometimes it is not, as illustrated in paragraphs A and B below. In paragraph A , the underlined verb *were* shows a shift in verb tense from present to past. This shift to the past is **not** appropriate, because the writer is still commenting in general about men in his country. The writer thinks that these men are generally wrong in their opinion. **General statements that are true in the present require the simple present tense,** so the writer should stay in the present tense by using the verb *are* instead of *were.*

> **A.** Many men in my country do not encourage their wives to work outside the home because they think women should not do anything but housework and child care. However, these men **were** wrong. They will never know what their wives can do or who their wives might become.

In paragraph B, the underlined verbs also show a shift from the present to the past. However, here, the shift to the past tense is appropriate because the writer shifts from a discussion of what is true in the present to a discussion of what it was like **before** personal computers became common. Shifting into the past tense is necessary in this situation to make the comparison between present and past.

> **B.** Personal computers have become very important tools in both homes and offices. At home, people use them for everything from writing letters to keeping records of their monthly budgets or for doing their income taxes. In the workplace, computers are used for word processing, sending messages, computer-aided design, writing software, locating reference material, and doing numerous other tasks. Before homes and offices **had** personal computers, individuals **had** to type and retype drafts of letters and other material. Engineers and others **had** to draft and design using pens, paper, and drawing boards. Students, researchers, and librarians **had** to search for reference materials manually. Producing and locating all this material **took**

much longer in those days than it does now. From writing to designing to communicating, computers have made our lives easier in both the home and the workplace.

Always keep in mind that, as a writer, you will usually use several different verb tenses in a piece of writing. Also, you will sometimes have the option of choosing between verb tenses, with this choice creating little difference in meaning. The two passages that follow, along with the notes below each one, will show you how various verb tenses can work together in sequence in a text. The first passage uses more verbs in the present time frame, while the second passage uses more verbs in the past time frame.

Passage 1

The following passage begins and ends in the present tense because the writer is presenting current facts about some of the benefits of television watching. However, the writer, who is a teacher, can also look back to the past or show actions that were true in the past yet are still true in the present by choosing appropriate verb tenses throughout the passage. The passage has been divided into eight parts. An explanation of the sequence of tenses the writer has chosen to use is at the end of the passage.

(1) Although television <u>has long been deplored</u> by parents as a waste of their children's time, well-informed college students in the 1990s <u>view</u> television as a supplementary source of knowledge inside and outside their classes. (2) Television <u>has affected</u> their lives ever since they <u>were</u> small. (3) Students who <u>want</u> to be up to date <u>keep up</u> with the news—via television. Not only <u>can they choose</u> from among a wealth of broadcasts, including Headline News, CNN, and the major networks, but also television news <u>offers</u> facts and the pictures to illustrate those facts, giving a three-dimensional impact to the news that a newspaper or *Newsweek* <u>cannot surpass</u>. (4) During the last big earthquake, it <u>was not</u> until I <u>turned on</u> CNN that I <u>understood</u> the full impact of the LA earthquake, even though I <u>had heard</u> about it on the radio. Seeing cars dangling over a precipice where a freeway <u>had been</u> or a closeup of a first-floor apartment that the earthquake <u>had reduced</u> to 18 inches <u>brought</u> it home in a way that its size, 6.6 on the Richter scale, <u>could not</u>. (5) Of course, I <u>am</u> a regular reader of the newspapers, but I <u>depend</u> on television for a "live" dimension that newspapers and magazines <u>cannot offer</u>. Good students in the 1990s <u>are</u> no different from me: They <u>rely</u> on television as an informant. (6) As a teacher, I <u>have added</u> television to the classroom since 1985 for the same reason that I <u>watch</u> it: its visual impact. (7) In an English 1 class, for example, I once <u>showed</u> a video clip of Martin Luther King's presentation when we <u>were studying</u> his speech "I Have a Dream." Seeing thousands of African Americans on the Washington Mall absorbing King's every word <u>made</u> the whole speech come alive for all of us in the room. I even <u>noticed</u> that some students <u>were moved</u> to

tears as they <u>watched</u>, which clearly <u>indicated</u> their interest in the broad-cast. (8) Because television <u>can offer</u> so much, good students <u>value</u> it as information technology, <u>use</u> it wisely, and, by watching it, <u>keep</u> themselves informed, both factually and pictorially.

Notes on Verb-Tense Sequencing in Passage 1

<u>Part (1):</u>   The writer starts with the present perfect tense in the passive voice *(has been deplored)* to show that over a period of time starting in the past and continuing into the present, parents have not approved of their children's watching television. She then shifts to the present tense *(view)* to state a current fact about the way college students view television watching.

<u>Part (2):</u>   The writer uses the present perfect tense *(has affected)* to show that the effect began in the past and is continuing in the present. The writer then shifts to the simple past tense *(were)* in referring to the students when they were children, because they are no longer children.

<u>Part (3):</u>   The writer uses all simple present-tense verbs in this part because she is making statements that are generally true in the present.

<u>Part (4):</u>   The writer shifts to past time in this part because she is referring to an example (the Los Angeles earthquake) that occurred in the past. In this part, the writer uses both the simple past tense *(was not, turned on, understood, brought, could not)* and the past perfect tense *(had heard, had been, had reduced)*. The verbs in the past perfect tense indicate actions and events that happened in the past <u>before</u> the time the writer turned on the television set to watch the news on the earthquake. In other words, the earthquake had already occurred when the writer began to watch TV news about it.

<u>Part (5):</u>   The writer shifts back to the simple present tense *(am, depend, cannot offer, rely)* in this part because she is finished with her example about the Los Angeles earthquake and, just as she did in part (3), is now making general statements that are true in the present about herself and about students.

<u>Part (6):</u>   The writer uses the present perfect tense *(have added)* to show that beginning in the past and continuing into the present, she has added television to her classroom. She shifts to the simple present tense *(watch)* to show that she generally watches TV in the present.

<u>Part (7):</u>   The writer shifts to past time because she is referring to an example (her experience teaching an English 1 course) that occurred in the past. In this part, the writer uses mostly the simple past tense *(showed, noticed, were moved* [passive voice]*, watched, indicated)* to show that these actions and events happened in the past and are fin-ished. However, she also uses the past progressive tense *(were studying)* to empha-

size the duration of time—that the action of studying Martin Luther King's speech went on over a period of time in her class—in contrast to a single moment in time when she showed the video clip.

Part (8): The writer shifts back to the simple present tense *(can offer, value, use, keep)* to conclude with statements that are generally true in present time.

Passage 2

The following passage is an essay introduction in which the writer summarizes an article by Eudora Welty before going on to write the essay, which is based on the Welty article. **The majority of verbs are in past time because they refer to Welty's experience in the past.** But we can see that the writer also sometimes uses the present tense and present perfect tense in this summary. In this passage, three verb tenses are used: the simple present, the simple past, and the present perfect. An explanation of why the writer uses these three tenses together in this paragraph is given at the end of the passage.

> In her article, "Listening," Eudora Welty <u>tells</u> how she <u>became</u> committed to reading and writing through listening. Welty <u>was</u> first <u>introduced</u> to the world of books when she was three years old. She <u>reports</u> that her mother <u>read</u> to her all day long, in every room of the house. Not only <u>did she develop</u> a love of books because of her mother's reading to her but she also <u>learned</u> to listen to what she <u>heard</u> and what she <u>read</u>. She <u>says</u>, "Ever since I <u>was</u> first <u>read</u> to, then <u>started</u> reading to myself, there <u>has</u> never <u>been</u> a line read that <u>I</u> <u>didn't *hear*</u>." She <u>feels</u> that her ability to listen to words <u>has influenced</u> her in her desire to write and her ability to write, as she <u>has</u> "always <u>trusted</u> this voice." Although Welty <u>does not say</u> it directly, it is clear that her mother <u>served</u> as an excellent role model because she <u>taught</u> her the love of reading.

Notes on Verb-Tense Sequencing in Passage 2

<u>Simple Present Verbs</u> *(tells, reports, says, feels, does not say, is)*
The writer uses the simple present tense in this passage to refer to what Eudora Welty says in her article. Even though Welty wrote the article in the past, it is common to use the simple present tense when using verbs that refer to what an author has written in an article. In other words, Welty *tells, reports,* and *says* or *does not say* certain things in her article that the author wants to refer to in the summary. Note that the writer could have chosen to use simple past tense for all of these verbs. But the writer must be consistent and put **all** of the verbs referring to what an authors says or writes in an article either in the present or in the past.

The verbs *feels* and *is* are also in the simple present tense. The verb *feel* is in the simple present because the writer is stating a current fact about how Welty feels in general at the present time about the effects of reading on her writing. The verb *is* is in the simple present because it refers to something that is clear to the writer now in the present.

<u>Simple Past Verbs</u> (*was introduced, was, did she develop, learned, heard, read, was read to, started, didn't hear, served, taught*)

The majority of the verbs in the passage are in the simple past tense because the writer is referring to Welty's childhood experience in which she was read to by her mother. This experience happened in the past and is finished as Welty is no longer a child now.

<u>Present Perfect Verbs</u> (*has influenced, has trusted*)

The writer uses the present perfect form of these two verbs to show that these actions occur over a period of time beginning in the past and continuing into the present. In other words, Welty, beginning in the past and up to the present time, has been influenced by her ability to listen to words and has trusted the voice inside her.

Improve Your Writing Style

Choose the most appropriate verb tense when the time reference of two verb tenses is similar yet not exactly the same.

Writers often have a choice of verb tenses that are similar but not exactly the same in meaning. Sometimes you may want to choose one tense over another for a specific reason. At other times, you may have options, with your choice of tense creating little difference in meaning. For you, as advanced writers, what is important is to be aware of the differences that can be created by the use of one verb tense over another. The sentences that follow illustrate some of the differences you should become aware of. Note differences both in time reference and in any other information each verb in the pairs of sentences that follow expresses.

1a. We <u>decided</u> to go to the movies. (simple past tense)
1b. We <u>have decided</u> to go to the movies. (present perfect tense)

Explanation of difference: In both sentences above, the decision to go to the movies has already been made. The difference is that the use of the present perfect tense in sentence 1b makes it clear that the decision was made close to the present time; that is, the decision has either just been made or has been made recently. Also, with sentence 1a, the meaning could be that *we decided to go to the movies and <u>already went</u>;* whereas in sentence 1b, the action of going to the movies has not yet been completed.

2a. It <u>rained</u> yesterday. (simple past tense)
2b. It <u>was raining</u> yesterday. (past progressive tense)

IMPROVE YOUR WRITING STYLE, cont.

Explanation of difference: In both sentences 2a and 2b, the event happened in past time. However, the use of the past progressive tense *was raining* in sentence 2b emphasizes the duration of time that it rained yesterday. The past progressive verb gives the impression that it rained over a period of time yesterday. In sentence 2a, in contrast, the verb in the simple past tense does not indicate whether or not it rained briefly or over a period of time. A time reference word, such as *all day (It rained all day)* or *briefly (It rained briefly)* would have to be used with the verb to indicate the length of duration.

3a. We <u>had eaten</u> when you came over to visit. (past perfect tense)
3b. We <u>ate</u> when you came over to visit. (past tense)

4a. We <u>had eaten</u> before you came over to visit. (past perfect tense)
4b. We <u>ate</u> before you came over to visit. (past tense)

Explanation of difference: In sentences 3a and 3b, the time that the eating took place in relation to the action of coming over to visit is different. In sentence 3a, the past perfect tense indicates that the action of eating had already happened before the action of coming over to visit. In sentence 3b, in contrast, the action of eating occurred at the same time or even slightly after the action of coming over happened. Note, however, that in sentences 4a and 4b, the action of eating in both cases was finished before the action of coming over to visit happened. The subordinating conjunction *before* in sentences 4a and 4b clearly indicates that the action of eating comes first in both cases.

5a. I <u>am studying</u> in the library. (present progressive tense)
5b. I <u>study</u> in the library. (simple present tense)

Explanation of difference: Notice that although both verbs are in present time, the exact meaning conveyed by each verb is different. In sentence 5a, the use of the present progressive tense shows that the action of studying is happening either exactly at the moment of speaking or for a period of time in the present that the writer considers temporary. In other words, sentence 5a could mean that the studying in the library is happening right now or for a period of time in the present—for example, *this week*—that is considered temporary and finite. In sentence 5b, in contrast, the use of the simple present tense indicates that the action of studying in the library is something that is done on a regular basis as a habit, for example *every night*.

PART III

EXERCISES FOR PRACTICE

EXERCISE 1 (Do this exercise on your own. Then check your answers with a classmate.)

Directions: Examine each verb tense in the following sentences to decide whether the sentence is correct (C) or incorrect (I). Cross out each incorrect verb and write the correct verb above it. Be prepared to explain why your choice of verb tense is correct.

have made

Example: ___I___ Since I have been a college student, I ~~made~~ many new friends.

___I___ 1. I was interested in physics since high school.

___I___ 2. Having computer skills is essential for a college freshman, and I decide to learn how to use a computer.

___I___ 3. Since she was a child, she likes sports, especially water sports, such as swimming and waterskiing.

___I___ 4. Mario graduate as a veterinarian in January of last year.

___C___ 5. Hector speaks Spanish and comes from Costa Rica.

___I___ 6. First, we went to Italy. Then we travel to Austria and Germany. Finally, we visit Spain.

___I___ 7. The professor had given an introduction to the course yesterday, the first day of class.

___I___ 8. There are rumors that college tuition is higher next year.

___I___ 9. By the time of the presidential election, the candidates will have campaigned in most, if not all, of the fifty states.

___I___ 10. In my opinion, voting in elections was very important.

EXERCISE 2 (Do this exercise on your own. Then check your answers with a classmate.)

Directions: First read the entire paragraph. Then fill in each blank with the correct verb tense of the verb in parentheses. For some blanks, more than one verb tense is possible. The first blank has been filled in for you.

One quality that _____helps_____ (help) students succeed in their studies is self-discipline. Self-discipline _____ (be) particularly important in college. I _____ (learn) a great deal about self-discipline by observing two of my friends. I have noted that my roommate Betsy _____ (plan) her time every night before she _____ (go) to bed. She _____ (write) down what she _____ (have) to do the next day and how much time she _____ (spend) doing each activity. First, she

_____ (schedule) time for attending classes and working. She also ___*sets*___

(set) aside time for socializing, running, studying, and eating. By having a timetable and sticking

to it, Betsy ____*is*____ (is) always able to accomplish a lot more than I can. Another

friend, Jo, _____ (discipline) herself by not doing anything unless she __*has completed*__

(complete) all of her homework and reading. One night last semester, I __*invited*__

(invite) her to go out to dinner, but she ____*refused*____ (refuse) because she _*didn't finished*_
hadn't

(not finish) her physics problem set. I wish I could be as disciplined as these two friends of mine

are. I ____*know*____ (know) that self-discipline is important if I want to be successful in col-

lege. Thus, next term I ___*will make*___ (make) an effort to discipline myself.

EXERCISE 3 (Do this exercise on your own. Then check your answers with a classmate.)

Directions: **Fill in the blanks in the following letter with the correct form of the verb given in parentheses. Pay particular attention to the sequence of tenses you use. For some blanks, more than one verb tense is possible.***

October 31, XXXX

Internship Office
Mighty Corporation
Hometown, CA 90001

Dear Sir or Madam:

I ___*read*___ (read) your advertisement in our campus newspaper yesterday and

*I'm writing* (write) to apply for a summer internship position. I _*have heard*_ (hear)

many wonderful things about your company and would be very interested in working for you.

I ___*graduated*___ (graduate) last June from Cal Poly Pomona with a B.S. in electrical

engineering. After graduating from college, I _*fulfilled*_ (fulfill) a lifelong dream of traveling

to Japan, the country of my parents' origin. Currently, I _*'m working*_ (work) on my

M.S. degree in electrical and computer engineering at Stanford University. I

*will complete* (complete) my degree next June, at which time I would like to work full

time for a company such as yours.

As you can imagine, the summer internships you offer are exactly what I

*'m looking* (look) for. The internship will not only be valuable to me in terms of profes-

sional experience, but, I believe, will also help me focus my studies in my second year of the

---

*   This exercise was adapted from one originally written by Jeffrey Hobbs. The authors
    would like to thank him for allowing them to use it.

M.S. program to reflect what I ___will___ (need) when I am working for the computer industry in the future. Because of its proximity to my university, Stanford, I ___have visited___ (visit) your company's Hometown branch a number of times. I am especially interested in working at this site because of its focus on research and development. In addition, as someone who is bilingual and bicultural (English and Japanese), I ___find___ (find) the idea of an internship with a multinational company such as yours particularly appealing.

I ___enclose___ (enclose) a copy of my resume for your consideration. Please do not hesitate to call me if you have any questions or wish to set up an interview.

Sincerely,

Peter E. Engineer

Peter E. Engineer

Graduate Student in Electrical and Computer Engineering, Stanford University

EXERCISE 4 (Do this exercise with a classmate.)

Directions: **The following paragraph, written by a student, has been edited so that the only errors are verb tense errors. First, read the paragraph. Then cross out each incorrect verb and write the correct verb above it. For some verbs, more than one option is possible. The first error has been corrected for you.**

came

I have a positive attitude toward writing in English. When I first ~~come~~ to America, I am very confused about using English, a new and strange language. But as time go by, my feeling toward the language begin to change. I force myself to write even though it was hard at first. I write a lot, and I become more confident each time I write. Now, although I am more confident about writing, I still have many problems to overcome. I find that writing takes a great deal of time and one has to be patient and disciplined in order to be good at it. At times, I was frustrated and impatient with my writing. In fact, sometimes I sit for hours and cannot write even a word. Nevertheless, despite my frustration and long hours of work, I tend to have a positive attitude toward writing in English. Even though English is not my native language, I have found that I simply like to write.

EXERCISE 5 (Do this exercise on your own. Then check your answers with a classmate.)

Directions: The following paragraph, written by a student, has been edited so that the only errors are verb-tense errors. First, read the paragraph. Then cross out each incorrect verb and write the correct verb above it. In some cases, more than one option is possible. The first error has been corrected for you.

function
Children of immigrants who do not speak English often ~~functioned~~ more like adults than children. As a child of immigrant parents myself, I have often had to act as an adult. Ever since my family arrived here five years ago, I take care of them in many ways. I have had to pay the rent, the utilities, the telephone, and any other bills. I translated letters from English to Italian for the whole family. When a family member was sick, I had gone along to the doctor to explain the problem and to translate the doctor's suggestions. I believe it has been good for me to do all these things because it prepared me for what I face when I am living on my own. Having adult responsibilities gave me the chance to understand what the world is like outside of my home. It provided me with hands-on training and is beneficial for me.

EXERCISE 6 (Do this exercise on your own. Then check your answers with a classmate.)

Directions: The following paragraph, written by a student, has been edited so that the only errors are verb-tense errors. First, read the paragraph. Then cross out each incorrect verb and write the correct verb above it. The first error has been corrected for you.

Luckily for me, at the very end of my first semester here at college, my grades changed for the better. My Chemistry 1A class last semester is one example. At the start of the semester, I did not understand the materials or the problems. I was confused when I read and *tried* ~~try~~ to solve problems. Even though I do the homework and go to all the laboratory sessions, my understanding did not seem to improve. In fact, on my first and second midterms, I receive a D and an F. After receiving those two grades, I start to realize that I had to change the way I was studying. I decide to put myself on a strict schedule and to go to the library every day after dinner. I continue to follow this plan until the end of the semester. Even now, I still cannot believe how well I had done on my final. I received a B on the final and a C for the semester. This is what I think happen. When I reviewed all the materials systematically, I am able to understand principles of chemistry that I did not understand before.

EXERCISE 7 (Do this exercise on your own.)

Directions: Choose an article in a newspaper or magazine. After reading the article, underline all the verbs in one or two paragraphs. Do you understand why the different verb tenses were used? If you are unsure of any of them, ask a classmate, a tutor, or your instructor.

PART IV

WRITING TOPICS

Select one or more of the following topics for writing and follow the steps in Appendix A.

Topic A: Write about a historical event that had or has had major effects, either positive or negative, on your country. First, explain the event. Then analyze its effects, making it clear whether you see these effects as positive or negative.

Topic B: Explain your field of study to people who are not familiar with it. In writing your response, think about the following questions, although you do not have to answer them all. What do specialists in your field study? What are some of the focuses or areas of study within your field? What do people in your field do as occupations and how does their work serve a purpose in the world? How did you personally become interested in this field of study? That is, what sparked your interest in it or appealed to you about it?

Topic C: Think about the positive role relaxation plays in our lives. What is your favorite place to relax and why?

PART V

CNN VIDEO ACTIVITY AND WRITING TOPIC

Students Create School Mural

Useful Vocabulary: mural   graffiti   deface   depict   intricate   hall

Before You Watch

This video segment describes a school project that
involves students in painting a mural in order to
curb graffiti and enhance the beauty of their school.

©CNN

A high school seeks to curb graffiti by
involving students in public art.

- List any public art that you have seen. Note what
  type of art it was and where you saw it.

- What are some places where you have noticed
  graffiti?

While You Watch

- Write down three reasons for creating the mural.

- Discover who came up with the idea of the mural.

After You Watch

  I. **Write a personal reaction.**

   Write a personal reaction of three to five
   sentences to what you saw in the video.
   What interested you most? Would you
   like to be involved in a project like this?

 II. **Share your reactions.**

   Answer the following questions either orally or in writing. Compare your answers with those
   of a classmate.

   1. What is the content of the mural?

   2. What seemed to be the reaction of the students (both students in general and those who
      helped paint the mural) to this project? What are some benefits of students working together
      on such a project?

   3. What are some other possible themes such a mural could have?

WRITING TOPIC

One purpose of the mural depicted in the video is to cover a wall with something student-created
in order to discourage students from defacing the wall with graffiti. To what extent is graffiti a
problem in your town or in your home country? What is being done to help deal with it?

Goals

- To learn the importance of mastering verb forms in writing
- To review seven problems ESL writers commonly encounter with verb forms
- To learn to form verbs correctly
- To develop confidence in using correct verb forms through practice with exercises and writing assignments

Verb Forms

University Hall at the University of Toledo in Ohio houses many of the main offices on campus.
Photo courtesy of Public Information Office.

Think about and discuss the following question:
What are the different departments or offices on
your campus that provide information and
resources for students who want to
improve their English skills?

PART I

WHAT YOU NEED TO KNOW ABOUT VERB-FORM ERRORS

In Part I, you will learn

- The definition of a verb-form error
- The importance of using verb forms correctly in writing
- Suggestions for mastering verb forms in writing

Definition of the Error (vf*)

A verb-form error **(vf)** is an error in the formation of the main verb or any part of a verb phrase. For example, the verb form in the following sentence is incorrect: *We have not yet estimate the cost of the trip.* Here, the past participle *estimated* is needed instead of the base form *estimate*. The form of the verb *enroll* is incorrect in the sentence *Mona has decided enrolling in three courses this semester.* The verb following *decide* must be *to enroll* (an infinitive) instead of *enrolling,* a gerund.

In the sentence, *The students confuse about the change in the homework assignment,* a verb-form error has occurred because a main verb has been incorrectly used instead of [be + the past participle]. The sentence should read *The students are confused about the change.* This kind of verb is sometimes called a stative passive.

Note that verb-form errors with modals and the conditional are not covered in this unit but rather in the units on modals and conditionals. Also, present and past participles used as adjectives are covered in Unit 14, "Word Forms."

Learning the following terminology will help you understand the material on verb forms contained in this unit.

an infinitive
　　to walk, to study, to speak
a base form
　　walk, study, speak (the infinitive without to)
a gerund or a present participle (the base form + ing)
　　walking, studying, speaking
a past participle
　　walked, studied, spoken
a simple past form
　　walked, studied, spoke
a verb phrase
　　has been speaking, has spoken, am speaking, will have spoken
　　(a main verb with any auxiliary verbs)

*vf = grading symbol for an error in verb form.

Importance of Mastering Verb Forms in Writing

Verb-form errors are global (more serious) errors and will usually significantly affect the reader's ability to understand the meaning of a text. Furthermore, problems with verb formation distract the reader because verbs are important content words that convey action in English sentences. Because readers in the academic and professional worlds expect verb formation to be correct, incorrect verb forms make a piece of writing, no matter how strong the content is, appear flawed to the reader.

Suggestions for Mastering Verb Forms in Writing

- Study grammar rules to avoid verb-form errors such as those that involve incorrect formation of part of a verb phrase. For example, the underlined verb in the sentence *He has send out several resumes* is incorrect. The writer of this sentence needs to learn that the formation of the present perfect is [*have/has* + past participle], not [*have/has* + base form]. If you are making such errors, study the rules for verb-phrase formation given in this unit.

- Memorize individual cases when working with verb-form errors that are not governed by rules, such as those involving verbals following verbs. You can memorize these forms just as you would memorize a new vocabulary word. For example, you might have to memorize the fact that certain verbs, such as *dislike*, are always followed by a gerund (the *-ing* form), as in *I dislike running*, while other verbs, such as *hope*, are followed by an infinitive, as in *I hope to run*. Still others, such as *like*, can be followed by either a gerund or an infinitive, as in *I like running* or *I like to run*. Use the guidelines for forming verbals in this unit to help you recognize and master these verb forms.

- Do not depend upon your ear to help you master verb formation because, in spoken English, it is often difficult to hear exactly how a verb is formed. For example, it is difficult to hear the difference between *talk* and *talked* in spoken English because the *-ed* ending is not stressed in speaking. Thus, listening to the spoken language will probably not help you learn that the correct verb phrase is *she has talked* rather than *she has talk*. Likewise, because auxiliary verbs are most often unstressed (not said loudly or clearly) in spoken English, your ear will probably not help you distinguish between the correct *I am going* and the incorrect *I going*.

- Become aware of gerunds, infinitives, main verbs, and verb phrases when you read. Written material—such as newspapers, magazines, journals, and textbooks—is an excellent resource for examples of correct verb formation.

Test Your Understanding of Verb Forms

Write answers to the following questions. Share your answers with another student.

1. How is a verb-*form* error different from a verb-*tense* error?

2. Why is it necessary to <u>memorize</u> the use of some verb forms?

Grammar Journal Entry 2: Verb Forms

Write a short entry in your grammar journal in response to the following questions.

1. Write about your most recent vacation from school or work. What did you do? Did you travel? If so, where? Overall, did you enjoy your vacation?

2. Underline all the verbs and verb phrases in the journal entry you have written above. Look at the verb forms you have used and check to see if the formation is correct. If you have questions about any of them, put a question mark above them and check them with your instructor, a classmate, or a tutor.

PART II

COMMON PROBLEMS, SELF-HELP STRATEGIES, AND GRAMMAR GUIDELINES

In Part II, you will study

- Seven common problems ESL writers encounter with verb forms
- Self-help strategies for controlling verb forms in your writing
- Grammar guidelines for verb formation

This section presents seven problems that ESL writers commonly encounter with verb forms. First, take the pretest to see what you already know about verb forms. In checking your answers, note that the pretest questions cover the same types of errors in the same order as the problems in this section. Then carefully study each problem and the examples that illustrate it, giving particular attention to those problems that correspond to the pretest questions you had difficulty with. Using the boxes to the left of each problem, check [✓] *yes, no,* or *don't know* to indicate to yourself which problems you should focus the most attention on in this unit and also when you write in English. Remember that becoming aware of the types of errors you most often make with verb forms will increase your chances of avoiding these errors in your writing.

Pretest: What Do You Already Know About Verb Forms?

Test your ability to recognize errors in verb form by finding and correcting the one verb-form error in each of the following sentences.

Answers on p. 291

1. Mario chosed to live in the dormitory rather than in an apartment.

2. The hikers had walk approximately 10 miles when they decided to set up camp.

3. Sometimes I totally confuse about English grammar.

4. The company did clearly deserved to obtain a large research grant to continue their innovative research.

5. An effective speaker tries look directly at his or her audience.

6. A grant writer hopes to presenting a convincing argument that clearly shows the value of a piece of research.

7. After finish work, Margarita likes to work out in the gym for at least an hour.

Seven Problems That ESL Writers Commonly Encounter with Verb Forms

yes	no	don't know	**PROBLEM 1**
☐	☐	☐	The main verb has been incorrectly formed.

                vf

Incorrect: My comment <u>hurted</u> my roommate's feelings.
Correct: My comment <u>hurt</u> my roommate's feelings.

                vf

Incorrect: She <u>flied</u> to Los Angeles for Chinese New Year.
Correct: She <u>flew</u> to Los Angeles for Chinese New Year.

Self-Help Strategy: If you find you do not know the forms of numerous irregular verbs in English, study lists of the most common irregular verb forms in an ESL grammar book. If, on the other hand, you just want to check the form of one particular verb, look the verb up in a dictionary. Most dictionaries list irregular verb forms under the definition of the base form of the verb.

yes   no   don't know   **PROBLEM 2**

☐   ☐   ☐   The past participle in a verb phrase has been incorrectly formed.

Note: The past participle is the last verb in a verb phrase.

vf

Incorrect: Ben did not want the teacher to know that he had not <u>study</u> for the quiz.
Correct: Ben did not want the teacher to know that he had not <u>studied</u> for the quiz.

vf

Incorrect: One of my colleagues was <u>fire</u> from his job because of a series of problems that could not be resolved.
Correct: One of my colleagues was <u>fired</u> from his job because of a series of problems that could not be resolved.

vf

Incorrect: The choir had already <u>sang</u> their last song before I got there.
Correct: The choir had already <u>sung</u> their last song before I got there.

Self-Help Strategy: Do not omit the *-ed* ending of a past participle when you write. The majority of verbs have past participles that end in *-ed*. This *-ed* ending is hard to hear in spoken English because it is not stressed and often is not a separate syllable.

yes   no   don't know   **PROBLEM 3**

☐   ☐   ☐   A main verb or an adjective has been incorrectly used instead of [*be* + past participle].

vf

Incorrect: I <u>confuse</u> about what you just said.
Correct: I <u>am confused</u> about what you just said.

vf

Incorrect: The store is <u>close</u> on Sundays.
Correct: The store is <u>closed</u> on Sundays.

vf

Incorrect: I <u>concerned</u> about getting a good grade on my chemistry midterm.
Correct: I <u>am concerned</u> about getting a good grade on my chemistry midterm.

vf

Incorrect: San Francisco <u>located</u> on the northern coast of California.
Correct: San Francisco <u>is located</u> on the northern coast of California.

Self-Help Strategy: Note that this type of construction is a form of the passive voice and is sometimes called the **stative passive.** Some stative passive constructions can be made active by changing the word order, while some cannot be made active.

- I am confused about what you just said. (stative passive)

  What you just said confuses me. (active voice)

- The store is closed on Sundays. (stative passive)
  (No active-voice construction is possible.)

- I am greatly concerned about getting a good grade on my chemistry midterm. (stative passive)

  Getting a good grade on my chemistry midterm concerns me greatly. (active voice)

- San Francisco is located on the northern coast of California. (stative passive)
  (No active-voice construction is possible.)

yes   no   don't know   **PROBLEM 4**

☐   ☐   ☐   An auxiliary verb and a main verb that do not go together have been used in a verb phrase.

vf

Incorrect: John felt he deserved his low grade because he <u>did not studied</u> enough.
Correct: John felt he deserved his low grade because he <u>did not study</u> enough.

vf

Incorrect: Tina was discouraged because she <u>was not progressed</u> very quickly.
Correct: Tina was discouraged because she <u>had not progressed </u>very quickly.
Correct: Tina was discouraged because she <u>was not progressing</u> very quickly.

vf

Incorrect: The employment office <u>does accepts</u> applications year round.
Correct: The employment office <u>accepts</u> applications year round.
Correct: The employment office <u>does accept</u> applications year round.
            (special emphatic use)

vf

Incorrect: The company <u>did received</u> my application for employment.
Correct: The company <u>received</u> my application for employment.
Correct: The company <u>did receive</u> my application for employment.
            (special emphatic use)

<table>
<tr><td>yes</td><td>no</td><td>don't know</td><td>**PROBLEM 5**</td></tr>
<tr><td>☐</td><td>☐</td><td>☐</td><td>The form of a verbal following a verb is incorrect.</td></tr>
</table>

Incorrect:	He decided *vf* <u>going</u> to the library tonight.
Incorrect:	He decided *vf* <u>go</u> to the library tonight.
Correct:	He decided <u>to go</u> to the library tonight.

Incorrect:	Matthew avoided *vf* <u>to discuss</u> that issue.
Incorrect:	Matthew avoided *vf* <u>discuss</u> that issue.
Correct:	Matthew avoided <u>discussing</u> that issue.

Incorrect:	The bystander helped me *vf* <u>pushed</u> my car to the side of the road.
Correct:	The bystander helped me <u>push</u> my car to the side of the road.

Self-Help Strategy: Keep in mind that the form of a verbal that follows a verb is not rule-based. Instead, you will need to memorize which forms of the verbal follow each verb on a case-by-case basis. You will find lists of the most common verbs and the verbals that follow them in the grammar guidelines in this unit.

<table>
<tr><td>yes</td><td>no</td><td>don't know</td><td>**PROBLEM 6**</td></tr>
<tr><td>☐</td><td>☐</td><td>☐</td><td>The infinitive has been incorrectly formed.</td></tr>
</table>

Incorrect:	It was hard for Naomi *vf* <u>to admitted</u> to her friends that she could not afford the high cost of college.
Correct:	It was hard for Naomi <u>to admit</u> to her friends that she could not afford the high cost of college.
Correct:	It was hard for Naomi <u>to have admitted</u> to her friends that she could not afford the high cost of college.

Incorrect:	Mike often forgets *vf* <u>to checks</u> his mail on Saturdays.
Correct:	Mike often forgets <u>to check</u> his mail on Saturdays.

Self-Help Strategy: Remember that infinitives consist of either [*to* + base form] with no *-ed* ending as in *to admit* or [*to* + *have* + past participle] as in *to have admitted* for the past form of the infinitive. Do not add an *-s* ending to an infinitive form.

yes   no   don't know   **PROBLEM 7**

☐   ☐   ☐   The base form of a verb has been used instead of a gerund or an infinitive.

                               vf
Incorrect: He says that <u>discuss</u> his problem would be too painful.
Correct: He says that <u>discussing</u> his problem would be too painful.
Correct: He says that <u>to discuss</u> his problem would be too painful.

           vf
Incorrect: <u>Study</u> all night does not always guarantee that a person will pass an exam.
Correct: <u>Studying</u> all night does not always guarantee that a person will pass an exam.

                 vf
Incorrect: It is easy <u>communicate</u> with him.
Correct: It is easy <u>to communicate</u> with him.

                     vf
Incorrect: He changed his way of <u>look</u> at them.
Correct: He changed his way of <u>looking</u> at them.

            vf
Incorrect: By <u>study</u>, we can learn these formulas.
Correct: By <u>studying</u>, we can learn these formulas.

Grammar Guidelines for Verb Forms

Rules for Verb-Phrase Formation

By learning the following rules for verb-phrase formation, you will increase your chances of avoiding verb-form errors when you write.

DO (do, does, did) + BASE FORM

Examples:
           I <u>do</u> not <u>know</u>.
           She <u>does</u> not <u>know</u>.
           She <u>did</u> not <u>know</u>.

HAVE (have, has, had) + PAST PARTICIPLE

Examples:

> I <u>have</u> already <u>left</u>.
> She <u>has left</u>.
> She <u>had</u> already <u>left</u> when I arrived.

BE (am, is, are, was, were, have been, has been, had been)
+ PRESENT PARTICIPLE

Examples:

> I <u>am sleeping</u>.
> She <u>is sleeping</u>.
> We <u>are sleeping</u>.
> She <u>was sleeping</u>.
> We <u>were sleeping</u>.
> We <u>have been sleeping</u> for an hour.
> She <u>has been sleeping</u>.
> She <u>had been sleeping</u> for an hour when I arrived.

Emphatic Use of Auxiliary Verbs in Verb Phrases

Sometimes, in order to make a sentence emphatic, an auxiliary verb is used in a verb phrase where it normally would not be needed. Although found in writing, emphatic sentences tend to be more common in speaking than in writing.

Examples:

> I wonder whether the employment office accepts applications year round? (in response) Yes, it <u>does accept</u> them year round.
>
> I discovered that the employment office <u>does accept</u> applications year round. (This sentence is emphatic because at some point previous to this statement, the writer did not know that the employment office accepted applications year round, and the writer is emphasizing that he or she <u>does know</u> now.)
>
> I do not think the company received your application for employment. (in response) Yes, the company <u>did receive</u> my application.

Guidelines for Choosing Verbals

In English, a verb can be followed by a verb form called a *verbal*. For example, in the sentence *He <u>decided to go</u> to the library*, the verb *decided* is followed by the verbal *to go*. A verbal following a verb may be an infinitive, a gerund, or occasionally a base form. There is no grammar rule, however, that will tell you which form of the verb will follow another verb. Some verbs are followed by a gerund, other verbs are followed by an infinitive, while still others can be followed by either. Thus, you will need to learn, on a case-by-case basis, which verbal should be used after a given verb.

Study these rules for adding verbals. Then study the lists of commonly used verbs and the verbals that follow them.

1. Some verbs must be followed by an infinitive.

_vf_
Incorrect: Paul agreed <u>going</u> to Sacramento tomorrow.

_vf_
Incorrect: Paul agreed <u>go</u> to Sacramento tomorrow.

Correct: Paul agreed <u>to go</u> to Sacramento tomorrow.

Note: Some verbs, such as <u>ask, choose, want</u>, or <u>expect</u>, can be followed by a noun or pronoun before the infinitive. In the following example, the noun _Isabel_ functions both as the direct object of _wants_ and as the subject of the infinitive.

Example: IBM wants _Isabel_ <u>to fly</u> to New York for an interview.

2. Some verbs must be followed by a gerund.

_vf_
Incorrect: Bill gave up <u>to study</u> for the exam.

_vf_
Incorrect: Bill gave up <u>study</u> for the exam.

Correct: Bill gave up <u>studying</u> for the exam.

3. Some verbs can be followed by either a gerund or an infinitive.

_vf_
Incorrect: Mia likes <u>sail</u> on Folsom Lake.

Correct: Mia likes <u>to sail</u> on Folsom Lake.

Correct: Mia likes <u>sailing</u> on Folsom Lake.

4. A small, commonly used group of verbs _(make, let, help, have)_ must be followed by a base form (the infinitive without _to_). These verbs always have a noun or pronoun between them.

_vf_
Incorrect: Please make the children <u>to go</u> upstairs.

_vf_
Incorrect: Please make the children <u>going</u> upstairs.

Correct: Please make the children <u>go</u> upstairs.

_vf_
Incorrect: Joseph let me <u>to carry</u> his suitcase.

Correct: Joseph let me <u>carry</u> his suitcase.

Note: The verb *help* may be followed by either a base form or an infinitive in current usage.

Example: Hien helped the elderly woman <u>cross</u> the street.

or

Hien helped the elderly woman <u>to cross</u> the street.

Commonly Used Verbs Followed by Infinitives, Gerunds, or Base Forms

VERBS FOLLOWED BY AN INFINITIVE

agree	deserve	need	seem
appear	endeavor	offer	tend
attempt	fail	plan	volunteer
consent	hesitate	prepare	wish
decide	hope	promise	
demand	intend	refuse	

Examples:

He hesitated <u>to call</u> me.

She promised <u>to write</u> soon.

We will attempt <u>to finish</u> the task by tomorrow.

Note: The following verbs **can** take a noun or pronoun before the infinitive.

ask	expect	need	promise
beg	intend	prepare	want
choose			

Examples:

I asked him <u>to go</u>.

I need you <u>to help</u>.

Note: Except in the passive voice, the following verbs **must** have a noun or pronoun before the infinitive.

advise	command	instruct	select
allow	convince	invite	teach
appoint	encourage	order	tell
authorize	forbid	permit	tempt
cause	force	remind	trust
challenge	hire	require	

Examples:

He challenged me <u>to participate</u> in the contest.

I will remind you <u>to get up</u> early.

She was advised <u>to leave</u>. (passive voice)

VERBS FOLLOWED BY A GERUND

admit	dislike	postpone	resent
avoid	enjoy	quit	resume
consider	finish	recall	risk
deny	imagine	recommend	suggest
discuss	miss	regret	

Examples:

I miss <u>seeing</u> you.
Barbara cannot risk <u>going</u>.

VERBS FOLLOWED BY EITHER A GERUND OR AN INFINITIVE

begin	like	remember	stop
continue	love	start	try
hate	prefer		

Examples:

I like <u>to hike</u>.
I like <u>hiking</u>.

VERBS FOLLOWED BY A BASE FORM

Note: Since these four verbs are very commonly used, memorize them along with the form of the verbal that must follow them.

make

have

let

help (This verb can also be followed by an infinitive.)

Examples:

I will let you <u>know</u>.
Could you help me <u>carry</u> these boxes?

Guidelines for Using Gerunds and Infinitives

The following guidelines for using gerunds and infinitives in a variety of situations (subject and object positions, as adjective complements, to show purpose) will help you in the majority of cases. However, all of the rules for using gerunds and infinitives are not fully treated in this text. If you want to know a particular rule in more detail, you may wish to consult an advanced ESL grammar book.

1. **Use an infinitive or gerund, not a base form, when a verbal functions as a subject or an object.**

    Examples:

    > To win (not *win*) the election is what he wants.
    > Reading (not *read*) is one of her hobbies.
    > We have benefited greatly from listening (not *listen*) to her lectures.

2. **Use a gerund, not a base form, as an object of a preposition.**

    Examples:

    > Pedro helped me by coming over to visit.
    > Martha talked me into helping her.

3. **Use an infinitive, not a base form, after many adjectives.**

    Examples:

    > I am sorry to see you so unhappy.
    > I am eager to get my B.S. degree.

    > (Some adjectives that are following by infinitives include *afraid, amazed, anxious, ashamed, careful, certain, content, delighted, determined, disappointed, eager, fortunate, glad, happy, hesitant, likely, pleased, proud, ready, reluctant, sad, shocked, sorry, surprised, upset.*)

4. **Use an infinitive, not a base form, to express a purpose.**

    Example:

    > He went to the teaching assistant's office to ask a question.
    > (The *to* is a shortened form of *in order to*.)

5. **Use a perfective infinitive [to + have + past participle] in cases in which the event or condition expressed by the infinitive is in the past.**

    Examples:

    > To have won the election fulfilled all his dreams. (He already won the election.)
    > I am sorry to have seen Mike so unhappy at the last meeting.
    > (I saw that Mike was unhappy at the last meeting, and I am sorry about this fact.)
    > It was thoughtful of you to have done that. (You already did something thoughtful, and the speaker is acknowledging it now.)

Improve Your Writing Style

Know How to Decide Whether to Use a Gerund or an Infinitive When Either Is Possible

Sometimes either a gerund or an infinitive verb form of a verb can be used. In some cases, the choice of one or the other will not change the meaning of the sentence, as in the examples below, which have equivalent meanings.

<u>Riding</u> a bicycle without a helmet is not advisable.
<u>To ride</u> a bicycle without a helmet is not advisable.

However, with certain verbs, the meaning can be affected by the choice of a gerund or an infinitive. The difference in meaning can be either very significant or minor, depending on the verb. With the verb *remember*, a significant difference in meaning results, depending on whether a gerund or infinitive follows it.

The customer remembered <u>to ask</u> about the store's return policy. (The meaning is that the customer remembered that she needed to ask and that she <u>did</u> ask about it.)
The customer remembered <u>asking</u> about the store's return policy. (The meaning is that the customer asked about the store's policy when she was in the store and at present the customer remembers having done so.)

The choice of a gerund or infinitive after the verb *stop* can also affect the meaning of a sentence. Note that an infinitive after the verb *stop* shows <u>the purpose</u> for stopping.

John stopped <u>smoking</u>. (The meaning is that he does not smoke anymore.)
John stopped <u>to smoke</u>. (The meaning is that the reason he stopped was to smoke a cigarette. It was his purpose to do so.)

The choice of a gerund or infinitive after the verb *prefer* can indicate whether or not an event is happening or has already happened or whether it is an event that could potentially happen.

David prefers <u>doing</u> research over teaching. (The meaning is that David *is currently doing* research and that he prefers it.)
David preferred <u>doing</u> research over teaching. (The meaning is that David <u>was doing research</u> at some time in the past and that he preferred it over teaching.)
David prefers <u>to do</u> research next semester. (The meaning is that David's preference for <u>the future</u> would be to do research rather than teach.)

> ### IMPROVE YOUR WRITING STYLE, cont.
>
> Generally speaking, gerunds are used when an action is already completed or in progress, while infinitives are more commonly used to show future time or the intention to do something. This fact is illustrated in the following newspaper headlines.
>
> Man to Sue Reckless Driver (The infinitive is a short form of *is going to sue* or *will sue* and shows a future intention.)
> Man Suing Reckless Driver (The gerund shows that the *suing* is already in progress, as in *is suing*.)

PART III

EXERCISES FOR PRACTICE

EXERCISE 1 (Do this exercise on your own. Then check your answers with a classmate.)

Directions: Examine each verb form in the following sentences to decide whether a sentence is correct (C) or incorrect (I). Then cross out each incorrect verb form and write the correct form above it.

comes
Example: __I__ Everyone should know where he or she are came from.

_____ **1.** I have live in the United States for two years.

_____ **2.** By exercise on a regular basis, an athlete can build a strong body, maintain muscle flexibility, and develop stamina.

_____ **3.** My instructor does not please with my lack of participation in class.

_____ **4.** I believe that I have a good chance of get into medical school.

_____ **5.** Scientists are currently try to find a cure for AIDS.

_____ **6.** Elizabeth has decided postpone taking the GRE until next summer.

_____ **7.** I did not expected you to call me so soon.

_____ **8.** Skip breakfast is not good for one's health.

_____ **9.** My best friend asked me to take a vacation and to came to California for a visit.

_____**10.** The government greatly concern about the high inflation rate.

EXERCISE 2 (Do this exercise on your own. Then check your answers with a classmate.)

Directions: Fill in each blank with the correct form (gerund, infinitive, or base form) of a verb of your choice. Use a verb form even if other parts of speech are possible. If necessary, add words in addition to the verb to complete the sentence grammatically.

Example: Jack plans <u>to go</u> the movies tonight after he finishes studying.

1. I avoided _____ my friend last night because I am angry at him.

2. Many students prefer _____ late at night rather than during the day.

3. By _____, we can work out our problems.

4. These boxes are too heavy for me. Could you help me _____ them?

5. The coach encouraged the team _____.

6. One of my goals is _____.

7. Many employees dislike _____.

8. _____ is one of my hobbies.

9. I consider myself good at _____.

10. A colleague let me _____ his notes when I was not able to attend a seminar last week.

11. It is easy _____ to the southern part of the country by train.

EXERCISE 3 (Do this exercise on your own. Then check your answers with a classmate.)

Directions: Fill in each blank space with the correct form of the verb in parentheses. Follow the model.

One of my very favorite activities is <u>to walk/walking</u> (walk) through the arboretum near my dormitory. After a stressful day of classes, I go there _____ (relax) and _____ (enjoy) the sight and smell of the trees. As I stroll along the path next to a small creek, I pass numerous tall trees including redwoods, oaks, and pines. I also pass a lake with ducks on it. The natural beauty and quiet of the area helps me _____ (relax). I enjoy _____ (walk) through the arboretum any time of the year, but on a hot summer day, it is especially refreshing. The shade from the trees keeps the area cool no matter how hot it is. I am always refreshed and ready _____ (continue) studying after a walk through the arboretum.

EXERCISE 4 (Do this exercise on your own. Then check your answers with a classmate.)

Directions: Use each of the following verbs in a sentence in the form [be + past participle]. Pay special attention to the form of the verb. Follow the model.

Example: **to be confused**
The voters <u>were confused</u> about several of the ballot propositions.

1. to be concerned

_____

2. to be located

_____

3. to be closed

_____

EXERCISE 5 (Do this exercise on your own.)

Directions: Practice using perfective infinitives by completing each blank with a perfective infinitive of the verb in parentheses. Follow the example.

Example: **When I was in Yosemite National Park I would like _to have seen_ (see) Nevada Falls, but it was too far to hike in one day.**

1. Mathias is thrilled _____ (complete) his bachelor's degree and _____ (find) a job immediately.

2. A bystander claimed _____ (witness) the accident that occurred last night.

3. The Smiths are happy _____ (move) to a new and bigger house.

4. _____ (swim) 10 miles was a great accomplishment for Janice.

5. I would love _____ (hear) John F. Kennedy speak when he was president of the United States.

EXERCISE 6 (Do this exercise on your own.)

Directions: The following is a job application cover letter. Correct the underlined verb-form errors. The first one has been done for you.

Dear Sir or Madam:

         to apply

  I am writing <u>for applying</u> for your internship position. I <u>am very interesting</u> in this position. I am a graduate student in the master's degree program in the Department of Biological and Agricultural Engineering. This department has a good reputation for its high level of research and the high quality of its students. I <u>am major</u> in food engineering, and my research project deals with nuclear magnetic resonance imaging (NMRI) <u>for study</u> bruises in apples. I <u>have take</u> NMRI classes, read many papers about NMRI, and <u>do</u> a lot of experiments using this technique. I greatly hope <u>expand</u> my practical experience in this area by <u>get</u> the internship with your company.

  I <u>have include</u> my resume for your review. I <u>do hope</u> <u>hearing</u> from you soon.

Sincerely,

Cheryl Young

Cheryl Young

EXERCISE 7 (Do this exercise on your own. Then check your answers with a classmate.)

Directions: The following paragraph, written by a student, has been edited so that the only errors are with verb forms. Test your knowledge of verb forms by finding and correcting the verb-form errors. Cross out each incorrect form and write the correct form above it. The first one has been done for you.

It takes a great deal of courage for a person to leave his or her family

        start

and ~~starts~~ life all over again in another country. The person must not only face many changes alone but also separate from friends and rely on letters as a means of share thoughts. The new environment and the new setting make even the bravest individual feels scared as he or she encounters many sudden changes and undergoes many kinds of struggles in a short period of time. Despite these difficulties, go abroad as an immigrant has many benefits. To go abroad gives a person the chance to see the world, to face new challenges, to make new friends, and gaining more knowledge about people and places. Before I came to the United States, I had many expectations. I thought that life in this country would be similar to life in my country. However, after be here for five months, I have came to the conclusion that life in the United States is entirely different from what I had expect.

EXERCISE 8 (Do this exercise on your own.)

Directions: Choose a short article in a newspaper or magazine. After reading the article, underline all the verbs (for example, main verbs, verb phrases, gerunds, infinitives) in two paragraphs. Can you understand why the different verb forms are used? If you are unsure of any of them, ask a classmate, a tutor, or your instructor.

PART IV

WRITING TOPICS

Select one or more of the following topics for writing and follow the steps in Appendix A.

Topic A: Discuss one of your goals, either short term or long term. Explain what the goal is and why you want to accomplish it.

Topic B: Explain how to do something that you enjoy doing. First, introduce the activity. Then explain the process of how to do it, step by step.

Topic C: Both the pace of life and how people view time and punctuality can vary from culture to culture. Compare the pace of life and people's attention to time in your culture of origin and American culture in order to determine to what extent they are similar or different. Then say which pace of life you are most comfortable with and why.

PART V

CNN VIDEO ACTIVITY AND WRITING TOPIC

Tai Chi—A Boon for the Elderly

Useful Vocabulary: martial art   meditation   endurance   frailty   fluidity   decline

Before You Watch

This video segment reports on an ongoing study on how seniors can benefit from practicing Tai Chi. Before watching the video, answer the following questions.

Tai Chi improves quality of life for the aging.

- Have you ever had any experience with Tai Chi or some other martial art? Explain.
- What are the benefits associated with doing any of the martial arts?

While You Watch

- Find out how the seniors in the video feel about learning Tai Chi.
- Find out what health benefits are reported for seniors participating in the study.

After You Watch

  I. Write a personal reaction.

  Write a personal reaction of three to five sentences to what you saw in the video. What interested you most? If you have not already studied Tai Chi, would you now be interested in it? Why?

II. Share your reactions.

  Answer the following questions either orally or in writing. Compare your answers with those of a classmate.

  1. How did the participants' balance and agility improve through practicing Tai Chi? Give examples.

  2. Did the people shown in this video fit the stereotypes you associate with the elderly?

  3. Can society as a whole benefit from the confidence, endurance, and control that can be gained from practicing Tai Chi?

WRITING TOPIC

Although the focus of this video is Tai Chi and its benefits for the elderly, most individuals would agree that physical activity is beneficial at any age. Discuss the mental and physical rewards of being active in sports or doing any form of physical activity.

Modals

Goals

- To learn the importance of mastering modals in writing
- To review three problems ESL writers commonly encounter with modals
- To learn to form and use modals correctly
- To develop confidence in using modals correctly through practice with exercises and writing assignments

Students at the University of California, Davis, study in Shields Library. Photo courtesy of Public Communications.

Think about and discuss the following question:
What are three important resources
your campus library offers
writing students?

WHAT YOU NEED TO KNOW ABOUT MODAL ERRORS

In Part I, you will learn

- The definition of a modal error
- The importance of using modals correctly in writing
- Suggestions for mastering modals in writing

Definition of the Error (modal*)

Modals are auxiliaries—such as *may, might, should, must, can,* and *could*—that add a specific meaning to a verb. In the sentences below, notice how the modal adds a specific meaning to the verb *exercise.*

I <u>exercise</u> at the gym regularly. (a fact)
   a. I <u>might exercise</u> at the gym tonight. (a possibility)
   b. I <u>should</u> exercise at the gym more often. (advice to myself)
   c. I <u>could have exercised</u> at the gym yesterday. (a past opportunity that I did not take advantage of)

A modal error **(modal)** is an error that involves the wrong choice of a modal, the wrong form of any part of a modal verb phrase, or the wrong time reference of a modal verb phrase. A modal verb phrase consists of a modal and all the verbs that appear with it, including the main verb. The modal verb phrase is underlined in the example below.

modal verb phrase
Example: I <u>should have exercised</u> at the gym last night.

Importance of Mastering Modals in Writing

Errors with modals involve verbs and are thus global (more serious) errors that can considerably affect a reader's ability to understand a text. Writers who are unable to use modals correctly in their writing will have limited ability to show the difference between facts, inferences, and possibilities in English—distinctions frequently made in academic and professional writing.

The following examples illustrate how modals can be used to show inferences and possibilities:

Example 1:   Someone I know has lived in the dorm for four years. (a fact) Because most students stay in the dorm for only one or two years, the person I know <u>must like</u> the dorm very much. (a logical inference based on the above fact)

*****Modal** = grading symbol for an error with a modal.

Example 2:   My roommate did not eat much at dinner last night. (a fact)
She <u>might be trying</u> to lose weight. or She <u>might not have been</u> very hungry. (logical inferences marked as possibilities by the modal *might*)

Another important function of modals is that they serve to <u>qualify</u> statements or adjust their degree of certainty. Compare the following three statements and notice how the underlined modal serves to lessen the degree of certainty of the statement.

Examples: This method <u>will</u> simplify the analysis of the data. (statement of fact)
This method <u>should</u> simplify the analysis of the data. (probability)
This method <u>may</u> simplify the analysis of the data. (possibility)

Thus, modals have specific and important functions in English, and being able to use them correctly increases a writer's ability to express his or her ideas clearly and precisely.

Suggestions for Mastering Modals in Writing

- Study the functions and forms of the different modals using the chart in this unit. Learn and understand what meaning each modal adds to the verb it accompanies. Learn the time reference of each form also.

- Be aware that some modals, like *must* or *can* and *could,* have more than one meaning depending on the context in which they are used. For example, the modal *must* can indicate a <u>requirement</u> as in the sentence *Passengers must fasten their seat belts during takeoff and landing.* Or it can indicate a <u>logical assumption</u> as in the sentence *Pat was not at an important meeting today. She must have forgotten.* You will find all of the different meanings for modals listed on the chart in this unit.

- Become aware of the use of modals in what you read. As you read books, articles, and other material, notice how writers use modals to add meaning to verbs in English.

Test Your Understanding of Modals

Write answers to the following questions. Share your answers with another student.

1. What are some examples of modals?

2. What makes modals important in academic and professional writing? What kinds of meaning can modals add to a sentence?

Grammar Journal Entry 3: Modals

Write a short entry in your grammar journal in response to the following questions.

1. What is something you feel you should have done recently but did not? Why weren't you able to do it?

2. Write two sentences with modals and underline the modal verb phrase. Explain what meaning the modal gives to the verb.

PART II

COMMON PROBLEMS, SELF-HELP STRATEGIES, AND GRAMMAR GUIDELINES

In Part II, you will study

- Three problems ESL writers commonly encounter with modals
- Self-help strategies for controlling modals in your writing
- Grammar guidelines for modals

This section presents three problems that ESL writers commonly encounter with modals. First, take the pretest to see what you already know about modals. In checking your answers, note that the pretest questions cover the same types of errors in the same order as the problems in this section. Then carefully study each problem and the examples that illustrate it, giving particular attention to those problems that correspond to the pretest questions you had difficulty with. Using the boxes to the left of each problem, check [✓] *yes, no,* or *don't know* to indicate to yourself which problems you should focus the most attention on in this unit and also when you write in English. Remember that becoming aware of the types of errors you most often make with modals will increase your chances of avoiding these errors in your writing.

Pretest: What Do You Already Know About Modals?

Test your ability to recognize errors with modals by finding and correcting the one modal error in each of the following sentences.

Answers on p. 291

1. I have not seen my next door neighbor for a week. She can be out of town.

2. In order to be successful, a person must has the determination to achieve his or her goals.

3. I cannot find my favorite pen. I must leave it at home.

Three Problems ESL Writers Commonly Encounter with Modals

yes   no   don't know   **PROBLEM 1**

☐   ☐   ☐   The wrong modal has been chosen to express the writer's intended meaning.

             modal

Incorrect: I <u>must have gone</u> to see my instructor during office hours, but I did not have time.

Correct: I <u>should have gone</u> to see my instructor during office hours, but I did not have time.

Note: *Should have gone* is correct because it shows <u>advisability after the fact</u>. *Must have gone* is incorrect because it shows that an <u>assumption</u> has been made <u>about the past</u>.

Self-Help Strategy: Review the chart in this section to learn the different meanings that modals can add to a sentence. Always keep in mind that the same modal can have more than one meaning, depending on the context in which it is used.

yes   no   don't know   **PROBLEM 2**

☐   ☐   ☐   The modal verb phrase has been incorrectly formed.

Note: Your instructor may mark this kind of modal error **modal (vf)** to indicate that the error is a modal <u>verb-form</u> error.

             modal (vf)

Incorrect: She <u>might studies</u> at the library tonight.

             modal (vf)

Incorrect: She <u>might to study</u> at the library tonight.

Correct: She <u>might study</u> at the library tonight.

             modal (vf)

Incorrect: I <u>could had submitted</u> the proposal, but I wanted to do some additional editing first.

Correct: I <u>could have submitted</u> the proposal, but I wanted to do some additional editing first.

Self-Help Strategy: Remember that you do not add an *-s* to a third person singular verb following a present modal (illustrated in the first example above and in the sentence *John may <u>give</u>* [not *gives*] *a short presentation at the meeting*). Also, carefully check the formation of past modals. These past modals should be in the format [modal + <u>have</u> + past participle] (illustrated in the second example above and in the sentence *John may <u>have</u>* [not *had*] *given a short presentation at the meeting*).

yes	no	don't know	**PROBLEM 3**
☐	☐	☐	The time reference of the modal verb phrase is incorrect.

Note: Your instructor may mark this kind of modal error **modal (vt)** to indicate that the error is a modal <u>verb-tense</u> error.

modal (vt)

Incorrect: My muscles are sore. I <u>should not exercise</u> so hard yesterday.

Correct: My muscles are sore. I <u>should not have exercised</u> so hard yesterday.

Grammar Guidelines for Forming and Using Modal Verb Phrases

Formation of Modal Verb Phrases

Present time

1. **modal + base form (infinitive without *to*)**

   Example:

   > What does he usually do for exercise?
   > He <u>might exercise</u> at the gym, but I am not sure that he definitely does.
   > (Time = present habitual)

2. **modal + be + present participle (*-ing* form)**

   Example:

   > What is he doing right now?
   > He <u>might be exercising</u> at the gym.
   > (Time = right now)

Future time

1. modal + base form (infinitive without *to*)

Example:

What is she going to do tomorrow night?
She <u>might exercise</u> at the gym.
(Time = future)

Past time

1. modal + have + past participle

Example:

What did he do last night?
He <u>might have exercised</u> at the gym.
(Time = past)

2. modal + have + been + present participle

Example:

What was he doing when you called last night?
He <u>might have been exercising</u> at the gym.
(Time = past with an emphasis on duration)

Note: The modals *ought to* and *have to* in the present and in the past have a preposition *to* in the modal verb phrase as illustrated below. The other modals do not have this preposition.

Examples:

We <u>ought to study</u> before the test. (present time)
We <u>have to study</u> before the test. (present time)
We <u>ought to have studied</u> more than we did. (past time)
We <u>had to study</u> hard before the test. (past time)

vs.

We <u>should study</u> before the test.
We <u>should have studied</u> hard before the test.

Meaning and Use of Modals

How to use the chart that follows:

A chart of the modals is provided on the following pages. In the left-hand column, you will find each modal listed. In the second column, you will see the functions most commonly expressed by each modal. These are the meanings that each modal can add to a verb. Note that some modals have more than one function. For example, *must* expresses necessity, as in the sentence *I must leave immediately,* or probability/assumption, as in the sentence *You have been working long hours. You must be busy.*

In the third column, you will find example sentences illustrating the functions of each modal in the present/future time frame. In the fourth column, you will find example sentences for each modal used in the past time frame. Study the third and fourth columns not only to understand what the modals mean but also to learn how to form each modal in the present and past. Note, for example, that the past of *can* is *could* (as in *I could do ten push-ups five years ago, but now I cannot*) while the past of *could* (meaning possibility) is *could have* + past participle (as in *Mary could have been at the party, although I didn't see her*). In particular, note that there are two different past forms for the modal *must,* each of which expresses a different meaning. For example, the past of the sentence *I must go* is *I had to go.* Here the modal *must* expresses necessity. On the other hand, the past of the sentence *You must be busy* is *You must have been busy.* Here, in contrast, the modal *must* implies probability/assumption.

FUNCTIONS AND FORMS OF MODALS

Modal	Function	Form in Present/Future	Form in Past
Can	To show ability	I can run 10 miles.	I could run 10 miles when I was in high school.
	To suggest a possibility or to give an option	Students can pre-enroll in classes or sign up at in-person registration.	
	To ask for or to give permission	Can I call you? You can leave when you have finished your exam.	
	To show impossibility	It cannot be Jim standing over there. He went away for the weekend.	
Could	To show past ability		I could run 10 miles when I was in high school.
	To ask a polite question	Could I call you?	

FUNCTIONS AND FORMS OF MODALS, cont.

Modal	Function	Form in Present/Future	Form in Past
Could (cont.)	To show possibility	Why isn't Maria here? She <u>could be</u> busy.	Why wasn't Maria at the party last night? She <u>could have been</u> busy.
	To show impossibility	He <u>could not be</u> here at the party. He is out of town.	He <u>could not have been</u> at the party last night. He was out of town.
	To suggest a possibility or to give an option	You <u>could try</u> going to Dr. Davidson to see if she can help you with your back problem.	
	To show a past opportunity that was not realized		I <u>could have asked</u> for help on the math problem set, but I wanted to do it myself.
May	To ask for or to give permission (formal)	<u>May</u> I <u>call</u> you? You <u>may leave</u> when you have finished your exam.	
	To show possibility	The instructor <u>may come</u> to class late today.	The instructor <u>may have come</u> to class late yesterday.
Might	To show possibility	The instructor <u>might come</u> to class late today.	The instructor <u>might have come</u> to class late yesterday.
Should	To show advisability	You <u>should try</u> that new restaurant downtown.	
	To show advisability after the fact		We <u>should have tried</u> that new restaurant downtown. (But we did not.) You <u>should not have said</u> that to Tom. (But you did.)

FUNCTIONS AND FORMS OF MODALS, cont.

Modal	Function	Form in Present/Future	Form in Past
Should (cont.)	To show obligation	I <u>should renew</u> my driver's license. It expires next month.	
	To show an obligation that was not carried out		I <u>should have renewed</u> my driver's license. (But I forgot to do so.)
	To show expectation	You <u>should receive</u> my letter in two days.	
	To show an expectation that was not realized		You <u>should have received</u> my letter two days ago. (But you did not.)
Ought to	To show advisability	Everyone <u>ought to</u> exercise regularly.	
	To show advisability after the fact		Francis <u>ought to have exercised</u> before his backpacking trip. (But he did not.)
	To show obligation	I <u>ought to register</u> to vote if I want to vote in the next election.	
	To show an obligation that was not carried out		I <u>ought to have registered</u> to vote by October 5. (But I did not register.)
	To show expectation	You <u>ought to receive</u> my letter in two days.	
	To show an expectation that was not realized		You <u>ought to have received</u> my letter two days ago. (But you did not.)
Had better	To show advisability	We <u>had better leave</u>. It is getting late.	

FUNCTIONS AND FORMS OF MODALS, cont.

Modal	Function	Form in Present/Future	Form in Past
Must	To show probability or to make a logical assumption	Janice <u>must be</u> out this evening. She does not answer her telephone.	Janice <u>must have been</u> out last night. She did not answer her telephone.
	To show necessity	I <u>must call</u> my parents tonight. I have not talked with them in a long time.	I was late for the meeting because I <u>had to call</u> my parents last night.
	To show prohibition	You <u>must not smoke</u> in the classroom at any time.	
Have to	To show necessity	Mike <u>has to make up</u> the physics lab he missed.	Mike <u>had to make up</u> the physics lab he missed.
	To show lack of necessity	I am glad that I <u>do not have to cook</u> tonight.	I <u>did not have to cook</u> last night.
Will	To indicate future time	We <u>will leave</u> for the airport at 7:00 AM tomorrow.	
	To make a promise or to show willingness	The federal government <u>will provide</u> assistance to the hurricane victims.	
	To state a general truth	The new car they have developed <u>will run</u> on either gasoline or ethanol. (**Note:** time = present)	
	To ask a polite question	Mike, <u>will</u> you <u>help</u> me with these heavy boxes? I cannot lift them myself. (**Note:** time = right now)	
Would	To ask a polite question	<u>Would</u> you please <u>call</u> me later tonight?	
	To indicate a repeated action in the past		When I lived in Los Angeles, I <u>would go</u> to the beach every weekend.

FUNCTIONS AND FORMS OF MODALS, cont.

Modal	Function	Form in Present/Future	Form in Past
Would (cont.)	To indicate future time in a sentence that is in the past		Mark promised that he <u>would help</u> me with my math homework.
Would rather	To show a preference	I <u>would rather go</u> to summer school than graduate late.	
Would like	To express a desire	I <u>would like to go</u> to medical school.	
	To express a desire that was not realized		I <u>would have liked</u> to have gone (OR to go) to medical school. (But I did not.)

Improve Your Writing Style

Use Modals to Adjust the Degree of Certainty or Degree of Obligation in Statements

Modals are frequently used to adjust the degree of certainty of a statement or the degree of obligation shown by an assertion. These functions are important in academic and professional writing because they allow the writer to be precise and accurate in making assertions. Note how the degree of certainty or obligation changes in the lists below.

Degree of Certainty	Modal	Example
Assertion of fact	none	Aspirin <u>reduces</u> pain.
Assertion showing capability	can	Aspirin <u>can reduce</u> pain.
Prediction showing certainty	will	Aspirin <u>will reduce</u> the pain.
Prediction showing probability	should	Aspirin <u>should reduce</u> the pain.
Prediction showing possibility	may	Aspirin <u>may reduce</u> the pain.
Prediction showing possibility	might	Aspirin <u>might reduce</u> the pain.
Prediction showing possibility	could	Aspirin <u>could reduce</u> the pain.

Degree of Obligation	Modal	Example
Assertion of fact	none	Students <u>use</u> the library.
Requirement	must	Students <u>must use</u> the library for this project.
Strong recommendation/advice	should	Students <u>should use</u> the library as much as possible.
Opportunity or option	can	Students <u>can use</u> the library if they wish.
Suggestion	could	Mark <u>could use</u> the library if he needed to.
Suggestion	might	Mark <u>might use</u> the library if he needs to.

PART III

EXERCISES FOR PRACTICE

EXERCISE 1 (Do this exercise on your own. Then check your answers with a classmate.)

Directions: To practice distinguishing between the present and past forms of modals, change the following sentences from present to past time. For some of the sentences, you will also need to change time words and phrases. Refer to the modals chart in this unit to ensure that you have chosen the correct past forms.

> **Example:** I do not see Monica at the reception, but she might arrive later.
> **Past:** *I did not see Monica at the reception, but she might have arrived later.*

1. Bob might be joking about his decision to quit school.

Past: _____

2. Lian could be finished by 3:00 PM this afternoon.

Past: _____

3. Max, who is on the track team, can run a mile in 4 minutes, 30 seconds.

Past: When he was on the track team, Max _____

4. Jill must be tired after working 10 hours today.

Past: _____

5. Because Lydia needs to get a good grade on her chemistry midterm, she must study this evening.

Past: _____

6. I should exercise regularly to get into shape for the backpacking trip.

Past: _____

7. You ought to send your roommate's parents a thank-you note when you get home.

Past: _____

8. My supervisor must be sick since she did not attend the office barbecue this afternoon.

Past: _____

9. Mary may not have time to call her parents tonight.

Past: _____

10. My roommate has to do the shopping this week.

Past: _____

EXERCISE 2 (Do this exercise on your own or with a classmate.)

Directions: Read the following sentences. Determine and write down what the meaning or function of the modal is in each sentence. Write the time frame of the statement also.

Example: I really **should** exercise more often. *(advisability; present or future)*

1. In most states, drivers **must** have liability insurance.

2. Analyzing your data in a different way **may** give you better results.

3. You **must** be tired after working at the office for 10 straight hours.

4. My supervisor is looking for someone who **can** translate a document from Japanese to English.

5. The study **could** have a considerable impact on the field of molecular biology.

6. When I was young, I **could** speak French, but I have forgotten most of it.

7. What a beautiful new sports car! It **must have** cost a lot of money.

8. I **should not have** spent so much time on the proposal because now I am behind on other important tasks.

9. Both of these factors **may** be important in explaining the recurrence of the disease.

10. Students **can** register either in person or over the phone.

EXERCISE 3 (Do this exercise on your own. Then check your answers with a classmate.)

Directions: Use a modal to express the underlined part of each of the following ideas. Note that by using a modal, you can often make your writing less wordy.

> **Example:**   I didn't see Bob at the library. <u>It's possible that I missed him.</u>
> *I might have missed him.*

1. I didn't see Judy at the library after 10 PM. <u>She probably left early.</u>

2. The sky is getting cloudy. <u>There is a chance of rain.</u>

3. Elena didn't come to class yesterday. <u>It was necessary for her to go to Sacramento.</u>

4. Linda received a gift from her aunt. <u>It is advisable for her to send a thank you note.</u>

5. We don't have much work to do today. <u>It is possible that our supervisor will allow us to leave early.</u>

6. My brother-in-law just bought a nice house in an expensive section of town. <u>I assume the house cost a lot of money.</u>

7. José was available to help over the weekend. <u>In retrospect, I realize that it would have been a good idea to have asked him to help.</u>

8. When I was young, <u>I knew how to play the piano</u>, but I have forgotten it since I have not played in many years.

9. <u>My housemate had time to wash the dishes last night</u>, but she went out instead.

10. <u>One option that we have is to camp out</u> on our way to the Grand Canyon.

EXERCISE 4 (Do this exercise on your own. Then check your answers with a classmate.)

Directions: Some of the following sentences contain errors in the use of modals. First, decide if a sentence is correct (C) or incorrect (I). If it is incorrect, cross out the incorrect form and write the correction above. Be able to explain to a classmate the meaning that the modal gives to the verb.

> *have (advisability)*
> **Example:**   <u> *I* </u>   I should not ~~had~~ told you about my problem because now you are worried.

_____ 1. My brother must had forgotten to call me.

_____ 2. My brother could have call me while I was at the library.

_____ 3. My brother may calls late tonight.

_____ 4. I did not have time to stop at the store because I must have stayed late at the office to finish my work.

_____ 5. Susan felt she could have worked out longer in the gym, but her coach advised her not to do so.

_____ **6.** I got a speeding ticket! I should not have be driving over the speed limit on the freeway.

_____ **7.** My roommate is in Hawaii applying for a job. It should be warm there even though it is winter here.

_____ **8.** Most people now realize that we must take action soon to save the environment.

EXERCISE 5 (Do this exercise with a classmate.)

Directions: **Underline each modal or modal verb phrase in the following paragraph. Then discuss with a classmate the meaning each modal gives to the sentence that contains it. The first two errors have been done for you.**

Grand Canyon National Park in Arizona is a paradise for nature lovers and outdoor enthusiasts. Visitors <u>will be</u> *shows future tense* awed by the fabulous view of the canyon—its vast depth and beautifully colored walls. The National Park Headquarters and Visitor Center is at the South Rim where visitors <u>can pick up</u> *suggests an option* information about the park. Visitors who have only a little time to spend can view the canyon from either the North Rim or the South Rim. People who have more time may want to see more of the Grand Canyon than just the North or South Rim. Such visitors can drive along parts of the rim or hike down into the canyon on various trails. In fact, hikers can walk or ride a mule all the way to the bottom of the canyon to the Colorado River. However, hikers must be sure to drink plenty of water to avoid dehydration, as the weather can be extremely hot and dry. At the bottom, hikers can stay at either Phantom Ranch, which consists of cabins or dormitories, or at an adjacent campground. Perhaps the best way to see the canyon, however, is to float down the Colorado River either on a rubber raft or in a wooden dory.

Seeing the canyon from this perspective is spectacular, but people who are afraid of white water should not take this trip since some of the Colorado River rapids are among the biggest in the world. For most visitors, a trip to the Grand Canyon should be a truly unforgettable experience.

EXERCISE 6 (Do this exercise on your own. Then check your answers with a classmate.)

Directions: **Fill in each blank with the correct modal verb phrase. The main verb and modal meaning are indicated in parentheses. The first blank has been filled in as an example.**

Writing a term paper last semester was very challenging for me. At the beginning of the term, I was looking forward to doing the research and writing the paper. But, unfortunately, I waited longer than I *should have waited* (wait/**advisability**) to get started. I _____ (start/**opportunity**) earlier, but for some reason I just kept waiting. I found myself working right up until the last minute. I know I _____ (proofread/**advisability**) the paper more carefully. I also _____ (add/**opportunity**) some illustrations if I had had more time. Because I started so late, I not only had to submit a less than satisfactory paper, but I also _____ (stay up/**necessity**) all night to finish it.

EXERCISE 7 (Do this exercise on your own.)

Directions: **Choose a short article in a newspaper or a magazine. Read the article, checking to see whether any modals have been used. If so, underline them and identify the meaning they give to the sentence.**

PART IV

WRITING TOPICS

Select one or more of the following topics for writing and follow the steps in Appendix A.

Topic A: You have been asked to give some advice to people who would like to visit your country of origin for the first time for a 2-week period. What suggestions do you have for them? For example, what do you think they might like to see and do? Should they go to one city or several? What should they take with them and/or how should they prepare for the trip?

Topic B: Write about a situation that you feel you did not handle as well as you could have. First, explain the situation. Then discuss what you think you could have done differently.

Topic C: Think about your cooking and eating habits. Who in your household currently does the cooking? What kinds of food do you generally eat? Do you consider your current eating habits healthful? Explain your answer.

PART V

CNN VIDEO ACTIVITY AND WRITING TOPIC
Young Man Fights Disability

Useful Vocabulary: to be disabled   to have a disability   to crawl   recovery   to be "hooked on" something   wishful thinking

Before You Watch

This video segment tells the story of Chris Ross, a young man who has lost the ability to walk because of an accident. Discuss the following questions with your classmates.

* Have you ever known anyone with a disability?
* How do you think having a disability affects a person both positively and negatively? How would it change your life if you had a disability?

While You Watch

* Think of a question you would ask Ross if you could talk to him.
* Consider to what extent you think Ross leads a full and satisfying life.

© CNN

Looking at the ocean "brings peace to a restless man."

After You Watch

I. **Write a personal reaction.**

Write a personal reaction of three to five sentences to what you saw in the video. What interested or surprised you about Chris Ross's story? What comments do you have?

II. **Share your reactions.**

Answer the following questions either orally or in writing. Compare your answers with those of a classmate.

1. What challenges does a person with a physical disability such as Ross's have to face? What does Ross mean when he says, "You have to crawl before you walk."?

2. Is Ross an optimistic or pessimistic person? What is his attitude toward his disability? What would your attitude be if you were Ross?

3. Do you consider Ross a successful person? Explain.

WRITING TOPIC

Many would view Chris Ross as a successful person. What are some of the characteristics of successful people? To what extent does Chris Ross meet these criteria despite his current physical disability?

Goals

- To learn the importance of mastering conditional sentences
- To review five problems ESL writers commonly encounter with conditional sentences
- To learn to form and use the conditional correctly
- To develop confidence in writing conditional sentences through practice with exercises and writing assignments

Conditional Sentences

Students at the University of California, San Diego, take notes during a lecture.
Photo courtesy of University Communications.

Think about and discuss the following question:
Why do instructors place so much importance on consistent class attendance?

PART I

WHAT YOU NEED TO KNOW ABOUT ERRORS WITH CONDITIONAL SENTENCES

In Part I, you will learn

- The definition of an error in a conditional sentence
- The importance of using the conditional correctly in writing
- Suggestions for mastering conditional sentences in writing

Definition of the Error (cond*)

An error with a conditional sentence **(cond)** occurs when a conditional sentence has been incorrectly formed or has not been used when it is needed. A conditional sentence usually consists of an *if* clause that states a condition and a result clause that shows the effect of that condition. An example of a conditional sentence is *If our school had more money for equipment* (the condition), *we would have a modern language laboratory* (the result).

Conditional sentences can express two types of conditions: factual (sometimes called *real*) and hypothetical (sometimes called *unreal*).

---

1. A factual conditional sentence is used to express a real situation.
   - **In the present:**

     If he goes to a movie (condition), he relaxes (result).
   - **In the future:**

     If he goes to a movie tonight (condition), he will relax (result).
2. A hypothetical conditional sentence is used to express an unreal or imagined situation.
   - **In the present or future:**

     If she were here (condition [which means she is not here]), we could leave (result).

     If he went to a movie (condition [which means he has not gone]), he would relax (result).
   - **In the past:**

     If he had gone to a movie (condition [which means he did not go]), he would have relaxed (result).

*****cond** = grading symbol for an error with a conditional sentence.

Importance of Mastering Conditional Sentences in Writing

Errors with conditional sentences are global and affect the meaning of individual sentences, parts of a paragraph, and whole paragraphs. The conditional has many important uses in formal writing.

For example, writers use conditional sentences to show cause-effect relationships (*If enrollment goes up* [condition], *classes become overcrowded* [result]); to speculate about a past event (*If I had studied the right chapters* [condition], *I would have at least received a B on my quiz* [result]); or to show a future possibility (*If the teacher lets class out early* [condition], *my friend and I will go for coffee* [result]). To be able to show such relationships, ESL writers need to master conditional sentences.

Suggestions for Mastering Conditional Sentences in Writing

- Learn the correct formation of the verb phrase for both the *if* clause (the condition) and the *result* clause of a conditional sentence.
- Check **both** clauses when revising to make sure that the verb phrase is correct in each.
- Be aware that native speakers often do not follow the rules for forming the conditional when they are speaking.

  Examples:

  The hurricane <u>could of</u> (*for* <u>could have</u>) done major damage if it had lasted longer.

  James would not have taken French if the university <u>did not require</u> (*for* <u>had not required</u>) it.

- Notice conditional sentences when you read; try to understand what they mean from the context.
- Memorize a set of hypothetical conditional sentences to use as a guide to form hypothetical conditional sentences correctly in your own writing. (See pages 75-76 in this unit for a guide.)
- Remember that, in a conditional sentence, a past verb form does not always mean past time.

  Example:

  If people used less water, we could conserve this precious resource. (The time expressed in this conditional sentence is the present.)

Test Your Understanding of Conditional Sentences

Write answers to the following questions. Share your answers with another student.

1. Write a sample conditional sentence and identify the condition clause and the result clause.

2. What are the two types of conditional sentences?

Grammar Journal Entry 4: Conditional Sentences

Respond to the following in your grammar journal.

1. If you were given the chance to change your life today, what would you do?

2. Write two example conditional sentences: one for the present/future hypothetical and the other for the past hypothetical. Check them with your instructor. Once you know they are correct, memorize them to use as keys for forming the hypothetical conditional when you are writing.

PART II

COMMON PROBLEMS, SELF-HELP STRATEGIES, AND GRAMMAR GUIDELINES

In Part II, you will study:

- Five problems ESL writers commonly encounter with conditional sentences
- Self-help strategies for controlling conditional sentences in your writing
- Grammar guidelines for conditional sentences

This section presents five problems that ESL writers commonly encounter with conditional sentences. First, take the pretest to see what you already know about conditional sentences. In checking your answers, note that the pretest questions cover the same types of errors in the same order as the problems in this section. Then carefully study each problem and the examples that illustrate it, giving particular attention to the problems that correspond to the pretest questions you had difficulty with. Using the boxes to the left of each problem, check [✓] *yes, no,* or *don't know* to indicate to yourself which problems you should focus the most attention on in this unit and also when you write conditional sentences in English.

Remember that becoming aware of the types of errors you most often make with conditional sentences will increase your chances of avoiding these errors in your writing.

Pretest: What Do You Already Know About Conditional Sentences?

Test your ability to recognize errors with conditional sentences by finding and correcting the one conditional error in each of the following sentences.

Answers on p. 291

1. If the weather improves, I would play tennis after finishing my homework.
2. The travel agent would never have fix the problem if we had not brought it to her attention.
3. Especially some good movies are playing at the foreign film theater, I would like to see one.
4. If I was you, I would not believe what she says because she likes to gossip.
5. If the ATM had not been working, Sheila would have been without any money when she arrived in San Diego. Also, she will feel very hungry after a few days of not eating very much.

Five Problems ESL Writers Commonly Encounter with Conditional Sentences

yes	no	don't know	**PROBLEM 1**
☐	☐	☐	The wrong verb or verb phrase has been used in one of the clauses of a conditional sentence.

	cond	*cond*
Incorrect:	If I <u>study</u> hard for my anthropology midterm, I <u>would pass</u> it.
Correct:	If I <u>study</u> hard for my anthropology midterm, I <u>will pass</u> it.
Correct:	If I <u>studied</u> hard for my anthropology midterm, I <u>would pass</u> it.

		cond
Incorrect:	I <u>would have gotten</u> to class earlier if the bus <u>did not come</u> late.
Correct:	I <u>would have gotten</u> to class earlier if the bus <u>had not come</u> late.

Self-Help Strategy: Consult the Guide to Forming the Verb Phrase in Conditional Sentences in this unit if you are unsure about which verb form to use in the verb phrase.

yes   no   don't know   **PROBLEM 2**

☐   ☐   ☐   The verb phrase in the conditional sentence has a verb-form error.

cond

Incorrect: If Christi <u>had not come</u> to class, she <u>would never had known</u> an essay draft was due.

Correct: If Christi <u>had not come</u> to class, she <u>would never have known</u> an essay draft was due.

       cond   *cond*

Incorrect: They <u>would have cook</u> dinner for us if we <u>had ask</u> them.

Correct: They <u>would have cooked</u> dinner for us if we <u>had asked</u> them.

cond

Incorrect: If she <u>had called</u> earlier, I <u>could of answered</u> her question.

Correct: If she <u>had called</u> earlier, I <u>could have answered</u> her question.

Note: *Have* often sounds like *of* in speaking but is not correct in formal writing.

Self-Help Strategy: Check the verb phrase in **both** clauses to make sure that you have not only chosen the correct verb for the conditional but also have not made any errors in verb form.

yes   no   don't know   **PROBLEM 3**

☐   ☐   ☐   A conditional sentence has not been used where one is needed.

cond

Incorrect: I know about the reading assignment. I <u>would have</u> done it.

Correct: <u>If</u> I had known about the reading assignment (condition), I would have done it (result).

cond

Incorrect: <u>Especially</u> Peter does not have a new job before quitting his old job, he might have a hard time finding a job in the future.

Correct: <u>If</u> Peter does not have a new job before quitting his old job (condition), he might have a hard time finding a job in the future (result).

yes	no	don't know	**PROBLEM 4**
☐	☐	☐	A hypothetical conditional sentence has not been used where one is needed.

Incorrect: I am a very disorganized person. For instance, I often cannot find my English
cond
homework because I have put it in my math notebook. If I <u>am</u> more organized
cond
(condition), I <u>will have</u> a separate color-coded folder for each class (result).

Correct: I am a very disorganized person. For instance, I often cannot find my English homework because I have put it in my math notebook. If I <u>were</u> more organized (condition), I <u>would have</u> a separate color-coded folder for each class (result). (The writer is referring to a hypothetical situation, not a real situation.)

yes	no	don't know	**PROBLEM 5**
☐	☐	☐	A conditional form has not been used in a later sentence to show an additional result of a condition that was stated in an earlier sentence.

Incorrect: If our instructor gave us a test today (condition), she would find that we have not
cond
yet mastered the conditional (result). We <u>will</u> probably all <u>fail</u>.

Correct: If our instructor gave us a test today, she would find that we have not yet mastered the conditional. We <u>would</u> probably all <u>fail</u>. (The conditional form must be used in the second sentence because it, too, is a result based on the condition in the preceding sentence. That is, *We would probably all fail if our instructor gave us a test today.*)

Self-Help Strategy: Use a conditional verb phrase in all the result clauses that are based on a particular condition, whether or not the *if* clause is repeated.

Grammar Guidelines for Conditional Sentences

A conditional sentence expresses either a real or a hypothetical condition and gives the result of that condition.

Factual Conditional Sentences: Meaning and Use

A real situation by definition exists or has a strong possibility of existing. Factual conditional sentences allow the writer to do the following:

1. To express a future possibility or make a prediction

> If we use the method Professor Jones suggested, we will probably get better results.
>
> If my neighbor plays loud music, I will complain to the manager.

2. To express a general fact or a habitual action

> If sugar is mixed with water, it dissolves. (general fact)
>
> If the elderly exercise regularly, they have a better chance of feeling healthy. (habitual action)
>
> (*When* or *whenever* can be substituted for *if* in these sentences.)

3. To make an inference

> If this compound contains carbon, it is organic material.
>
> If that book is the latest edition, I bought the wrong one.
>
> (*When* or *whenever* cannot be substituted for *if* in these sentences.)

4. To give a command or instructions

> If your laboratory experiment fails, try it again tomorrow.

Hypothetical Conditional Sentences: Meaning and Use

A hypothetical situation does not exist or is not likely to exist. Hypothetical conditional sentences allow the writer to do the following:

1. To express what might happen in the present or future as the result of a given condition. In the writer's mind, it is not very likely that the situation will exist or the event will happen.

Examples:

> If my neighbor started to play loud rock music, I would complain to the apartment manager. (I have little reason to believe she will start playing rock music, but this action is the one I would take.)

> If instructors taught fewer classes, they could write more comments on their students' papers. (Teachers would no doubt write more comments on papers, but it is highly unlikely that teachers will have the number of classes they teach reduced.)

Note: In both the example sentences above, the factual conditional can be used. However, when using the factual conditional, the writer sees the situation as more likely to exist or the event as more likely to happen; that is, the writer is talking about a future possibility or making a prediction.

2. **To express an impossible or counterfactual condition and the result of that condition.**

Examples:

If I were you, I would move out of that apartment. (I am not you, but this is what I would do in this situation.)

If George Washington saw the White House today, he would not recognize it. (George Washington cannot return to life to see the White House today, but since the 1700s, the White House has completely changed.)

Note: The factual conditional cannot be used in the example sentences above because these conditions cannot be made possible or true.

3. **To imagine what could have happened in a past situation but never did.**

Example: If Sang had not reviewed the conditional before the quiz, he would have lost ten points. (Sang did review it and he did not lose ten points.)

Guide to Forming the Verb Phrase in Conditional Sentences

Factual Conditional Sentences: Forming the Verb or Verb Phrase

In factual conditional sentences, the sequence of tenses varies according to the meaning of the conditional sentence.

1. **To express a future possibility or make a prediction**

Condition Clause	Result Clause
present tense present progressive tense present perfect tense	will, can, should, could, may, might + base form

Examples:

If countries <u>do not conserve</u> their resources, they <u>will regret</u> it later.
If Andreas <u>is telephoning</u> me right now, he <u>will get</u> a busy signal.

Note: A conditional sentence with the modal *will* expresses the strongest possibility, a prediction. The other modals indicate a lesser degree of possibility.

Examples:

If you <u>have not bought</u> your ticket, you <u>may not get</u> a seat.

If Mina <u>is not attending</u> class regularly, she <u>could fail</u> the course.

If the letter <u>has not come</u> by now, it <u>might not arrive</u> at all.

2. To express a general fact or a habitual action

Condition Clause	Result Clause
same tense	same tense

Examples:

If a caterpillar <u>matures</u>, it becomes a <u>chrysalis</u>. (fact)

Whenever my roommate <u>studied</u> late, I <u>stayed up</u> too. (habitual action)

Note: *When* and *whenever* are often used instead of *if* to express a habitual action.

3. To make an inference

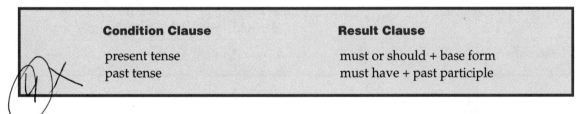

Condition Clause	Result Clause
present tense	must or should + base form
past tense	must have + past participle

Examples:

If the store <u>is</u> already closed, it <u>must be</u> later than we thought.

If Nam really <u>did lose</u> his wallet instead of misplacing it, he <u>must have felt</u> very nervous.

4. To give a command or instructions

Condition Clause	Result Clause
present tense	imperative
past tense	
present perfect tense	

Examples:

> If you <u>miss</u> the lecture, <u>go</u> to see the teacher.
> If you <u>missed</u> the lecture, <u>go</u> to see the teacher.
> If you <u>have missed</u> the lecture, <u>go</u> to see the teacher.

Hypothetical Conditional Sentences: Forming the Verb or Verb Phrase

In hypothetical conditional sentences, the time of the sentence is not related to the verb tense used. For example, in the sentence *If I were you* (condition), *I would go* (result), *were* does not signal past time but, instead, a condition that is contrary to fact. The same is true for the sentence *If I had been there* (condition), *she would not have won* (result); in this sentence, *had been* does not signal an event that happened before another in the past but rather is used to speculate about an event that has already taken place in the past.

1. **To express a present or future hypothetical or contrary-to-fact situation.**

   Note: In the condition clause, when the simple past form or the past progressive form is used, *were* is used for all forms of *be*.

Condition Clause	Result Clause
simple past form	would, could, might + base form
	would, could, might + be + base form + *ing*
past progressive form	would, could, might + base form
	would, could, might + be + base form + *ing*
could, would + base form	would, could, might + base form

Examples:

> If I <u>were</u> you, I <u>would save</u> more money.
> If Tran <u>lived</u> at home instead of in the dormitory, she <u>would have</u> a quiet place to study.
> If Abdul <u>cleaned</u> his apartment every week, he <u>would not always</u> <u>be complaining</u> about how messy it is.
> If Sheila <u>were not working</u> in the dining hall, she <u>could not afford</u> college.
> If Ara <u>were working</u> in San Francisco, he <u>would not be spending</u> so much time driving to his job.
> If Mike <u>could find</u> his library card, he <u>would start</u> his term paper.

Note: In the example sentences above, *were to* + a preposition may be used for the simple past form of the verb, as in *If Tran <u>were to live</u> at home* or *If Abdul <u>were to</u> <u>clean</u> his apartment every week.*

2. To express a hypothetical situation in the past

Condition Clause	Result Clause
past perfect form	would, could, might + have + past participle would, could, might + have + been + base form + *ing*
past perfect progressive form	would, could, might + have + past participle would, could, might + have + been + base form + *ing*

Examples:

If Gail <u>had turned</u> her lab report in on time, she <u>would have received</u> the full ten points on it.

If Lan <u>had not refused</u> to lend us his car, we <u>could have been driving</u> to the beach right now.

Natasha <u>might have enjoyed</u> the movie if she <u>had not been concentrating</u> so hard on understanding what the actors were saying.

If Ameleset <u>had been paying</u> attention in class, he <u>would not have been asking</u> his friends how to do the assignment last night.

Improve Your Writing Style

Know How to Mix Conditional Types

It may sometimes be necessary to mix conditional types. The most common mixing involves a past condition and a present result.

Example: If I had eaten breakfast this morning, my stomach would not be growling. (I did not eat breakfast earlier this morning, so my stomach is growling now.)

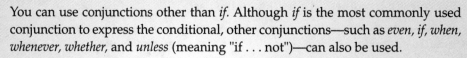

Improve Your Writing Style

Vary Your Conditional Sentences

You can use conjunctions other than *if*. Although *if* is the most commonly used conjunction to express the conditional, other conjunctions—such as *even, if, when, whenever, whether,* and *unless* (meaning "if . . . not")—can also be used.

Examples:

> Whether it rains or not, I will still go to the movies.
> (I will go [result] regardless of the weather [condition].)
> Unless I find my keys, I cannot unlock my bike.
> (I must have my keys [condition] to unlock my bike [result].)
> (If I do not find my keys, I cannot unlock my bike.)

You can write conditional sentences without *if*. A conditional sentence can be formed without using *if* by reversing the subject and the verb in the *if* clause. This formation is most commonly used with *had* and *should* but may also be used with *were*.

Examples:

> Had I known the test was today, I would have studied the chapter.
> Should the telephone ring while I am out, please answer it.
> Were I closer to the front, I could hear the speaker better.

PART III

EXERCISES FOR PRACTICE

EXERCISE 1 (Do this exercise on your own. Then check your answers with a classmate.)

Directions: Read each sentence and then answer the questions based on it to test your understanding of the structure and meaning of conditional sentences. The first one has been done for you.

1. If Lucia has enough vacation time and money, she will go to Hawaii for a vacation.

    a. Does Lucia have enough money yet? _no_

    b. Will she go to Hawaii for a vacation? _yes, when she has enough time and money_

    c. What is the time expressed in the statement? _future_

2. If Jim were 16 years old, he would be able to drive.

    a. Is Jim 16 yet? _no_

    b. Can he drive? _no_

    c. What is the time expressed in the statement? _present_

3. If my coworker had not asked me to keep the news a secret, I would have told you that she had gotten another job and is leaving New Orleans.

   a. Did the coworker ask to have the news kept a secret? _____

   b. Did I tell you her news? _____

   c. What is the time expressed in the statement? _____

EXERCISE 2 (Do this exercise with a classmate.)

Directions: **Test your understanding of the time frame of the conditional by reading the following conditional sentences. Check which time you think is expressed in each sentence.**

1. If I have time, I watch videos.

   ☒ present   ❑ past   ❑ future

2. If I have time, I will watch a video.

   ❑ present   ❑ past   ☒ future

3. If I had time, I would watch a video.

   ☒ present   ❑ past   ❑ future

4. If I had had time, I would have watched a video.

   ❑ present   ☒ past   ❑ future

5. If I hadn't watched a video, I would not be so far behind on my paper.

   ❑ present   ☒ past   ❑ future

6. If I had been you, I would have started my paper earlier.

   ❑ present   ❑ past   ❑ future

EXERCISE 3 (Do this exercise on your own. Then check your answers with a classmate.)

Directions: **Test your understanding of the meaning and formation of conditional sentences by deciding whether each sentence is correct (C) or incorrect (I). Then cross out the errors and correct them.**

Example: _I_   If the teacher had not been ill, he would ~~had~~ *have* come to class.

   _C_   Bob would have received a better grade if he had attended class regularly.

_I_   1. If I have a car, I would not ask my friends to take me shopping.

_I_   2. If Margaret had slept more, she would not have trouble staying awake during the chemistry lecture yesterday.

_____ C 3. When it is hot outside, I drink plenty of water. *2 senses*

_____ 4. If I will go to Los Angeles next week, I will see all my friends.

_____ 5. If Peter went to the bookstore later today, he can buy two tapes for the price of one.

_____ 6. If Edith had not had to turn in her paper today, she would had skipped class.

_____ 7. If the weather is nice, Marcella always took a walk after dinner.

_____ 8. If I could found a ride home this weekend, I would give my parents a surprise visit.

_____ 9. If the teacher had not stopped us right at 10 o'clock, I would have been able to finish the test.

_____ 10. If I were going to a junior college, I would be living at my parents' home.   *I'd live*

EXERCISE 4 (Do this exercise on your own. Then check your answers with a classmate.)

Directions: Complete each conditional sentence below by giving the correct form of the verb indicated in parentheses. If you are having problems, review what you learned in Part II.

> **Example:**   If the weather is nice tomorrrow, the teacher _will hold_ (hold) class outside.

1. If the city _____ (expand) the parking space downtown, we would not have had to park so far away from the movies.

2. When my roommate _____ (snore) loudly, I cannot sleep.

3. Celebrities often get very depressed if their names _____ not _____ (appear) in the news.

4. If we _____ not _____ (have) to take an exam on the conditional, we might not have learned it.

5. Maya _____ not _____ (pass) her driving test unless she calms down.

6. If it _____ (be) winter, all these trees would be covered with snow.

7. Had it not rained, the farmers _____ (lose) all their crops.

8. If the airplane had not had a mechanical problem, we _____ probably _____ (arrive) in Tucson by now.

9. We _____ (lie) on the beach in Mexico right now if we had been able to get our visas on time.

10. I _____ (try) to find more opportunities to speak English if I were you.

EXERCISE 5 (Do this exercise on your own. Then check your answers with a classmate.)

Directions: **Fill in the blanks with the correct form of the conditional. The first one has been done for you.**

If I _were_ (be) you, I would not eat so much candy. It is not good for your digestive system. Furthermore, my mother says that recent studies have shown that if mice are given a diet high in sugar, they _will dev_ (develop) chronic fatigue syndrome. On the other hand, when these same mice had the opportunity to eat sugar or protein, they instinctively _chose_ (choose) protein over sugar. However, my mother also tells me that if I _had been_ _were_ (be) part of that study, I would never have chosen the healthy food but would have gone straight for the candy. It seems that mice have better sense than humans. If I have a craving for candy, I _will consult_ (consult) a mouse before going out and buying a bag of butterscotch toffees.

EXERCISE 6 (Do this exercise with a classmate.)

Directions: **Practice your understanding of the formation and meaning of conditional sentences by completing the following sentences.**

hand in —   **Example:**   If I were the instructor of this class, _I would let the students out early today_.

1. If Jennifer did not have to be in class right now, _____

2. I would have gotten to class earlier if _____

3. If I had gotten enough sleep last night, _____

4. I would complain about this class if _____

5. If Vincent has time later, _____

6. If I had had time during the weekend, _____

7. If I had a little extra money, _____

8. If students are given too much to learn, _____

9. If the tuition were raised, _____

10. Even if the sales representative had lowered the price of the car by $1000, _____

If past, would + v sano to present
plu parf , would have + pp past
sleeps , will   future

EXERCISE 7 (Do this exercise on your own and then read your sentences out loud to a classmate.)

Directions: **Write answers to the following questions.**

1. If you have a problem, whom do you usually share it with?   _____

   _____

2. If today were Thursday, where would you probably be right now?   _____

   _____

3. Given the chance to make the decision again, would you choose to attend the same school or
   to have the same job?   _____

   _____

EXERCISE 8 (Do this exercise with a classmate.)

Directions: **The following paragraph, adapted from a student's essay about what students
should consider when they choose a major, contains errors in the use of the conditional. Test your knowledge of the meaning and formation of the conditional by
circling and correcting these errors. The first one has been done for you.**

Another point students should consider when they choose a major is not whether it
will make them rich but whether it will at least ensure them enough income to support
themselves and their families. It is true that liberal arts majors often get lower-paying

are

jobs than do science majors; however, if people ~~were~~ interested in the liberal arts, they
should study those majors. Even though the jobs they get might not enable them to buy
big houses or fancy cars, the jobs would allow them to support themselves easily. For
instance, my cousin, who majored in English, now writes novels and is going to publish
his first novel in July. Although he has experienced many hardships as a writer, he still
has enough income to support his family. He likes writing very much and wants to write
as long as he lives. Even though his parents wanted him to become a doctor, it would
have been hard for my cousin if he majored in biology. He would probably be very
uncomfortable and feel pressured and stressed in his classes. If he then get a job he
did not like in that field, he might earn a high salary but he might have found himself
with an ulcer. If we looked at my cousin as an example, it becomes clear that students
must choose a major that is mentally satisfying, not a major that guarantees a big
income.

WRITING TOPICS

Select one or more of the following topics for writing and follow the steps in Appendix A.

Topic A: If you had the power to change anything in your country or in the United States, what would you most like to change and why? (Alternatively, you could choose to change something in your school or workplace.)

Topic B: Ask five of your friends this question, "If you could travel anywhere in the world, where would you go and why?" Write their responses in a short report and discuss whether or not you feel they are making the right choice. Also include the place you would most like to visit.

Topic C: Think about the growth in distance education via the computer. What are some of the advantages and drawbacks of this type of education, in which the student does not go to class but rather sits in front of a computer to learn?

PART IV

CNN VIDEO ACTIVITY AND WRITING TOPIC

Island Paradise Suffers

Useful Vocabulary: erosion   microcosm   waste potential   pollution   contentious

Before You Watch

This video segment shows, on a smaller scale, how the effects of humans and nature on the environment of a small island can teach us about these same effects on a worldwide scale.

- What are some environmental problems caused by nature that you are aware of?
- What are some environmental problems caused by tourism?

While You Watch

- Write down the natural causes of environmental problems on this island.
- Write down environmental problems caused by humans on this island.

As microcosms of larger land areas in the world, small islands reflect worldwide environmental problems.

After You Watch

I. **Write a personal reaction.**

Write a personal reaction of three to five sentences to what you saw in the video. What interested you most? Were you surprised at the extent of the problems on just one small island? Explain your answer.

II. **Share your reactions.**

Answer the following questions either orally or in writing. Compare your answers with those of a classmate.
  1. What are the major environmental problems facing this island? Which do you think are the most serious?
  2. What environmental problems are facing your country or the place where you live?
  3. Do you think global conferences make much difference in solving environmental problems? Why or why not?

WRITING TOPIC

One of the islanders in this video hopes that people will see the relationship between the environmental problems that small islands are facing and those larger nations face. What environmental problems does your country or the place in which you live face? What is being done about them or what should be done about them?

Goals

- To learn the importance of mastering passive voice in writing
- To review four problems ESL writers commonly encounter with the passive voice
- To learn to form and use the passive voice correctly
- To develop confidence in using the passive voice through practice with exercises and writing assignments

Passive Voice

Students at St. Louis Community College congregate between classes. Photo courtesy of St. Louis Community College.

Think about and discuss the following question:
What are three benefits of relaxing with
your friends and classmates
outside of class?

PART I

WHAT YOU NEED TO KNOW ABOUT ERRORS WITH THE PASSIVE VOICE

In Part I, you will learn

- The definition of an error with the passive voice
- The importance of using the passive voice correctly in writing
- Suggestions for mastering the passive voice in writing

Definition of the Error (pass*)

An error with the passive voice **(pass)** occurs when a verb in the passive voice has been incorrectly formed or when the passive voice has been used where the active voice is needed.

In English, a verb can be used in either the active voice or the passive voice. In the sentence *The bookstore sells computer supplies*, the verb is in the active voice because the subject is doing the action. In the sentence *Our teachers will be moved to temporary offices this spring*, the verb is in the passive voice because the subject is being acted upon. The doer of the action is not named; "by someone" is understood. However, in the sentence *Our Spanish textbook was written by my teacher*, the doer of the action—"by my teacher"—is named. The writer chooses whether or not to name the doer of the action depending on how important it is for the reader to have that information.

Even when the passive voice has been correctly formed in a sentence, a problem with the passive voice may still occur because the active voice may be preferable to the passive voice in that sentence. In that case, your instructor may use an alternative symbol, **wk pass** (for weak passive).

The verb *be* + the past participle, as in the sentence *The lake is situated halfway between the two towns*, is sometimes considered a passive construction (called the stative passive). Errors in this type of formation are treated in Unit 2, "Verb Forms."

Importance of Mastering the Passive Voice in Writing

Errors with the passive voice are global (more serious) errors and can affect the meaning of individual sentences, parts of a paragraph, and whole paragraphs. In formal writing, knowing how to use the passive voice correctly is very important. Although a sentence in the passive voice may be grammatically correct, it may not be the best choice in a piece of writing. Rather, the decision of whether or not to use

*__pass__ = grading symbol for an error with the passive voice.

the passive voice should be based upon whether the subject of the sentence is doing the action or being acted upon. Of equal importance in the piece of text is the focus on the topic; active or passive voice is chosen to maintain the focus on the topic being discussed.

Knowing how to form the passive voice correctly is very important for an ESL writer. If the passive voice is incorrectly formed in a sentence, the reader will try to supply its correct form but may be confused about whether the writer intended to use the active or passive voice.

In academic and professional writing, the writer uses both active and passive voice; therefore, it is essential that ESL writers master the use and formation of the passive voice.

Suggestions for Mastering the Passive Voice in Writing

- Memorize how to form the passive voice so that you can do so automatically. (If you have any doubts about the formation of the passive voice in the tense or verb form you want to use, consult the charts in Part II of this unit.)

- Make sure the verb you have chosen can be used in the passive voice by checking your ESL dictionary (or a standard dictionary) to find out whether or not the verb is transitive (takes a direct object and can be made passive, like the verbs *collect, teach,* or *follow*) or intransitive (does not take a direct object and cannot be made passive, like the verbs *arrive, exist,* or *stay*).

- Compare the way the two voices are used when you are reading textbooks, the newspaper, or magazine articles. In particular, try to determine why the author used the passive instead of the active voice and whether you think its use is effective.

- If you need to write a scientific paper or a laboratory report, examine similar papers in that field or any sample papers the instructor has provided so that you can see the balance of active and passive voice. If you are in doubt, ask your instructor or a teaching assistant for help.

Test Your Understanding of the Passive Voice

Write answers to the following questions. Share your answers with another student.

1. What two voices can verbs take in English?
2. What kinds of verbs cannot be made passive and why?

> ## Grammar Journal Entry 5: The Passive Voice
>
> *Write a short entry in your grammar journal in response to the following.*
>
> 1. What is the best gift that has ever been given to you and why?
> 2. Write two sample sentences: one in the active voice and the other in the passive voice. Label each one correctly.

PART II

COMMON PROBLEMS, SELF-HELP STRATEGIES, AND GRAMMAR GUIDELINES

In Part II, you will study

- Four problems ESL writers commonly encounter with the passive voice
- Self-help strategies for controlling the passive voice in your writing
- Grammar guidelines for the passive voice

This section presents four problems that ESL writers commonly encounter with the passive voice. First, take the pretest to see what you already know about the passive voice. In checking your answers, note that the pretest questions cover the same types of errors in the same order as the problems in this section. Then carefully study each problem and the examples that illustrate it, giving particular attention to those problems that correspond to the pretest questions you had difficulty with. Using the boxes to the left of each problem, check [✓] *yes, no,* or *don't know* to indicate to yourself which problems you should focus the most attention on in this unit and also when you write passive constructions in English. Remember that becoming aware of the types of errors you most often make with the passive voice will increase your chances of avoiding these errors in your writing.

Pretest: What Do You Already Know About the Passive Voice?

Test your ability to recognize errors with the passive voice by finding and correcting the one error with the passive voice in each of the following sentences.

Answers on p. 291

1. Some math problems can be solve very easily.

2. The speaker's question directed at the younger members of the audience.

3. Despite the efforts of the United Nations, peace still is not existed in the world.

4. Many animals are disappearing in the wild. Today, zoos play an increasingly important role in keeping endangered animals from becoming extinct. Furthermore, zoos can be visited to see and enjoy these animals.

Four Problems ESL Writers Commonly Encounter with the Passive Voice

yes	no	don't know	**PROBLEM 1**
☐	☐	☐	The passive voice has been incorrectly formed.

	pass
Incorrect:	Some pronunciation problems <u>can be fix</u> easily.
Correct:	Some pronunciation problems <u>can be fixed</u> easily.

	pass
Incorrect:	Your grades <u>will sent</u> next week.
	pass
Incorrect:	Your grades <u>will being sent</u> next week.
Correct:	Your grades <u>will be sent</u> next week.

Self-Help Strategy: Refer to the chart in this section to see if you have formed the passive voice correctly of the verb tense you are using.

yes	no	don't know	**PROBLEM 2**
☐	☐	☐	The passive voice is needed instead of the active voice.

	pass
Incorrect:	A new air conditioner <u>install</u> next week.
Correct:	A new air conditioner <u>will be installed</u> next week. (The air conditioner cannot install itself but must be installed by someone.)

yes   no   don't know   **PROBLEM 3**

☐   ☐   ☐   The passive voice has been used with a verb that cannot be made passive.

pass

Incorrect: Male dominance over females still <u>is existed</u> in some countries.
Correct: Male dominance over females still <u>exists</u> in some countries.

pass

Incorrect: A power failure <u>was occurred</u> last month.
Correct: A power failure <u>occurred</u> last month.

Self-Help Strategy: If you are unsure whether a verb is transitive or intransitive, check the verb in a dictionary.

yes   no   don't know   **PROBLEM 4**

☐   ☐   ☐   The passive voice has been used where the active voice would be more effective.

Note: Although this problem is probably more common to native speakers than to ESL writers, you still need to be aware of ineffective use of the passive voice. An alternate symbol for this kind of problem with the passive is **wk pass**—weak passive. (The weak passive is treated more completely in composition textbooks for native speakers.)

Ineffective Use of the Passive Voice

In the following short paragraph, the passive voice has been used ineffectively. There is no focus on who had the problem with organization or what the weakness was.

Listing my ideas in an unorganized form is a second weakness of mine in
pass
writing. Organization <u>was</u> not adequately <u>taught</u> by my high school. My
pass   pass
thoughts <u>were scribbled</u> in list form and <u>were accepted</u> by my instructors.

Revised Paragraph with the Active Voice

In the revised paragraph below, the writer uses the active voice, and the paragraph focuses on how the writer wrote in a disorganized fashion.

Listing my ideas in an unorganized form is a second weakness of mine in writing. My high school English teachers did not adequately teach organization. Instead of following a prescribed method of prewriting, like brainstorming or clustering, I merely scribbled out my thoughts in list form and my instructors accepted them.

Grammar Guidelines for Forming and Using the Passive Voice

A proficient writer knows when to choose the active or the passive voice. In expository writing, the active voice is generally a better choice than the passive voice except in cases where the writer wants to emphasize what has happened rather than who or what caused the action. In scientific and technical writing, the passive voice is often preferred so that the emphasis is on the experiment or the phenomenon, not on the researcher(s).

Remember that while a sentence with the passive voice may be grammatically correct, the writer chooses either the active or passive voice to effectively express what he or she wants to say. The following guidelines can help you decide how to form and when to use the passive voice in expository writing.

Formation of the Passive Voice

Passive Form of Verb Tenses

The passive voice is formed by using the form of the helping verb *to be* in whatever tense the writer selects and then adding the past participle. The present and past perfect progressive as well as the future progressive and the future perfect progressive are not used in the passive voice.

Verb-Tense Formation in Passive Voice	Example
Present	
am, is, are + past participle	Mail <u>is delivered</u> to the residence hall every day except Sunday.
Present progressive	
am being, is being, are being + past participle	A new addition <u>is being added</u> to the library.
Past	
was, were + past participle	The grades <u>were posted</u> by the teaching assistant at 3:00 PM.
Past progressive	
was being, were being + past participle	When I arrived at Wellman Hall, the corrected problem sets <u>were</u> just <u>being distributed.</u>
Present perfect	
has been, have been + past participle	I think the money <u>has</u> already <u>been sent</u> electronically by the bank.
Past perfect	
had been + past participle	All the food <u>had been eaten</u> when I arrived at the potluck dinner.
Future	
will be + past participle	The tests <u>will be given back</u> on Thursday.
Future perfect	
will have been + past participle	By the time you arrive at the concert hall, all the free tickets <u>will have been given out</u>.

Passive Form of Modal Verb Phrases

In a modal verb phrase, the passive is formed by adding *be* + the past participle after the modal for the present tense and *have been* + the past participle after the modal for the past tense.

Modal Verb-Tense Formation in Passive Voice	Example
Present	
modal + be + past participle	Revision for spelling <u>can</u> easily <u>be done</u> on a computer.
	Problems with reservations <u>should be reported</u> to the restaurant manager.
Past	
modal + have been + past participle	It is possible that the train <u>could have been delayed</u>.
	I think she <u>should have been elected</u> chair of the committee.

Passive Voice of Conditional Verb Phrases

In a conditional sentence, the passive voice can be used in the condition clause, the result clause, or both. To correctly form the passive voice in a conditional sentence, use the guidelines to forming the passive voice of verb tenses and modal verb phrases in this section. The chart below shows examples of the passive voice in conditional sentences.

Conditional Verb-Phrase Formation in the Passive Voice	Example
Note: Use the passive of the appropriate verb tense or modal verb phrase.	
Factual conditional	If Ben makes a mistake, he <u>is corrected</u> by his friend.
Hypothetical conditional (present or future)	If the computer software <u>were shipped</u> tonight, it would arrive tomorrow. (<u>was</u> becomes <u>were</u> in the *if* clause)
Hypothetical conditional (past)	If the dam <u>had</u> not <u>been constructed</u>, we would have had a flood last spring.

Passive of Infinitives and Gerunds

Infinitives in the Passive Voice	Example
Present infinitive	
to + be + past participle	She arranged for the make-up test <u>to be given</u> Monday.
Perfect infinitive	
to + have been + past participle	The results were supposed <u>to have been sent</u> yesterday.
Gerunds in the Passive Voice	**Example**
being + past participle	He did not like <u>being called</u> Jim instead of James.
	<u>Being awakened</u> in the middle of the night by a telephone call upset George.
	After <u>being told</u> to go from one office to another, Phil finally found where to turn in his application.

Common Uses of the Passive Voice

1. **To express something that happened to the subject**

   The new electric car <u>was released</u> in Sacramento last month [by the Honda dealer].

   Note: The agent, or doer of the action, may or may not be mentioned, depending upon whether the agent is known or how important it is to know the agent. In the example sentence above, the writer can choose to either mention the Honda dealer or not.

2. **To explain how something was done or what methodology was used**

   The specimens <u>were analyzed</u> and the results <u>were recorded</u>.
   The requested forms <u>were completed</u> and <u>sent</u> to the physician yesterday.

3. **To describe a process**

   Water <u>can be purified</u> by heating it to the boiling point.
   Each letter <u>should be drafted, typed</u>, and <u>proofread</u> before it <u>is sent</u> out.

Improve Your Writing Style

Avoid Wordiness by Effective Use of the Active Voice

You can use the active voice to avoid wordiness. A passive construction can sometimes make a sentence wordy—which, of course, will affect the writer's style negatively.

Examples:

It is stated by the author that Mondays are depressing. (passive voice, 10 words)

The author states that Mondays are depressing. (active voice, 7 words)

You can reduce the passive verb phrase to avoid wordiness and to vary your style.

Examples:

The specimens <u>were analyzed</u> and the results <u>were recorded</u>.

The specimens <u>were analyzed</u> and the results <u>recorded</u>.

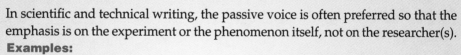

Improve Your Writing Style

Know How to Use the Passive Voice in Scientific and Technical Writing and Factual Reporting

In scientific and technical writing, the passive voice is often preferred so that the emphasis is on the experiment or the phenomenon itself, not on the researcher(s).

Examples:

The dragonflies were mounted and then kept at 2 degrees Celsius for four hours.

The software should be installed on a reformatted hard disk.

In reporting, the passive voice is also preferred in some cases.

Examples:

More thunderstorms <u>were expected</u> to hit the Southland late Sunday, but the rainfall <u>was expected</u> to be considerably less than that of last week's storm. More showers and thunderstorms <u>were predicted</u> through Wednesday, with a heavy surf advisory until 10 AM today. An 84-year-old man <u>was killed</u> early Saturday morning when high waves knocked him off his surfboard and he <u>was swept</u> under.

The president <u>was reported</u> to have suffered a fall last night at the hotel where he was staying. At this time, no details <u>have been released</u> to the press. The president <u>will be transported</u> by helicopter to a military hospital later this morning for an examination. At that time, his press secretary will hold a press conference.

In the above examples, the passive voice has been used to keep the focus on the subject or to protect the confidentiality of the sources.

PART III

EXERCISES FOR PRACTICE

EXERCISE 1 (Do this exercise on your own. Then check your answers with a classmate.)

Directions: Fill in the correct form of the passive voice. Use the verb tense indicated. If you are unsure, consult the charts in Part II.

1. **Present:**

   All of the participants in the race _____ (invite) to the awards ceremony.

2. **Present progressive:**

   Applications for part-time jobs _____ (accept) from now until the end of the month.

3. **Past:**

   Volkan told me that the store _____ (close), so I did not go.

4. **Present perfect:**

   Do you know whether or not the package _____ (send)?

5. **Past perfect:**

   The officer announced that the suspects _____ (arrest) for the crime.

6. **Future:**

   Stanley does not need to worry about buying a plane ticket; it _____ (take care of) by his company.

7. **Future perfect:**

   By the time I get home, I hope that the dishes _____ (wash) by my roommates.

8. **Infinitive:**

   Johnson expects _____ (lay off) next month because the store is experiencing financial problems. (present infinitive)

   The building was expected _____ (complete) by now, but only the foundation has been laid. (perfect infinitive)

9. **Gerund:**

   Marilyn did not anticipate _____ (charge) tax when she bought groceries.

10. **Modal:**

    I am afraid that the date _____ (might, change). (present time)

    Do you think this box _____ (might, deliver) to my house by mistake? (past time)

11. **Conditional:**

    If the English test _____ (can, postpone), I would be very relieved as I do not know the material that well.

EXERCISE 2 (Do this exercise on your own. Then check your answers with a classmate.)

Directions: Change the underlined verbs or verbals in the following sentences from the active voice to the passive voice if possible. Make other changes in the sentences as necessary. Be particularly careful to use the correct formation of the passive voice for the verb tense you are using. If you are not sure, consult the charts in Part II.

> **Example:**
>
> The Red Cross <u>collected</u> canned food and clothes for the earthquake victims. (active, 12 words)
>
> Canned food and clothing <u>were collected</u> for the earthquake victims by the Red Cross. (passive, 14 words)
>
> **Note:**   The sentence in the active voice is less wordy, but if the writer wants to emphasize what was collected by the Red Cross, the sentence in the passive voice should be used.

1. Most restaurants <u>accept</u> credit cards.

   _____

2. They <u>must have torn</u> down the bookstore since I was there in March.

   _____

3. The teacher expects the students <u>to do</u> the assignment before class.

   _____

4. If the temperature <u>had dropped</u> last night, snow <u>would have fallen</u>.

   _____

5. The news anchor <u>interrupted</u> the program for a special bulletin on the approaching storm.

   _____

6. By the time I get home, the letter carrier <u>will have delivered</u> the mail.

   _____

7. At the end of the school year, teachers and students <u>are ready</u> for summer vacation.

   _____

8. The university press <u>has published</u> Dr. Robertson's book.

   _____

9. If <u>removing</u> his shopping cart from the park upsets the homeless man, let him keep it there.

   _____

10. Although I <u>had invited</u> six people for dinner, only three came.

    _____

11. More students would have taken advantage of the field trip if the instructor <u>had announced</u> it earlier.

    _____

12. Tom <u>must have broken</u> his foot in the accident as he is wearing a cast.

    _____

EXERCISE 3 (Do this exercise on your own. Then check your answers with a classmate.)

Directions: In each of the sentences below, there is an error in the formation of the passive voice. Correct it by writing in the correct answer above the sentence.

was being spoken

Example: When I was walking in the streets of Taiwan, Chinese ~~was speaking~~ all around me.

1. We constantly being asked by the government for more taxes.

2. My conversation with her conducted in Vietnamese.

3. Are you sure that company is still existed?

4. Juan has the honor of having awarded the prize for the best attendance.

5. A solid friendship create between them because of their common interest in soccer.

6. My fear about speaking English in public was contributed to my shyness.

7. This English class offer only to nonnative speakers.

8. When the announcement was been made, some students were not there.

9. Some English words derived from Latin.

EXERCISE 4 (Do this exercise with a classmate.)

Directions: The writer of this paragraph has elected to use some verbs in the passive voice. The paragraph, as written, works well. Read the whole paragraph. Then underline each passive construction. With your classmate, discuss whether or not you might want to make any changes from the passive to the active voice. The first one has been underlined for you.

Although riding the train <u>has been</u> negatively <u>labeled</u> as nostalgic in our car-dependent society and many trains have long ceased to exist, a short commuter train ride can be a unique trip into the past—and a beautiful ride. On a recent short train trip, I was thrilled by the variety of bird life in the salt marsh the train passed through. In fact, the train was virtually ignored by the stately white egrets, shiny red-winged blackbirds, and plump mallard ducks. As we moved out of the marsh and glided along the water's edge, we were greeted by fishermen out to try their luck for the day. Farther from shore lay the oil tankers, and behind them, in the distance, the bay was decorated with white sails. As we approached the city, I wondered whether there was anything left to be seen. To my surprise, I found myself looking into people's backyards, catching glimpses of downtown streets, and, best of all, being treated to a panoramic view of the highway. There cars were creeping along, bumper to bumper, while out on the tracks, we peacefully glided by, rocking gently on the rails. I like to think that as our whistle tooted, it may have been heard by a driver out there who wished he or she were riding on the train.

PART IV
WRITING TOPICS

Select one or more of the following topics for writing and follow the steps in Appendix A.

Topic A: What is one of the most important discoveries that has been made and how, in your opinion, have humans benefited by it?

Topic B: Now that computers are so widely used in the workplace, some workers do not have to go to the job site but can work at home via computer either every day or for part of the work week. Would you consider taking such a job if it were offered to you? Why or why not?

Topic C: In recent years, public art—art that is displayed in public places such as airports or parks—has become increasingly popular. What, in your opinion, is the value of such art for the public?

PART V

CNN VIDEO ACTIVITY AND WRITING TOPIC

Alternative Museums Showcase Social Issues

Useful Vocabulary: alternative museum (as in "alternative learning" or "alternative school")
social issue   showcase   interactive   dysfunctional

Before You Watch

This video segment presents a new approach to the use of museums. Before learning about this approach, answer the following questions and share your answers with a classmate.

- What museums have you visited in the past year, or what are some famous museums in your country?

- What purposes do museums serve?

While You Watch

- Look for at least four kinds of alternative museums and what they present.

- Think about which of the exhibits shown in the video you would most like to visit.

Some museums are turning from art to social issues.

After You Watch

I. **Write a personal reaction.**

Write a personal reaction of three to five sentences to what you saw in the video. What interested you most? Would you go to these museums? Why or why not?

II. **Share your reactions.**

Answer the following questions either orally or in writing. Compare your answers with those of a classmate.

1. List the kinds of alternative museums you heard about in the video. If you remember their locations, include them also.

2. Do you agree with the narrator who says that this new use of museums will help them be more interesting to the society as a whole?

3. One woman stated that she thinks social issues are inappropriate themes for a museum. What is your opinion?

WRITING TOPIC

At the end of the video, the narrator states that ". . . as society's troubles become more visible, museums will do their part to educate and enlighten." Is this an effective way to educate the public about social issues? Present arguments for other ways to "educate and enlighten" the public about troublesome issues for society.

Goals

- To learn the importance of mastering relative, adverbial, and noun clauses in writing
- To review four problems ESL writers commonly encounter with relative clauses, eight problems with adverbial clauses, and nine problems with noun clauses.
- To learn to form and use relative, adverbial, and noun clauses correctly
- To develop confidence in using relative, adverbial, and noun clauses through practice with exercises and writing assignments.

Relative, Adverbial, and Noun Clauses

An instructor at Dekalb College in Decatur, Georgia answers a student's question during class.
Photo courtesy of Public Relations.

Think about and discuss the following question:
When is it appropriate to ask questions during class?

PART I

WHAT YOU NEED TO KNOW ABOUT RELATIVE, ADVERBIAL, AND NOUN CLAUSE ERRORS

In Part I, you will learn

- The definition of a clause error
- The importance of using dependent clauses correctly in writing
- Suggestions for mastering relative, adverbial, and noun clauses in writing

Definition of the Error (cl*)

A clause error (**cl**) is an error in which the formation of a relative, adverbial, or noun clause is incorrect. These three dependent clauses are treated in this unit.

Types of Clauses and Their Definitions

Note: All clauses, whether dependent or independent, must have a subject and a verb.

An **independent** or **main clause** can stand alone as a sentence because its meaning is complete.

Example: Last year my university had an enrollment of 15,000 students.

A **dependent** or **subordinate** clause cannot stand alone but must work together with an independent clause to complete its meaning.

Example: Although last year my university had an enrollment of 15,000 students (dependent clause), this year the number of students has increased by 10 percent (independent clause).

Examples of the Three Types of Dependent Clauses Covered in This Unit:

The student who came late [relative clause] missed an important part of the lecture.
Although living in a foreign country is interesting [adverbial clause], I want to return to Japan after I get my degree.
Melissa thought that she had missed the deadline for her paper [noun clause].

---

*cl = grading symbol for an error with a dependent clause.

Although sentences marked clause (**cl**) may also have other errors, your instructor may choose not to mark them. In the sentence *There is questions concerning the possible dangers of this machines may cause*, a relative clause is needed after *dangers (dangers <u>that this machines may cause</u>)*. In addition, the sentence contains a subject-verb agreement error *(there <u>is</u> questions)* and a singular/plural error *(this <u>machines</u>)*. However, the most serious problem is the relative clause error.

Importance of Mastering Relative, Adverbial, and Noun Clauses in Writing

The dependent-clause errors covered in this unit are global (more serious) errors. In the sentence *Although my parents expect me to do well in school, but I am not always dedicated to my studies*, the reader mentally has to delete *but* from the sentence because the coordinating conjunction *but* is not used after an adverbial clause that starts with the subordinating conjunction *although* or *even though*.

Meaning may also be highly affected by dependent clause errors as in the following sentence: *The doctor examined the patient had a bad headache*. Because the relative pronoun *who* is missing from the dependent clause, the reader is unsure who had the headache, whether it was <u>the patient</u> who had a bad headache or <u>the doctor</u> who examined the patient.

Readers of formal written English expect writers in the academic and professional worlds to have good control of clauses. Thus, ESL writers who are having difficulty with relative, adverbial, or noun clauses will want to give high priority to reducing these errors in their writing.

Suggestions for Mastering Relative, Adverbial, and Noun Clauses in Writing

- Determine whether your dependent clause errors are with relative, adverbial, or noun clauses by examining your essays. If you cannot determine them yourself, ask your instructor or a tutor to help you discover the kind(s) of dependent clause errors you are making.

- Use an advanced ESL grammar book to find a more detailed analysis of dependent clauses if you need a more detailed explanation than this unit provides.

- Study specific rules in this unit once you know what your clause errors are.

- Read extensively in English. Although you may not notice it at first, reading will help you become more familiar with both independent and dependent clauses and improve your ability to use them correctly in your own writing.

Test Your Understanding of Relative, Adverbial, and Noun Clause Errors

Write answers to the following questions. Share your answers with another student.

1. What are three types of dependent clause errors that ESL writers may make?

2. Why should ESL writers pay particular attention to dependent clause errors?

Grammar Journal Entry 6: Relative, Adverbial, and Noun Clauses

Respond to the following in your grammar journal.

1. What has been your most embarrassing moment in English? Describe it and explain what made it so painful for you.

2. Pick up a magazine or book that you are currently reading. See if you can pick out three dependent clauses on a page. Write them in your grammar journal.

PART II

COMMON PROBLEMS, SELF-HELP STRATEGIES, AND GRAMMAR GUIDELINES

In Part II, you will study

- Problems ESL writers commonly encounter with relative, adverbial, and noun clauses
- Self-help strategies for controlling dependent-clause errors in your writing
- Grammar guidelines for relative, adverbial, and noun clauses

This section presents problems that ESL writers commonly encounter with relative, adverbial, and noun clauses. As you study each type of dependent clause, take the pretest to see what you already know about using relative, adverbial, and noun clauses. In checking your answers, note that the pretest questions cover the same types of errors in the same order as the problems in this section. Then carefully study each problem and the examples that illustrate it, giving particular attention to those problems that correspond to the pretest questions you had difficulty with. Using the boxes to the left of each problem, check [✓] *yes, no,* or *don't know* to indicate to yourself which problems you should focus the most attention on in this unit and also when you are using relative, adverbial, and noun clauses in English. Remember that becoming aware of the types of errors you most often make with relative, adverbial, and noun clauses will increase your chances of avoiding these errors in your writing.

Part A: ✗ Relative Clauses

> **Note:** Your instructor may mark this error **(rel cl).** Relative clauses are also sometimes called adjective clauses.

Pretest: What Do You Already Know About Relative Clauses?

Test your ability to recognize relative clause errors by finding and correcting the one relative clause error in each of the following sentences.

Answers on p. 292

1. The people live in Florida are used to warm, sunny weather for much of the year.
2. In high school, the students who their cars were illegally parked would get a ticket.
3. After college, David wants to find a job which he will need to use mathematics.
4. One chemistry experiment in particular that I did it in Chemistry 2A gave me the idea that I might want to major in chemistry in college.

Four Problems ESL Writers Commonly Encounter With Relative Clauses

yes	no	don't know	**PROBLEM 1**
☐	☐	☐	The relative clause is missing.

rel cl

Incorrect: [Alienation is noticeable among people come] from different cultural backgrounds.

Correct: Alienation is noticeable among people <u>who</u> (or <u>that</u>) come from different cultural backgrounds.

rel cl

Incorrect: [There are more than one in three marriages will end] in divorce.

Correct: There are more than one in three marriages <u>that</u> (or <u>which</u>) will end in divorce.

Correct: More than one in three marriages will end in divorce. (No relative clause is needed here.)

yes	no	don't know	**PROBLEM 2**
☐	☐	☐	The formation of a relative clause is incorrect because the wrong relative pronoun or the wrong form of it has been used.

rel cl

Incorrect: I just met [the people who their house] I am planning to rent for the summer.

Correct: I just met the people <u>whose house</u> I am planning to rent for the summer.

rel cl

Incorrect: Cases have been found [that] even good students resort to cheating in college due to competition and the pressure to get good grades.

Correct: Cases have been found <u>in which</u> even good students resort to cheating in college due to competition and the pressure to get good grades.

yes	no	don't know	**PROBLEM 3**
☐	☐	☐	The preposition is missing when needed in a relative clause.

rel cl

Incorrect: Whenever I get into [a situation which it is hard] to make a decision, I try to look at it from different perspectives.

Correct: Whenever I get into a situation <u>in which it is</u> hard to make a decision, I try to look at it from different perspectives.

rel cl

Incorrect: The person [whom] I was supposed to return the key is not home.

Correct: The person <u>to whom</u> I was supposed to return the key is not home.

Correct: The person <u>whom</u> I was supposed to return the key <u>to</u> is not home.

yes	no	don't know	**PROBLEM 4**
☐	☐	☐	A noun or a pronoun has been unnecessarily repeated in a relative-clause.

rel cl

Incorrect: The people [whom I have met them] in my class are very friendly.

Correct: The people <u>whom I have met</u> in my class are very friendly.

Grammar Guidelines for Relative Clauses

Relative clauses are adjective clauses formed with the relative pronouns *who, whom, whose, which,* or *that* or with the relative adverbs *when, where,* or *why.* To use relative pronouns correctly, you need to be aware of how they function in a relative clause.

1. *Who, that,* and *which* **can function as the subject of a relative clause.** *Who* **refers to people,** *that* **refers to people and things, and** *which* **refers only to things.**

Examples:

The teacher called out the names of those students <u>who</u> (or *that*) were absent. (*Who* [or *that*] refers to students and is the subject of the relative clause.)

The book <u>that</u> (or <u>which</u>) was left on the table is no longer there. (*That* [or *which*] refers to the book and is the subject of the relative clause.)

2. *Whom, that,* and *which* **can function as a direct object in a relative clause.** *Whom* **refers to people,** *that* **refers to people and things, and** *which* **refers only to things.**

Examples:

The student <u>whom</u> (or <u>that</u>) they have chosen to be editor of the class newspaper does not want the job. (*Whom* [or *that*] refers to the student and is the direct object of *have* chosen in the relative clause. In spoken English, *who* can be used, but it should not be used in formal, written English.)

I think the gift <u>that</u> (or <u>which</u>) I found will please Samuel. (*That* [or *which*] is the object of *found* and refers to the gift.)

Notes

- *Whom, that,* and *which* may be omitted when they function as direct objects if the writer wishes to do so. (I think the gift I found will please Samuel.)

- In the relative clauses in rules 1 and 2 above, *that* is preferable to *which* in current American English.

3. *Whom* **and** *which* **can function as the object of a preposition in a relative clause.** *Whom* **refers to persons and** *which* **refers to things.**

Examples:

The person for <u>whom</u> these plane reservations were made never picked up the tickets. (*Whom* is the object of the preposition *for* and refers to the person.)

The history class in <u>which</u> Adela enrolled requires a term paper. (*Which* is the object of the preposition *in* and refers to the history class.)

4. *Whose* **functions as a possessive pronoun in a relative clause and refers to people or things.**

Examples:

The person <u>whose</u> books are on the table will be back soon. (Whose shows that the books belong to the person.)

Eric fixed my car as well as the car <u>whose</u> transmission was broken. (*Whose* shows that the transmission belongs to the car.)

5. Relative clauses can also be connected to the nouns they modify with the relative adverbs *when, where,* and *why.*

Examples:

> The restaurant <u>where</u> we ate is only open for dinner.
> Tell me the reason <u>why</u> you had so much difficulty with the exam.
> I will never forget the time <u>when</u> the teacher got mad at us in class.

In the example sentences given so far in this section, the information added to the sentence by the relative clause is essential, meaning that it is necessary to identify the noun or to distinguish the noun from others of the same type. However, if the relative clause adds additional or extra information to the sentence, it is set off by commas. The first is called a **restrictive** relative clause and the second a **nonrestrictive** relative clause. The sentences below contain nonrestrictive relative clauses. In nonrestrictive relative clauses, *that* is not interchangeable with *who, whom,* or *which.* (Note: Sometimes these clauses are called essential or nonessential.)

Examples:

> My mother, <u>who</u> is 91 years old, lives in a retirement community.
> The University of California, <u>which</u> is a public school, has nine campuses.
> My math professor, <u>who</u> loves to cook, invited us all to dinner at his house.
> Thomas Jefferson, <u>whose</u> home was in Virginia, always loved to return there.
> Pepe's restaurant, <u>where</u> we often eat, has an excellent buffet.
> My fall schedule, <u>which</u> I arranged very carefully, is not working.

Improve Your Writing Style

Vary Your Writing Style by Reducing Relative Clauses

In rule 2 in this section, you learned that *whom, that,* and *which* can be omitted if they function as direct objects. If *who, that,* or *which* is a subject and the main verb is *to be,* the relative clause can be reduced as follows:

To a Past Participle

Long form: The book <u>that was left on the table</u> is no longer there.

Reduced: The book <u>left on the table</u> is no longer there.

To a Noun

Long form: My math professor, <u>who is a Harvard graduate</u>, is a very hard grader.

Reduced: My math professor, <u>a Harvard graduate</u>, is a very hard grader.

IMPROVE YOUR WRITING STYLE, cont.

To a Prepositional Phrase

Long form: The woman <u>who is in the red car</u> is not wearing a seat belt.

Reduced: The woman <u>in the red car</u> is not wearing a seat belt.

To an Infinitive

Long form: The packages <u>that are to be sent</u> are on the table.

Reduced: The packages <u>to be sent</u> are on the table.

To a Participial Phrase

Long form: The revised lab manual, <u>which includes six new experiments</u>, has come in.

Reduced: The revised lab manual, <u>including six new experiments</u>, has come in.

Part B. Adverbial Clauses

Note: Your instructor may mark this error (**adv cl**).

Pretest: What Do You Already Know About Adverbial Clauses?

Test your ability to recognize adverbial clause errors by finding and correcting the one adverbial clause error in each of the following sentences.

Answers on p. 292

1. Although Henry hates grammar, but he studies it anyway.
2. We have purchased one of those pens while we like them.
3. When Meena got a prescription, she went to the doctor.
4. Because of the rain has stopped, we can go on our picnic.
5. Especially I see shoes, I want to buy them.
6. While you were at the movies. Alexander called to ask about the homework assignment.
7. Many travelers fly business class, because they like the wider seats.
8. While he will be working in Australia, we will visit him.

Eight Problems ESL Writers Commonly Encounter with Adverbial Clauses

yes   no   don't know   **PROBLEM 1**

☐   ☐   ☐   An adverbial clause is connected to an independent clause with a subordinating conjunction <u>and</u> a coordinating conjunction.

adv cl

Incorrect: <u>Even though</u> my mother is trying to learn English, <u>but</u> she finds studying it difficult.

Correct: <u>Even though</u> my mother is trying to learn English, she finds studying it difficult.

Note: An alternative way of phrasing this sentence would be: My mother is trying to learn English, <u>but</u> she finds studying it difficult.

In the preceding corrected sentences, note that you have the option of using either a subordinating or a coordinating connector but not *both*.

yes   no   don't know   **PROBLEM 2**

☐   ☐   ☐   A subordinating conjunction with the wrong meaning has been used in an adverbial clause.

adv cl

Incorrect: Bob refuses to wear a tie <u>while</u> the restaurant requires one.

Correct: Bob refuses to wear a tie <u>even though</u> the restaurant requires one. (An adverb of contrast has been used where an adverb of concession is needed.)

Self-Help Strategy: Make sure that the connector you have chosen gives the correct meaning to the sentence. Refer to Grammar Guideline 3 on page 115 for help.

yes   no   don't know   **PROBLEM 3**

☐   ☐   ☐   The connector is correct but is attached to the wrong clause.

adv cl

Incorrect: He broke the window <u>because</u> he had to pay for it.

Correct: <u>Because</u> he broke the window, he had to pay for it.

Self-Help Strategy: Carefully consider the logical relationship that you want to establish between clauses so that you put the connector with the clause to which it belongs.

yes	no	don't know	**PROBLEM 4**
☐	☐	☐	A prepositional phrase has been used instead of a subordinating conjunction in an adverbial clause.

adv cl

Incorrect: Pierre could not travel to Mexico<u>because of</u> his visa had expired.

Correct: Pierre could not travel to Mexico <u>because</u> his visa had expired. (*Because of* is a prepositional phrase. Example: Marlene refused to raise her hand in class because of her shyness.)

Note: A prepositional phrase cannot be used in place of a conjunction to connect two clauses, but it can function as a transition to link one sentence to another. Prepositional phrases commonly used as transitional words are *in addition to, because of, in spite of, in contrast with, in contrast to,* and *in comparison with.*

Example:

Dimitri broke his leg while skiing. <u>Because of his accident</u>, he has to use crutches. (*Because of his accident* connects information in the first sentence to new information in the following sentence.)

yes	no	don't know	**PROBLEM 5**
☐	☐	☐	An adverb has been used instead of a subordinating conjunction in an adverbial clause.

adv cl

Incorrect: <u>Especially</u> my aunt likes hamburgers, we always buy one for her.

Correct: <u>Because</u> my aunt likes hamburgers, we always buy one for her.

Note: <u>Especially</u> is an adverb.   **Example:**   I am especially tired on Mondays.

yes	no	don't know	**PROBLEM 6**
☐	☐	☐	An adverbial clause is a fragment.

adv cl

Incorrect: [While the store was still open.] Harriet bought some soft drinks.

Correct: <u>While the store was still open</u>, Harriet bought some soft drinks. (An adverbial clause is dependent and cannot stand alone as a sentence.)

yes   no   don't know   **PROBLEM 7**

☐   ☐   ☐   The adverbial clause is not followed by a comma or a comma has been used where it is not needed.

                  adv cl

Incorrect: <u>While we were on vacation</u> my brother stayed in our house.

Correct: <u>While we were on vacation,</u> my brother stayed in our house.

                            adv cl

Incorrect: Marjorie likes Davis, <u>because it is a small university town</u>.

Correct: Marjorie likes Davis <u>because it is a small university town</u>.

yes   no   don't know   **PROBLEM 8**

☐   ☐   ☐   One of the future tenses has been used in an adverbial clause of time.

                  adv cl

Incorrect: [When we *will get* home,] we will call you.

Correct: <u>When we get home,</u> we will call you.

                  adv cl

Incorrect: [After we *will have finished*] dinner, we will go for a drive.

Correct: <u>After we have finished dinner,</u> we will go for a drive.

Note: The future tense is not used in adverbial clauses of time. It can only be used in the independent clause.

Grammar Guidelines for Adverbial Clauses

Adverbial clauses are dependent clauses that begin with a subordinating conjunction and show a relationship to the independent (main) clause, such as reason *(because)*, concession *(although, even though)*, or time *(as, while, when). If* clauses are treated separately in Unit 4: "Conditional Sentences."

1. **An adverbial clause can be placed before or after the independent clause, usually without changing the meaning of the whole sentence.**

   Examples:

   <u>Because Kanya is interested in protecting the environment,</u> she recycles paper, glass, and aluminum.
   Kanya recycles paper, glass, and aluminum <u>because she is interested in protecting the environment</u>.

   <u>When the end of the semester is near</u>, students and teachers often begin to feel nervous about final exams.
   Students and teachers often begin to feel nervous about final exams <u>when the end of the semester is near</u>.

2. **Put a comma after a subordinate clause that introduces a sentence. Do not use a comma before a subordinate clause that follows the independent clause. (Exceptions:** *While, whereas, although, even though,* **and** *though* **are usually separated from the independent clause with a comma.)**

   Examples:

   While I was busy registering for my classes and buying my books, my friend Kerry was enjoying her vacation in Canada.

   The dog finally stopped barking after his owner came home and fed him.

   Our town voted not to ban leaf blowers, whereas most other towns in our area already have regulations against them.

   When I was particularly tired one day, I got angry at my boss.

3. **Subordinating conjunctions are used according to the meaning the writer wants to convey.**

contrast	while, whereas	Some people like coffee while others prefer milk.
concession	although, even though, despite the fact that	Although the building looks safe, it has not been checked for asbestos.
result	so . . . that	Hiroshi is so happy he got his verb tenses right in an essay that he is telling everyone.
purpose	so that in order that	My brother booked his flight early so that he would be sure to get on it.
reason	because, since	Jason got a parking ticket because the time on the meter had expired.
time or order	after, as soon as, before, when, while, until, whenever, as, as long as	While my sister was working outside, someone telephoned her. The teacher will give us back our essays as soon as she finishes correcting them.
condition	if, even if, unless, when, whenever	If you study hard enough, you should pass the test.
place	where, wherever	Wherever I travel, I usually meet someone who can speak English.

Improve Your Writing Style

Vary Your Writing Style by Reducing Adverbial Clauses

You can reduce adverbial clauses to add variety to your sentences.

An adverbial clause beginning with *so that* or *because* can be reduced to an infinitive phrase when it has the same subject as the independent clause.

Examples:

> Maren took good notes <u>so that she could share them with her sick roommate</u>.
>
> Maren took good notes <u>to share them with her sick roommate</u>.

An adverbial clause can be reduced to a participial phrase when it has the same subject as the independent clause.

Examples:

> <u>While she was studying</u>, Amy discovered she had not yet read an assigned chapter.
>
> <u>While studying</u>, Amy discovered she had not yet read an assigned chapter.

An adverbial clause can be reduced to an absolute phrase. (An absolute phrase = a noun or pronoun + a present or past participle.)

Examples:

> <u>After he finished his lecture</u>, the professor encouraged the students to ask questions.
>
> <u>His lecture finished</u>, the professor encouraged the students to ask questions.

CAUTION: Do not reduce every adverbial clause but rather use some reduced and some full-length adverbial clauses to provide sentence variety.

Part C: Noun Clauses

Note: Your instructor may mark this error **(n cl)**.

Pretest: What Do You Already Know About Noun Clauses?

Test your ability to recognize noun clause errors by finding and correcting the one noun clause error in each of the following sentences.

Answers on p. 292

1. She got a job so quickly is amazing.
2. We were worried you lost.
3. Christy needs to face up to that she is not prepared for the exam.

4. The city council supports that as many bicycle paths as possible should be built in the city.

5. Barry needs to find out his supervisor wants him to proceed on the project.

6. Matthew promised that he go to the potluck.

7. Marcel is not sure what was the assignment for tomorrow.

8. Her professor prefers that Marta writes a thesis.

9. The students were surprised That the exam was going to be given on Monday.

Nine Problems ESL Writers Commonly Encounter with Noun Clauses

yes   no   don't know   **PROBLEM 1**

☐   ☐   ☐   A noun clause has not been used as a subject of a sentence or as an adjective complement where it is needed.

Note: An adjective complement is a "that" clause which follows a phrase such as "it is necessary, it is unfair, it is common" or a "that" clause which follows an adjective, as in "The mother felt embarrassed that her child was screaming during the movie."

n cl

Incorrect: [Famous athletes and entertainers earn millions of dollars a year] seems unfair.

Correct: That famous athletes and entertainers earn millions of dollars a year seems unfair. (Here the noun clause is used as a subject.)

Correct: It seems unfair that athletes and entertainers earn millions of dollars a year. (Here the noun clause is used as an adjective complement and the dummy subject "it" is used as the subject.)

n cl

Incorrect: Karen is afraid lose money in the stock market.

Correct: Karen is afraid that she will lose money in the stock market. (Note also correct: Karen is afraid of losing money.)

yes   no   don't know   **PROBLEM 2**

☐   ☐   ☐   A noun clause has not been used as an object of a verb.

n cl

Incorrect: I dreamed [the midterm difficult.]

Correct: I dreamed (that) the midterm would be difficult.

n cl

Incorrect: I wonder [the university provides e-mail free of charge to all students.]

Correct: I wonder whether the university provides e-mail free of charge to all students.

n cl

Incorrect: Their acquaintances assume [them as passive, unsociable, and boring.]

Correct: Their acquaintances assume (that) they are passive, unsociable, and boring. (Note also correct: Their acquaintances assume them to be . . .)

yes	no	don't know	**PROBLEM 3**
☐	☐	☐	A noun clause has been used immediately after a phrasal verb without inserting a noun phrase like "the possibility that," "the idea that," or "the fact that."

> **Note:**   A phrasal verb is a verb plus a particle. See Problem 3d in Unit 15, "Prepositions," for more information on phrasal verbs.

n cl

Incorrect: We are concerned [about that there will be a food shortage.]
Correct: We are concerned <u>about the *possibility that* there will be a food shortage</u>.

n cl

Incorrect: We will just have to put up [with that this apartment is noisy.]
Correct: We will just have to put up <u>with *the reality that* this apartment is noisy</u>.

yes	no	don't know	**PROBLEM 4**
☐	☐	☐	A phrase such as "the possibility that," "the idea that," or "the fact that" has not been used before the noun clause when the main verb or an adjective with a preposition requires such a phrase.

n cl

Incorrect: Franklin D. Roosevelt [concealed that he could not walk without support.]
Correct: Franklin D. Roosevelt <u>concealed *the fact* that he could not walk without support</u>.

n cl

Incorrect: We can no longer [dispute that the earth is round.]
Correct: We can no longer <u>dispute *the theory* that the earth is round</u>.

yes	no	don't know	**PROBLEM 5**
☐	☐	☐	A noun clause has not been used as the object of a preposition.

n cl

Incorrect: Helen did not agree [with they said.]
Correct: Helen did not agree <u>with what they said</u>.

yes	no	don't know	**PROBLEM 6**
☐	☐	☐	The verb tense in a noun clause in reported speech is incorrect.

n cl

Incorrect: [She said she go] to Hawaii for spring break.
Correct: <u>She said (that) she was going</u> to Hawaii for spring break.

n cl

Incorrect: [The author stated she has worked] in Mexico City as a nurse 10 years ago.
Correct: <u>The author stated (that) she had worked</u> in Mexico City as a nurse 10 years ago.

yes   no   don't know   **PROBLEM 7**

☐ ☐ ☐   A noun clause that is a reported question has been incorrectly formed because either the wrong connecting word or incorrect word order has been used.

> **Note:**   This error is also covered in Unit 8, "Word Order."

n cl

Incorrect: The researcher hopes to discover [that the function of this chemical is.]
Correct: The researcher hopes to discover <u>what</u> the function of this chemical <u>is</u>.

n cl

Incorrect: The researcher hopes to discover [what is the function of this chemical.]
Correct: The researcher hopes to discover <u>what</u> the function of this chemical <u>is</u>.

yes   no   don't know   **PROBLEM 8**

☐ ☐ ☐   The subjunctive form of the verb (base form) has not been used in a noun clause that expresses a demand, recommendation, requirement, advice, or expectation.

n cl

Incorrect: His friends [recommended John to take] the course.

n cl

Incorrect: His friends [recommended that John takes] the course.
Correct: His friends recommended (that) John <u>take</u> the course.
Correct: His friend recommended (that) John <u>should take</u> the course.

> **Note:**   The use of "should" in this situation is optional and is more common in British English than American English.

yes   no   don't know   **PROBLEM 9**

☐ ☐ ☐   The noun clause is a fragment.

n cl

Incorrect: Pat already told his boss. [That the report would be a little late.]
Correct: Pat already told his boss <u>(that) the report would be a little late</u>.

Grammar Guidelines for Noun Clauses

1. **Like all clauses, noun clauses contain a subject and a verb. Noun clauses, like single-word nouns, function as subjects of sentences or as objects of verbs or prepositions. They are introduced by the connecting word *that*, or, if they are derived from information questions, are introduced by connecting words such as *what, why, where, whether,* or *how*. Examples of other connecting words are *whatever, whether, how long,* and *how often*.**

Examples of noun clauses as subjects:

<u>That eating broccoli can help prevent cancer</u> has been suggested by numerous studies.

<u>That you have graduated</u> makes the whole family proud.

<u>How the experiment was done</u> baffles me.

Examples of noun clauses as objects:

The students have been complaining <u>(that) the room is too cold</u>.

She asked me <u>where I lived</u>.

I am not sure <u>how the experiment was done</u>.

The professor cannot understand <u>why the students did not do well on the lab assignment</u>.

The TA looked at <u>what I had written</u> and made some suggestions for improvement.

2. **A noun clause can follow an adjective. These structures are called adjective complements.**

   Examples of adjective complements:

   It is obvious <u>that John did not prepare for the meeting</u>.

   It was necessary <u>that we attend the meeting</u>.

   (In the above two examples, the noun clause can also be used as a subject as in *That we attend the meeting was necessary.*)

   I am sure <u>that you were invited to the party</u>.

3. **The connecting word *that* can be omitted when the noun clause is in the object position. Note that omitting *that* may make your writing seem less formal.**

   Examples:

   On New Year's Eve, the couple announced (that) they were getting married.

   I doubt (that) the experiment has been properly designed.

4. **Phrasal verbs as well as adjectives that take prepositions must be followed by a noun phrase + that, such as *the fact that, the idea that, the possibility that, the notion that.***

   Examples:

   The tourists <u>complained about *the fact*</u> that the tour bus was not air-conditioned.

   The mayor is <u>worried about *the fact*</u> that so many homeless are in her city.

5. **Certain verbs must also be followed by a noun phrase + that. Such verbs include *accept, conceal, discuss, dispute, disregard, overlook, hide,* and *support.***

   Examples:

   The employees <u>disputed *the fact*</u> that their vacation time had been cut.

   The hikers completely <u>disregarded *the possibility*</u> that it might snow.

6. **Two main groups of verbs-—verbs of indirect speech and verbs of mental activity—are frequently followed by noun clauses.**

   Common verbs of indirect speech: *admit, announce, claim, complain, confess, declare, explain, hint, mention, remark, report, say, state, swear.*

   Common verbs of mental activity: *assume, believe, conclude, decide, discover, doubt, dream, feel, find out, forget, guess, hope, hear, imagine, indicate, know, learn, notice, pretend, question, realize, recall, regret, remember, think, understand.*

   Noun clauses used with verbs of indirect speech:
   Examples:
   > The witness reported <u>(that) he had seen two people</u>.
   > The professor explained <u>(that) he wanted the assignment done by May 1</u>.

   Note: Some verbs of indirect speech must be followed by an indirect object before the noun clause as in the following examples:

   > The president informed <u>his staff</u> (that) he would be out of town for a week.
   > She told <u>me</u> (that) she needed help moving.

   Noun clauses used with verbs of mental activity:
   Examples:
   > I have always believed <u>(that) it is beneficial to think positively</u>.
   > Amir doubts <u>(that) he will be admitted to Harvard Medical School</u>.

7. **In noun clauses following verbs of indirect speech, the verb tense in the noun clause changes to past time when the tense of the main verb changes to past.**

   Examples:
   > She <u>says</u> (that) she <u>will go</u> to the party.
   > She <u>said</u> (that) she <u>would go</u> to the party.

   > Mark <u>says</u> (that) the plane <u>took off</u> ten minutes ago.
   > Mark <u>said</u> (that) the plane <u>had taken off</u> ten minutes previously.

8. **Noun clauses in reported questions are common and may be introduced with question-word connecting words such as *who, where, whether,* or *how.* Note that the word order in these noun clauses is [connecting word + subject + verb].**

   Examples of noun clauses in reported questions:
   > She asked me <u>where I lived</u>.
   > She asked me <u>whether I had Tom's e-mail address</u>.
   > I do not know <u>what the answer is</u>.
   > I wonder <u>what the next lecture will cover</u>.

9. **The subjunctive form of the verb (the base form) is used in a noun clause after verbs expressing an idea, such as a *demand, recommendation, requirement, advice,* or *explanation.* The base form is always used and is not affected by tense or number.**

   Common verbs followed by noun clauses in subjunctive form: *ask, advise, beg, demand, forbid, insist, order, prefer, propose, require, recommend, request, suggest, urge.*

Examples:

The board recommended (that) he <u>resign</u>.

The board recommended (that) he <u>should resign</u>. (The use of *should* is more common in British than American English.)

We suggest (that) Alex <u>be</u> the chairman.

We suggested (that) Alex <u>be</u> the chairman.

Improve Your Writing Style

Know When to Use *That* in a Noun Clause

It helps your reader if you include the word *that* in noun clauses even when it is technically not needed to make the sentence grammatically correct. Note that including *that* is especially helpful in situations in which the noun following the initial verb could also possibly be an object of the verb.

Acceptable: We concluded the experimental design was flawed.

Better: We concluded <u>that</u> the experimental design was flawed.

Acceptable: The gardener found out the problem with the grass was solved.

Better: The gardener found out <u>that</u> the problem with the grass was solved.

Note: For details on omitting *that*, see Item 3 in Grammar Guidelines for Noun Clauses in this unit.

Improve Your Writing Style

Know Variations on Noun Clauses

Improve your writing style by using variations on noun clauses.

A noun clause used as a subject: <u>That he can walk again after his accident</u> is a miracle.

Variation: <u>His being able to walk again after his accident</u> is a miracle.

Variation: <u>For him to be able to walk again after his accident</u> is a miracle.

Variation: <u>His ability to walk again after his accident</u> is a miracle.

A noun clause used as an adjective complement: Charles is afraid <u>that he will lose his money</u>.

Variation: Charles is afraid <u>of losing his money</u>.

PART III

EXERCISES FOR PRACTICE

PART A: Exercises on Relative Clauses

(Do these exercises on your own. Then check your answers with a classmate.)

EXERCISE 1

Directions: **Fill in the blanks with the correct relative pronoun** *who, whom, whose, which,* *that.* **In some cases, more than one answer is possible.**

1. Mark thanked the tutor __who__ had worked with him for the whole semester.

2. Dr. Ruiz is the professor __whose__ economics course I am planning to take next semester.

3. The person with __whom__ I share a locker is over there.

4. The backpack __that__ is on the chair is mine.

5. Portland is a city __whose__ residents tend to be environmentally aware.

EXERCISE 2

Directions: **Combine each of the following sets of sentences into one sentence using a relative clause.**

> **Example:**
>
> The trail guide stayed behind with the hikers. The hikers were too tired to hike any farther.
>
> The trail guide stayed behind with the hikers who were too tired to hike any farther.

1. Genetic engineering is a relatively new technology. It is expected to help immensely in agriculture.

_____

2. The man is a lawyer. I am renting his house.

_____

3. The people were late. We were waiting for them.

_____

4. She borrowed a bicycle. Its tires were slightly flat.

_____

5. Today Michael plans to do the lab experiment. He was unable to do the experiment last week.

_____

6. The student was asked to make a speech at commencement. The student got the highest grades in the class.

_____

7. Some bike riders do not stop at stop signs. ~~These bike riders~~ may be given either a warning or a ticket.

_____

EXERCISE 3

Directions: Identify any problems with relative clauses in the following sentences. If a sentence is correct, write C. If it is incorrect, write I and correct the error. The first correction has been made for you.

with
__I__ 1. The person ᴧwhom I went to the movies fell asleep during the film.

_____ 2. A student who plagiarizes on a paper will fail the paper and possibly the whole course in which he wrote the paper.

__C__ 3. The man whom I met last night and who immigrated to the Unted States a year ago speaks English well.

_____ 4. I wrote a thank-you note to the people whom I visited their home over the Christmas holidays.

_____ 5. The instructor teaches that course is very well organized.
who

PART B: Exercises on Adverbial Clauses

(Do these exercises on your own. Then check your answers with a classmate.)

EXERCISE 1

Directions: Read the material below and fill in the blanks with subordinating conjunctions from the list to create correct adverbial clauses. You may need to use a specific conjunction more than once, and you will not use all of the conjunctions on the list.

| after | as soon as | even though | when | whereas |
| although | because | so that | whenever | while |

1. The day _____ I received my first midterm back in math, I decided that I had to improve my study habits _____ I would not end up failing the class.

2. One of the reasons I feel I did poorly, _____ I had studied, was that my roommates had a big, noisy party the night before the exam _____ I was in my room trying to prepare for it.

whom/that
who / whose

3. Unfortunately, I joined them. However, _~~as soon~~ when/after_ the party was over, I tried to do as much as I could to review for the upcoming exam, but I really needed more time than I had.

4. The serious students did very well, _whereas_ my friends and I, who had partied too much, placed way below the mean on the exam.

5. _Although_ the final exam counts for 50 percent of the grade and I have only a D and a C+ so far, I think I will have to move into the library so that I can stay away from parties.

EXERCISE 2

Directions: **Find the adverbial clause error in each of the following sentences and correct it. The first one has been done for you.**

1. When my parents ~~will~~ buy me a car, I will not have to ask for rides from my friends.

2. Beverly did not ask her tutor for help, Although she needed it.

3. Even though I like to watch television, But I can only watch the news and my favorite game show during the semester.

4. She cannot get good grades whereas she doesn't study.

5. Especially I have been attending college, my parents are giving me more independence.

6. My car often breaks down when I really need it.

7. After Roger has cleaned his apartment, he will go play tennis.

PART C: Exercises on Noun Clauses

(Do these exercises on your own. Then check your answers with a classmate.)

EXERCISE 1

Directions: **Complete the following sentences using a noun clause or adjective complement.**

1. The doctor suggested that _I should did some exercise_ .

2. The instructor observed that _from she didn't the class_ .

3. The student did not fully understand what _the instructor said_ .

4. Peter's teacher recommended that _he studied more_ .

5. It is obvious to everyone that _this is an interesting chapter_ .

6. _it is obvious that my brother_ bothers me.

7. The department requires that _____ .

8. The committee does not know whether _____.

9. The researcher explained that _he didn't find the answer he was looking for_.

10. The news reporter stated that _____.

EXERCISE 2

Directions: Decide whether or not the following sentences are correct (C) or incorrect (I). For incorrect sentences, find the error and correct it.

Although

_____ 1. That the potluck dinner was already over. We were disappointed. _because_ - - -

_____ 2. The school requires that every student takes 15 units each semester. _check rule_

__C__ 3. Elizabeth hopes that her grant will be approved soon.

_____ 4. What are you doing is not my business.

_____ 5. The magicians did so many tricks amazed the audience.

_____ 6. Mr. Smith's manager knows him one of the best workers. _who to be_

_____ 7. The young mother worries her child get lost. _that he's will would_

__C__ 8. Many residents feel that the city has grown too quickly.

_____ 9. The students had no idea the answer. _was_

_____10. The study group could not determine what was the answer. _what_

PART D: Exercises on Adjective, Noun, and Adverbial Clauses

(Do these exercises on your own. Then check your answers with a classmate.)

EXERCISE 1

Directions: Examine the six clause errors that are marked with a star in the paragraph that follows. Rewrite each incorrect sentence correctly below the paragraph. The first one has been done for you.

*Some couples are childless have made a decision not to have children. It is clear that this type of family is rapidly growing in the United States. These couples choose to be childless for various reasons. *However, I personally have a hard time understanding people choose to live without children.

Many couples think that this world is not "good enough" for children to grow up in. *Other couples think they not have enough time and money to raise children. Still others want to focus on developing their careers rather than on raising children.

For me, having children is one of the most essential parts of life. *Because I have always wanted children. It would be hard for me to view a career as being more important than having a family. I am sure I would feel disappointed with my life when I got older if I did not have children or grandchildren. I understand that the world is overpopulated, but having children is one of our basic instincts. *Although I do not want many children, ~~but~~ I certainly hope to have one or two of my own. I believe that children are our future. Although I recognize that having children is not for everyone, *I recommend that everyone who wants to ~~has~~ children.

  have

1. Some couples who (or that) are childless have made a decision not to have children.

2.

3.

4.

5.

6.

EXERCISE 2 Sentence Combining Exercise

Directions: Combine each of the following pairs of sentences into one sentence by using a relative, noun, or adverbial clause. Follow the model. Note that there will often be more than one possible answer.

> **Example:**
>
> No notes will be allowed during the examination.
> This announcement surprised the students.
> *The announcement that no notes will be allowed during the examination surprised the students.*
>
> or
>
> *The students were surprised that no notes would be allowed during the examination.*
>
> or
>
> *Although the announcement surprised the students, no notes will be allowed on the examination.*

1. Mark is currently taking chemistry.

   Chemistry is not a requirement for his major.

   _____ *which is* _____

2. Her grandfather is in a nursing care facility and often gets lonely.

   She tries to visit him at least once a week. ☞

   because _____

3. Her skis are bright yellow with a purple design.

   She just bought them this season.

whenever//
where branch/

4. Jackson gets very stressed out at work.

He always asks for a day off to calm down.

5. London is a very old city.

This fact attracts many visitors.

PART IV

WRITING TOPICS

Select one or more of the following topics for writing and follow the steps in Appendix A.

Topic A: Write about a current news event. First, summarize the news item. Then explain why it is of interest to you or why it is of particular importance.

Topic B: Choose a problem currently facing society that you are interested in (such as the homeless, gangs, drugs, or teenage pregnancies). Explain what the problem is and its possible causes. Then suggest some possible solutions.

Topic C: Describe the scene in the photograph using as much detail as possible. Would you like to live in a city such as this one? Why or why not?

PART V

CNN VIDEO ACTIVITY AND WRITING TOPIC

Can Fish Oils Prevent Lung Disease?

Useful Vocabulary: chronic   inflammation   bronchitis   fatty acids   asthma

Before You Watch

This video highlights a research study on the relationship between the consumption of fish oils and the prevention of lung disease. Discuss the following questions with a classmate.

- What are some major lung diseases and their causes?

- Eating whole grain foods is said to be beneficial in preventing colon cancer. What are some other dietary recommendations for good health that you are aware of?

A new study touts the benefits of fish oils.

While You Watch

- Find out why the medical doctor interviewed in this video segment is concerned about smokers' reaction to this new information.

- Listen to see how the researcher responds to this doctor's concern.

After You Watch

I. **Write a personal reaction.**

   Write a personal reaction of three to five sentences to what you saw in the video. What interested you most? What did you think of the advice given at the end of the video?

II. **Share your reactions.**

   Answer the following questions either orally or in writing. Compare your answers with those of a classmate.

   1. What were the concerns of the medical doctor about the use of fish oils to treat lung ailments, and were these concerns valid? Did the researcher adequately answer these concerns?

   2. If you smoke, will you begin to consume more dark-meat fish on the basis of what you heard in this report? If you don't smoke, would you recommend this remedy to smokers you know?

   3. In your opinion, did the media give a thorough, balanced report on this study?

WRITING TOPIC

This video focuses on the interplay between what people eat and their health. As children, we often hear statements like, "Eat your carrots so that you'll have good eyesight." What are some examples of other dietary recommendations that you are aware of? To what extent do you believe they are just "folk wisdom" or that they indeed have some scientific basis?

Goals

- To learn the importance of mastering sentence structure in writing
- To review seven problems ESL writers commonly encounter with sentence structure
- To learn rules for correct sentence structure
- To develop confidence in using correct sentence structure through practice with exercises and writing assignments

Sentence Structure

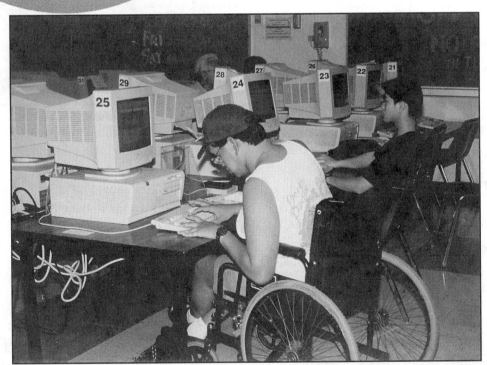

Students use the computer lab during open hours at Mount San Antonio College in Walnut, California.
Photo Courtesy of the President's Office.

Think about and discuss the following question:
How can you use the Internet to get information for a writing assignment?

WHAT YOU NEED TO KNOW ABOUT SENTENCE-STRUCTURE ERRORS

In Part I, you will learn

- The definition of a sentence-structure error
- The importance of correct sentence structure in writing
- Suggestions for mastering sentence structure in writing

Definition of the Error (ss*)

A sentence-structure error **(ss)** is an error in which part of the grammatical structure of a sentence is incorrect. There are several types of sentence structure errors, including missing sentence parts, unnecessary repetition of the subject of a sentence, two clauses joined that do not fit together in a sentence, or problems with parallel structure. Fragments (sentences that are less than complete) and run-on sentences (sentences that are more than complete) are sentence boundary problems, which are also addressed in this unit. As you work through this unit, remember that a complete sentence in English must have at least a subject and a verb.

You need to be aware that sentences marked **ss,** or sentence structure, may also have other errors, but your instructor may choose not to mark them. For instance, an overall problem with sentence structure occurs in the sentence *By assisting to a person who doesn't needs help can be embarrassing* in that the sentence does not have a subject (*Note: By assisting to a person who doesn't needs help* is not a sentence subject; it is an introductory phrase). However, the sentence also contains a subject-verb agreement error *(a person who doesn't <u>needs</u> help)* and a preposition error *(by assisting <u>to</u>)*. However, the most serious problem with the sentence is its incorrect sentence structure.

Importance of Mastering Sentence Structure in Writing

Sentence-structure errors are global (more serious) errors. As such, they not only cause readers great difficulty in understanding a piece of writing but also are highly noticeable to readers. In the sentence, *A person who does not exercise regularly is not because they don't care their health,* the reader has to go back and mentally change the sentence to *A person's failure to exercise regularly may not indicate a lack of concern about his or her health* to make it correct and to be able to comprehend it. Thus, the reader must edit the text while reading its content. Sentence-structure

*ss = grading symbol for an error in sentence structure.

errors are also highly noticeable to readers of formal written English because writers in the academic and professional worlds are expected to have good control of sentence structure. Thus, ESL writers who are making sentence-structure errors will want to give high priority to reducing these errors in their writing.

Suggestions for Mastering Sentence Structure in Writing

- Try to determine if there is a pattern in the sentence-structure errors you are making. Examine your essays and ask yourself whether your sentence-structure errors are of one particular type or of several different types. If you cannot determine whether your errors are similar to any of the types covered in this unit, you will need to ask your instructor or a tutor to help you understand the kind(s) of sentence-structure errors you are making.

- Once you know what your sentence-structure problems are, study the specific rules in this unit. Then, if you know you have a tendency to omit the verb *to be* in your sentences, for example, you can begin to consciously monitor your writing for this error.

- If possible, try to figure out why you are making sentence structure errors. For example, perhaps you are having difficulty with leaving out or repeating the subject of a sentence because such a structure is permitted in your native language.

- Read extensively in English. Although you may not notice its impact on your writing immediately, reading will help you become more familiar with English sentence structure and help improve your ability to write correct sentences in English.

Test Your Understanding of Sentence-Structure Errors

Write answers to the following questions. Share your answers with another student.

1. What are two different kinds of sentence-structure problems?
2. Why do sentence-structure errors make a piece of writing particularly difficult for the reader to comprehend?

> ### Grammar Journal Entry 7: Sentence Structure
>
> *Write a short entry in your grammar journal in response to the following questions.*
>
> 1. Write about your career plans and goals. If you are a student, discuss what ideas you have about your future career. If you are already working, discuss whether or not you are satisfied with your current position or whether you hope to do something different.
> 2. Underline or highlight five sentences in your response to question 1. Then mark the subject and the verb in each sentence. If the sentence has other parts that you can identify (for example, a prepositional phrase or an object), mark those also.

PART II

COMMON PROBLEMS, SELF-HELP STRATEGIES, AND GRAMMAR GUIDELINES

In Part II, you will study

- Seven problems ESL writers commonly encounter with sentence structure
- Self-help strategies for controlling sentence structure in your writing
- Grammar guidelines for correct sentence structure

This section presents seven problems that ESL writers commonly encounter with sentence structure. First, take the pretest to see what you already know about sentence structure. In checking your answers, note that the pretest questions cover the same types of errors in the same order as the problems in this section. Then carefully study each problem and the examples that illustrate it, giving particular attention to those problems that correspond to the pretest questions you had difficulty with. Using the boxes to the left of each problem, check [✓] *yes, no,* or *don't know* to indicate to yourself which problems you should focus the most attention on in this unit and also when you write in English. Remember that becoming aware of the types of errors you most often make with sentence structure will increase your chances of avoiding these errors in your writing.

Pretest: What Do You Already Know About Sentence Structure?

Test your ability to recognize errors in sentence structure by finding and correcting the one sentence-structure error in each of the following sentences.

Answers on p. 292

1. In my opinion, speaking in English easier than writing in English.

2. Is a very interesting point you have raised.

3. My summer internship, for example, it is one way for me to obtain valuable work experience.

4. My parents are first-generation immigrants to the United States, and they communicate mostly native language.

5. I think that some people do not want to help others in an emergency is because of that they do not want to interfere in other people's lives.

6. At present, I am finishing a project and also I start a new one.

7. If you are working as an attorney, the problem is not the quantity of work itself it is the responsibility you feel for defending your clients' interests.

Seven Problems ESL Writers Commonly Encounter with Sentence Structure

yes   **no**   **don't know**   **PROBLEM 1**

☐   ☐   ☐   The verb *to be* is missing.

ss

Incorrect: [My cousin probably a very rich man] in Vietnam since he owned many houses and drove a fancy car.

Correct: My cousin <u>was</u> probably a very rich man in Vietnam since he owned many houses and drove a fancy car.

ss

Incorrect: [There many majors] to choose from on this campus.

Correct: There <u>are</u> many majors to choose from on this campus.

Self-Help Strategy: Be particularly careful not to omit the verb *to be* when it is needed in English, particularly if the verb *to be* does not exist or is used in a different way in your native language.

yes   no   don't know   **PROBLEM 2**

☐   ☐   ☐   The subject of a sentence or clause is missing.

                                        ss
Incorrect: [When we meet new people and start living in a totally new environment are scary.]

Correct: <u>Meeting</u> new people and <u>living</u> in a totally new environment is scary.

> **Note:**   In the incorrect sentence above, the adverb clause beginning with *when* cannot be the subject of the verb *is.* Thus, the sentence does not have a subject.

                                        ss
Incorrect: [When realized his son was frequently skipping class,] Mr. Simon was angry.

Correct: [When <u>he</u> realized his son was frequently skipping class,] Mr. Simon was angry.

                          ss
Incorrect: [Is an interesting class] in which I am learning a great deal.

Correct: <u>It</u> is an interesting class in which I am learning a great deal.

Self-Help Strategy: Make sure all verbs have subjects when you are making statements in English. The verb *to be* sometimes requires the "dummy subject" *it* as in the example above or in the structure [*it is* + adjective]. (*<u>It is easy</u> to park on campus. <u>It is useful</u> to have a dictionary.*)

Note: Verbs in the imperative or command form have an implied subject *you,* as in the sentence *Feel free to leave early* (the implied subject is *you*).

yes   no   don't know   **PROBLEM 3**

☐   ☐   ☐   The subject of a sentence has been unnecessarily repeated.

                                        ss
Incorrect: [<u>My roommate</u> when <u>he</u> is not busy] with his school work, he is working a part-time job.

Correct: When <u>he</u> is not busy with his school work, <u>my roommate</u> is working a part-time job.

Self-Help Strategy: Remember that, in conversation, English speakers sometimes repeat the subject of a sentence as in the incorrect example above. In formal writing, however, this kind of repetition is incorrect.

yes	no	don't know	**PROBLEM 4**
☐	☐	☐	Words in a sentence are missing.

Note: Missing subjects are covered in Problem 2.

Incorrect: They don't want their children to grow up [in a broken family father's or mother's love.] ^{ss}

Correct: They don't want their children to grow up in a broken family <u>without</u>a father's or mother's love.

Incorrect: He also knew that he didn't possess [enough power to against the current government.] ^{ss}

Correct: He also knew that he didn't possess enough power to <u>fight</u>against the current government.

yes	no	don't know	**PROBLEM 5**
☐	☐	☐	Two clauses or a clause and a phrase have been used that do not fit together grammatically.

Note: This error is sometimes called *mixed sentence structure.*

Incorrect: [As my brother said to my mother that he did not feel like having a family.] ^{ss}

Correct: My brother said to my mother that he did not feel like having a family.

Correct: As my brother said to my mother, he does not feel like having a family.

Incorrect: [In the article, "Vitamin C Under Attack," by Mario Nevares, explains some possible negative effects] of taking large doses of vitamin C. ^{ss}

Correct: <u>In the article, "Vitamin C Under Attack," Mario Nevares explains</u>some possible negative effects of taking large doses of vitamin C.

yes	no	don't know	**PROBLEM 6**
☐	☐	☐	A parallel structure has not been used when needed.

Note: Your instructor may mark this kind of error **ss (not //)**.

Incorrect: My advisor told me to check out a journal from the library [and that reading it
        ss (not //)
    as soon as possible was necessary].

Correct: My advisor told me <u>to check out</u>a journal from the library and <u>to read</u>it as soon as possible.

Incorrect: Most successful students are skilled at taking notes, summarizing, [and are
        ss (not //)
    able to read critically].

Correct: Most successful students are skilled at <u>taking</u>notes, <u>summarizing,</u> and <u>reading</u> critically.

yes	no	don't know	**PROBLEM 7**
☐	☐	☐	A sentence boundary problem has occurred. Either the sentence is a fragment (sentences that are less than a complete sentence) or a run-on sentence (sentences that are more than a complete sentence).

Note: Your instructor may mark these errors **ss (frag)** for a fragment or **ss (ro)** for a run-on sentence.

ss (ro)

Incorrect: [On the river rafting trip, please bring clothes that will dry quickly and keep you warm polyester and wool are the best.]

Correct: On the river rafting trip, please bring clothes that will dry quickly and keep you warm. <u>Polyester and wool are the best</u>.

ss (frag)

Incorrect: [After having had the experience of traveling abroad.] An individual has a broader perspective on the world.

Correct: After having had the experience of traveling abroad, an individual has a broader perspective on the world.

Grammar Guidelines for Sentence Structure

Understanding English Sentences

If you learn the following important information about English sentence structure, you will be able to avoid many of the sentence-structure problems illustrated above. English sentence structure is complex and is not covered in full detail in these guidelines.

1. A sentence is a group of words that can stand by itself as a complete idea. It must have at least a subject and a main verb in order to be complete. For example, the sentence *Cats meow* is complete because *cats* is the subject and *meow* is the main verb. Some verbs require objects or complements to follow them in order to make the sentence complete. For example, *The wall is red* is a complete sentence because it has a subject *(the wall)* and a verb *(is)*. But it also needs a complement to make it complete *(red)*. The sentence, *John gave a speech* is a complete sentence because it has a subject *(John)* and a verb *(gave)*. But it also needs a direct object *(a speech)* to make it complete.

2. Sentences are sometimes defined as having a subject and a predicate. The predicate is the verb and all of its complements (such as adverbs, direct and indirect objects, auxiliary verbs, prepositional phrases).

subject   predicate
The wall / is red.
subject   predicate
John / gave a speech.

Note: A verb in the imperative, or command form, does not have a stated subject in English because the subject *you* is implied, as in the sentence, *Please <u>give</u> me your e-mail address,* where the verb *give* is a command. This is the only type of verb that does not need a stated subject in a sentence in English.

3. Standard word order for sentences in English is [subject-verb-object] or [subject-verb-complement]. For more information on word order in sentences, see Unit 8, "Word Order," in this textbook.

4. A sentence must have at least one independent clause. A dependent clause is not a complete sentence even though it has a subject and a verb. However, when a dependent clause is connected to an independent clause, the entire structure is a complete sentence. When you write sentences of more than one clause, make sure that the two clauses you have chosen fit together correctly. If not you will have a mixed construction or a sentence-structure error, as illustrated in Problem 5 above. See Unit 5 in this textbook, "Relative, Adverbial, and Noun Clauses," for more information on dependent clauses and how they work together with independent clauses.

> New York is on the east coast of the United States.
> (independent clause = complete sentence)
> While New York is on the east coast of the United States.
> (dependent clause = *not* a complete sentence)
> While Los Angeles is on the west coast, New York is on the east coast of the United States.
> (one independent clause and one dependent clause = complete sentence)

5. The subject of a sentence can be one of the following:
- a noun (*the book; Maria; an engineer*)
- a pronoun (*it; she; he*)
- a noun clause (*what the engineer said; that you were late*)
- a gerund or infinitive (*reading; to read*)

Note: A prepositional phrase (*in the article by Leon Smith; at the movies*) <u>cannot</u> serve as a sentence subject.

6. The verb in a sentence can be one main verb or a main verb in a verb phrase. For more information on verb phrases, see Unit 2, "Verb Forms," in this textbook.

> Norman <u>bicycles</u> to work everyday. (main verb)
> Norman <u>has been bicycling</u> to work everyday for a year.
> (verb phrase: main verb with two auxiliary verbs preceding it)

Avoiding Sentence Boundary Problems

A complete sentence begins with a capital letter (upper case) and ends with a punctuation mark (a period or full stop, a question mark, or an exclamation point), as shown in the following examples:

> Employees generally have a four-day weekend for Thanksgiving.
> Do employees have a four-day weekend for Thanksgiving?
> I am so happy that this coming weekend is a four-day weekend!

A fragment is less than a sentence. The sentence that follows is not complete because it is a dependent clause and needs to be connected to an independent clause to make it a complete sentence.

(Fragment)	Even though employees generally have a four-day weekend for Thanksgiving.
(Revision)	Even though employees generally have a four-day weekend for Thanksgiving, some will have to remain on call for emergencies.

Avoid fragments by making sure that your sentences have at least a subject and a main verb and one independent clause.

A run-on sentence is more than a sentence. The sentence that follows is a run-on because it consists of two independent clauses without any punctuation. These clauses must be separated by a punctuation mark or be joined with a connecting word.

(Run-on)	Living away from home for the first time has been a learning experience for me I have become a much more independent and self-sufficient person.
(Revision)	Living away from home for the first time has been a learning experience for me. I have become a much more independent and self-sufficient person.
(Revision)	Living away from home for the first time has been a learning experience for me, <u>for</u> I have become a much more independent and self-sufficient person.

A comma splice is a type of run-on sentence in which two independent clauses are incorrectly separated with a comma instead of a period or semicolon.

(Comma splice)	One option is to listen to music, another option is to watch a video.
(Revision)	One option is to listen to music; another option is to watch a video.
(Revision)	One option is to listen to music. Another option is to watch a video.
(Revision)	One option is to listen to music, <u>while</u> another option is to watch a video.
(Revision)	One option is to listen to music, <u>but</u> another option is to watch a video.
(Revision)	One option is to listen to music; <u>however,</u> another option is to watch a video.

Avoid run-on sentences and comma splices by making sure that complete sentences (independent clauses) end with either a period, question mark, or exclamation mark or by making sure that two independent clauses are joined by a connecting word (for example, *and, but, for, after, before, while, because*) or by a semicolon.

Using Parallel Structure

Whenever one or more items in a sentence are joined by the words *and, but, or, nor, yet*, these parts of the sentence should be parallel in structure. That is, they should have the same grammatical form (for example, all infinitives, all noun clauses, or all prepositional phrases).

Examples of Parallel Structure

Verbs (infinitives):
I like to <u>swim, to surf,</u> and <u>to waterski</u>.

Verbs (base forms):
I like to <u>swim, surf,</u> and <u>waterski</u>.

Verbs (gerunds):
I enjoy <u>swimming, surfing,</u> and <u>waterskiing</u>.

Verbs (present participles):
While he was <u>thinking about</u> the class lectures and <u>reviewing</u> some articles, he got an idea for his term paper.

Prepositional phrases:
Nowadays, computers are used heavily <u>by many people</u> and <u>in many different ways</u>.

Noun clauses:

Professor Allen has promised <u>that the exam will be graded by 5 PM</u> and <u>that the scores will be posted outside his office by 5:30 PM</u>.

Adjectives:

The teacher is <u>friendly</u> and <u>helpful</u> but somewhat <u>disorganized</u>.

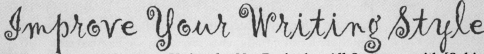

Improve Your Writing Style

Improve Sentence Variety by Not Beginning All Sentences with [Subject + Verb] Structure

Although every complete sentence needs to have a subject and a verb, the subject does not always have to be the first word in a sentence in English. You can improve sentence variety in your writing by using other kinds of structures at the beginning of some of your sentences. Some of these structures are illustrated in the examples that follow.

A time word or phrase

<u>Yesterday</u>, we decided to go on a hike in the mountains.

An infinitive phrase to show purpose

<u>To avoid being indoors all day</u>, we decided to go on a hike in the mountains.

A dependent clause

<u>Because the weather was so beautiful</u>, we decided to go on a hike in the mountains.

A prepositional phrase

<u>In my hometown</u>, many beautiful hiking trails attract visitors and residents alike.

An adverb

<u>Certainly</u>, I can see your point.

A transitional word or phrase

<u>On the other hand</u>, I can see you have a point, even though I do not fully agree.

PART III

EXERCISES FOR PRACTICE

EXERCISE 1 (Do this exercise on your own. Then check your answers with a classmate.)

Directions: The following sentences contain sentence-structure errors. First, decide whether a sentence is correct (C) or incorrect (I). Then correct the incorrect sentences by rewriting the complete sentence correctly below the original sentence.

> **Note:** The sentences in this exercise cover all the different types of sentence-structure errors presented in this unit. For exercises on sentence boundaries and parallel structure only, see Exercises 2 and 3.

_I_ 1. Molecular genetics a field that is progressing very quickly.

Molecular genetics is a field that is progressing very quickly.

_____ 2. To know their native language should be proud instead of embarrassed.

_____

_____ 3. She wonders whether studying so hard worth it.

_____

_____ 4. Engineering 10, it is the course that I spend the least time on.

_____

_____ 5. Room 100 Smith Hall is one of the largest classrooms on my campus it can hold around 500 students.

_____

_____ 6. As grow up, many children develop attitudes they will later have as adults.

_____

_____ 7. To improve her writing skills, Laura keeps a daily writing journal and reads as much as possible.

_____

_____ 8. Astronauts need to be prepared for every obstacle that could encounter in space.

_____

_____ 9. When she has spare time, Antonia likes to take bike rides, read novels, and visiting her friends.

_____

_____10. The office is well equipped has a lot of antique furniture.

_____

_____11. By putting up posters of beautiful landscapes has made me feel more relaxed in my office.

_____

EXERCISE 2 (Do this exercise with a classmate.)

A. Directions: Some of the following sentences have parallel-structure problems. Correct any problems in parallel structure by rewriting the incorrect sentences. The first correction has been done for you.

1. That Jack arrived late to the meeting and his not being prepared angered his supervisor.

   That Jack arrived late to the meeting and that he was not prepared angered his supervisor.

2. I hope to introduce you to Dr. Wood, my thesis advisor and who chairs the Chemistry Department.

3. In college, what classes you take and when you take them is generally your own decision.

4. His summer job involves washing laboratory equipment, to set up new experiments, and recording some basic data.

5. Growing up in a large family and working parents resulted in Elizabeth's not getting much individual attention from her parents.

6. If my visitor had not been to San Francisco, I would have spent a day there walk on the Golden Gate Bridge, lingering in Chinatown, visit the Japanese Tea Garden in Golden Gate Park, and do many other things.

B. Directions: Complete the following sentences in your own words. Make sure you use parallel structure.

1. Three things I enjoy doing in my free time are _____.

2. In my opinion, a good teacher has the following characteristics: _____.

3. Several good places to go for a bicycle ride in or near the city I live in are_____.

C. Directions: Complete the following list of suggestions, making sure that the items listed under the bullets are parallel in structure.

Ways to Avoid Feeling Homesick in a New Environment
- Stay active (or By staying active)
-
-
-

EXERCISE 3: (Do this exercise on your own. Then check your answers with a classmate.)

Directions: **Four of the following sentences have sentence boundary problems, while one is correct. Correct the incorrect sentences. Circle the number of the sentence that is correct.**

1. The most useful class I took was statistics, it was very challenging for me.

2. Thus far, school is more fun than work however I find the studies quite hard.

3. Statistics is a very useful class for me as I will need the material to analyze my research data.

4. Chicago is such an interesting city I love going there.

5. Another reason why some people do not exercise regularly. Simply a lack of time.

Exercise 4: (Do this exercise on your own.)

Directions: **Choose at least five sentences from one of your textbooks, a journal, a newspaper, or a magazine. Examine each sentence carefully and look at its structure. Try to notice how the sentences are constructed, including how each sentence begins, how each is punctuated, where the subject and main verb are, and whether the sentence is made up of one clause or more than one.**

PART IV

WRITING TOPICS

Select one or more of the following topics for writing and follow the steps in Appendix A.

Topic A: Write about something you have always thought about doing but have never done, perhaps because the opportunity never presented itself or you were afraid or reluctant to carry out your plans. Explain what you have wanted to do and why you would like or would have liked to do it.

Topic B: Most individuals would agree that we learn not only in formal classroom situations but that much of our learning also goes on outside of school. Write about an important learning experience that you have had outside of the classroom. Explain the experience and what you learned from it.

Topic C: The lifestyle of elderly members of society can vary from culture to culture. For example, in some cultures, the elderly live with family members, while in other cultures they remain on their own or live in retirement communities. Describe the lifestyle of the elderly in your culture of origin. Do you think they live satisfying lives?

PART V

CNN VIDEO ACTIVITY AND WRITING TOPIC

Breaking the Color Barrier in Baseball

Useful Vocabulary: color barrier   legacy   inspiration   integrate   integration   civil rights

Before You Watch

This video segment tells the story of Jackie Robinson, who broke the color barrier in major league baseball and worked all his life to promote civil rights for African Americans.

- What are your favorite sports to play and watch?
- Think about the sports you have seen on TV. To what extent are the teams integrated?

While You Watch

- Listen for and jot down what Jackie Robinson did after retiring from baseball.
- What is Jackie Robinson's wife doing now to carry on his legacy?

In 1947 Jackie Robinson accepted the challenge of integrating major league baseball teams.

After You Watch

I. **Write a personal reaction.**

Write a personal reaction of three to five sentences to what you saw in the video. What interested you most? What would you have liked to learn more about?

II. **Share your reactions.**

Answer the following questions either orally or in writing. Compare your answers with those of a classmate.

1. List some personal characteristics of Jackie Robinson that were mentioned in the video.
2. From information given in this video, do you think that Jackie Robinson was a sufficiently important baseball player to have a baseball season dedicated to his memory?
3. In her speech, Jackie Robinson's wife urged Americans to continue promoting civil rights, the work that Jackie had begun. How important do you think this work is?

WRITING TOPIC

Like Hollywood movie stars, sports figures are in the limelight and have an impact on society. What are some of the impacts, both positive and negative, that sports stars have on us as a society? Explain your answer.

Goals

- To learn the importance of mastering word order in writing
- To review seven problems ESL writers commonly encounter with word order
- To learn rules for correct word order
- To develop confidence in using correct word order through practice with exercises and writing assignments

Word Order

A tutor helps a student at the learning center at Oakton Community College in Des Plaines, Illinois.
Photo courtesy of College Relations.

Think about and discuss the following question:
Where can you go on campus for
help with your writing when an
instructor is not available?

PART I

WHAT YOU NEED TO KNOW ABOUT WORD-ORDER ERRORS

In Part I, you will learn

- The definition of a word-order error
- The importance of using word order correctly in writing
- Suggestions for mastering word order in writing

Definition of the Error (wo*)

A word-order error **(wo)** is one in which the order of words in a sentence is incorrect or awkward. For example, in the sentence *The basketball team was exhausted <u>completely</u> after the game,* the word *completely* is in an incorrect position in the sentence; it should come before the adjective *exhausted.* In the sentence *Mary <u>yesterday</u> went to the library,* the word *yesterday* is in an awkward position in the sentence; it usually comes at the beginning or the end of the sentence.

Importance of Mastering Word Order in Writing

Word-order errors are global (more serious) errors because in some cases they can affect the organization of a whole sentence. For example, in the sentence *Spanish language speak many people in Latin America,* the word order, which is not English word order, affects the whole sentence, making it difficult for the reader to understand. Some word-order errors, however, may not be as serious and may not affect the reader's understanding of the overall sentence. For example, in the sentence *Mary lent to John the book,* the word order is incorrect, but the reader can still easily understand the message. Nevertheless, incorrect or awkward word order, whether serious or less serious, will distract the reader and make a piece of writing difficult to read, particularly if the error is frequent.

Suggestions for Mastering Word Order in Writing

- Keep in mind that not all ESL writers have problems with English word order. Some writers, however, tend to experience problems with word order when using certain grammatical structures, such as indirect questions, adverbs, or adverbial phrases. If you are having problems with word order in these cases, you will find the grammar guidelines and self-help strategies in Part II of this unit helpful.

*wo = grading symbol for an error in word order.

- Think about the word order used in your native language in order to become aware of any patterns that you might be incorrectly transferring into English. In English, the basic word order is [subject + verb + object] as in *Gene + is reading + the newspaper*, or [subject + verb + complement] as in *Gene + is + happy*. In some languages, such as Japanese and Korean, the basic word order is [subject + object + verb]. In other languages, such as Tagalog, the basic word order is [verb + subject + object]. Even if your native language has the same basic word order as English does, there still may be other differences. For example, although Spanish and English have the same basic word order [subject + verb + object], word-order differences still occur. In Spanish, adjectives often come after the noun they modify, while in English, they usually come before the noun they modify, as in *These black shoes belong to Jessica.*

- Keep in mind that in some cases—for example, with adverbs—you will have options with word order. Notice how the adverb *sometimes* can be placed in three different locations in the sentences *Sometimes I go to the movies, I go to the movies sometimes,* and *I sometimes go to the movies.* This means that, in these cases, you as the writer will choose which word order you want to use.

- Remember that perhaps the best way to master English word order is by reading extensively. You can focus on the word order used in your textbooks as well as in the books, magazines, and newspapers that you read.

Test Your Understanding of Word Order

Write answers to the following questions. Share your answers with another student.

1. Why can word-order errors be either serious or less serious?

2. What is the basic word order of English? Is word order always fixed in English? Explain.

Grammar Journal Entry 8: Word Order

Write a short entry in your grammar journal in response to the following questions.

1. Describe a place that you frequently go to. It could be a cafe, restaurant, supermarket, store, park, or other location. Explain what the place looks like, what people do there, and why you like to go there.

2. Are there any differences in word order that you can identify between English and your native language? Write a simple sentence in your language and label the basic word-order patterns that you see. Include at least subject, verb, and object. You can include nouns and adjectives if you wish.

COMMON PROBLEMS, SELF-HELP STRATEGIES, AND GRAMMAR GUIDELINES

In Part II, you will study

- Seven problems ESL writers commonly encounter with word order
- Self-help strategies for controlling word order in your writing
- General guidelines for English word order

This section presents seven problems that ESL writers commonly encounter with word order. First, take the pretest to see what you already know about word order. In checking your answers, note that the pretest questions cover the same types of errors in the same order as the problems in this section. Then carefully study each problem and the examples that illustrate it, giving particular attention to those problems that correspond to the pretest questions you had difficulty with. Using the boxes to the left of each problem, check [✓] *yes, no,* or *don't know* to indicate to yourself which problems you should focus the most attention on in this unit and also when you write in English. Remember that becoming aware of the types of errors you most often make with word order will increase your chances of avoiding these errors in your writing.

Pretest: What Do You Already Know About Word Order?

Test your ability to recognize word-order errors by finding and correcting the one word-order error in each of the following sentences.

Answers on p. 293

1. I do not remember when is the job application due.
2. The meeting has been postponed because the chairperson is getting the flu over.
3. O'Hare airport in Chicago is busy extremely.
4. The roses red long-stemmed are the loveliest.
5. My department awarded to me a certificate of commendation.
6. The movies at the downtown six-screen cinema change always on Fridays.
7. We left the laboratory because we did not have time to finish the experiment at 7:00 PM.

Seven Problems ESL Writers Often Encounter with Word Order

yes	no	don't know	**PROBLEM 1**
☐	☐	☐	The word order is incorrect in an indirect question that makes up a noun clause.

> **Note:** This error is also covered in Unit 6, "Relative, Adverbial, and Noun Clauses," in the section on noun clauses.

wo

Incorrect: When I came home, I wondered [where were my roommates].
Correct: When I came home, I wondered <u>where my roommates were</u>.

wo

Incorrect: I don't know [what did the instructor say] about the next lab assignment.
Correct: I don't know <u>what the instructor said</u> about the next lab assignment.

wo

Incorrect: The article does not clearly explain [how was the experiment performed].
Correct: The article does not clearly explain <u>how the experiment was performed</u>.

yes	no	don't know	**PROBLEM 2**
☐	☐	☐	The pronoun that accompanies a two-word verb (such as *hand in, pick up, throw out*) has been incorrectly placed.

> **Note:** These verbs are often called *phrasal verbs,* and the prepositions that go with these verbs are called *particles.*

wo

Incorrect: I don't like these posters anymore. I have decided to [throw out them].
Correct: I don't like these posters anymore. I have decided to <u>throw them out</u>.

wo

Incorrect: Any student who misses a quiz cannot [make up it].
Correct: Any student who misses a quiz cannot <u>make it up</u>.

Self-Help Strategy: Review the word-order guidelines in this section for information on when two-word verbs can and cannot be separated. Keep in mind that you will need to memorize, on a case-by-case basis, whether each two-word verb is always separable, optionally separable, or never separable. An ESL dictionary will indicate whether or not a phrasal verb is separable.

yes	no	don't know	**PROBLEM 3**
☐	☐	☐	An adverb that modifies an adjective has been incorrectly placed.

                     wo
Incorrect: The mayor had become [aware more] of his position in the town.
Correct: The mayor had become <u>more aware</u> of his position in the town.

              wo
Incorrect: I felt [exhausted completely] after the all-day hike.
Correct: I felt <u>completely exhausted</u> after the all-day hike.

yes	no	don't know	**PROBLEM 4**
☐	☐	☐	An adjective that modifies a noun has been incorrectly placed.

          wo
Incorrect: The [notebook blue] is Jerry's.
Correct: The <u>blue notebook</u> is Jerry's.

             wo
Incorrect: The [blue large notebook] is Jerry's.
Correct: The <u>large blue notebook</u> is Jerry's.

Self-Help Strategy: Remember that adjectives come *before* the nouns they modify in English. See the word-order guidelines later in this section for cases in which more than one adjective modifies a noun.

yes	no	don't know	**PROBLEM 5**
☐	☐	☐	The word order is incorrect after a verb that has both a direct object and an indirect object.

                           wo
Incorrect: The president of the company [gave to Jenna a special assignment].
Correct: The president of the company gave a <u>special assignment to Jenna</u>.
Correct: The president of the company gave <u>Jenna a special assignment</u>.

          wo
Incorrect: Matt [bought for me a present].
Correct: Matt bought <u>a present for me</u>.
Correct: Matt bought <u>me a present</u>.

yes   no   don't know   **PROBLEM 6**

☐   ☐   ☐   An adverb has been incorrectly placed.

                   wo

Incorrect: I went [yesterday] to the movies with Johan.
Correct: I went to the movies with Johan <u>yesterday</u>.
Correct: <u>Yesterday</u> I went to the movies with Johan.
Correct: I went to the movies <u>yesterday</u> with Johan.

                   wo

Incorrect: [Poorly,] Bill did that cleaning job.
Correct: Bill did that cleaning job <u>poorly</u>.

yes   no   don't know   **PROBLEM 7**

☐   ☐   ☐   Adverbial phrases or clauses at the end of a sentence are not in the correct order.

Note: In English more than one adverbial phrase or clause can occur at the end of a sentence. Some of these adverbial phrases or clauses can also occur at the beginning of the sentence. However, usually only one adverbial clause or phrase can occur at the beginning of a sentence.

                   wo

Incorrect: Mark lifts weights [to keep in shape every morning].
Correct: Mark lifts weights <u>every morning to keep in shape</u>.
Correct: <u>Every morning</u>, Mark lifts weights <u>to keep in shape</u>.
Correct: <u>To keep in shape</u>, Mark lifts weights <u>every morning</u>.

                   wo

Incorrect: We left the movie [because it was boring before it was over].
Correct: We left the movie <u>before it was over because it was boring</u>.

                   wo

Incorrect: I walked [this morning to the cafeteria].
Correct: I walked <u>to the cafeteria this morning</u>.
Correct: <u>This morning</u>, I walked <u>to the cafeteria</u>.

Grammar Guidelines for Word Order

Basic Word Order in English

     Subject + verb + object   or   **Subject + verb + complement**
   (Gene + is reading + the newspaper.)   (Gene + is + happy.)

Word Order in Indirect Questions

Always use statement word order (not direct-question word order) for noun clause indirect questions. In other words, do not invert the subject and the verb as you would when asking a direct question.

Direct-question word order: Invert the subject and first auxiliary verb.

Examples:

Where <u>have you</u> been living?
<u>Did Paul</u> pass the midterm?

Indirect-question word order: Do not invert the subject and verb.

Examples:

I don't know where <u>you live</u>.
I wonder whether <u>Paul passed</u> the midterm.

Some common phrases followed by noun-clause indirect questions include those in italics in the sentences below.

I wonder where the post office is.
I don't know whether (or not) Tom will be coming to the potluck.
I cannot remember why my supervisor wants to meet with me.
I do not understand what the lecture was about.
I am not sure if the meeting is tomorrow or the next day.
Could you please tell me what your date of birth is.
I asked where the nearest pay phone was.

Word Order for Noun and Pronoun Object Placement with Two-Word (Phrasal) Verbs

Using two-word verbs can be challenging because some two-word verbs cannot be separated, meaning the object must always come after the verb and its particle. Some two-word verbs can be optionally separated, meaning the object can either come after the verb and particle or between it. Other two-word verbs must always be separated, meaning the object must come between the verb and particle. You can review the word order guidelines in this section for more detailed information on two-word verbs, but keep in mind that you will need to memorize on a case-by-case basis whether each two-word verb is always separable, optionally separable, or never separable. Also remember that an ESL dictionary will indicate whether or not a phrasal verb is separable.

Examples:

Half of the voters <u>sided with</u> the governor on the controversial issue. (cannot be separated)
Marsha <u>filled up</u> the beaker. or Marsha <u>filled</u> the beaker <u>up</u>. (can be optionally separated)

John finally decided to <u>ask</u> Christy <u>out</u>. (must be separated)

If a phrasal verb can be separated and it has an object pronoun, this pronoun will always be located between the verb and the particle. If the phrasal verb is not separable, the pronoun will come after the verb.

1. **Always separated: The object or object pronoun comes between the verb and its particle.**

   Examples:

   > Martha <u>talked</u> her father <u>into</u> letting her use the car.
   > Martha <u>talked</u> him <u>into</u> letting her use the car.

2. **Can be separated: The object comes either after the verb and particle or between the verb and particle. An object pronoun always comes between the verb and its particle.**

   Examples:

   > Jake said he wanted <u>to think over</u> the situation.
   > Jake said he wanted <u>to think</u> the situation <u>over</u>.
   > Jake said he wanted <u>to think</u> it <u>over</u>.

3. **Never separated: The object or object pronoun comes after the verb and its particle.**

   Examples:

   > Katya <u>takes after</u> her mother.
   > Katya <u>takes after</u> her.

Word Order for Adjectives That Modify Nouns

Adjectives come **before** the nouns they modify in English.

Examples:

> the <u>red</u> roses
> a <u>cloning</u> technique
> a <u>football</u> field
> an <u>excellent</u> proposal

When more than one adjective modifies a noun, use the following guide to decide on the order of adjectives.

1	2	3	4	5	6	
(number) +	(general comment) +	(size) +	(shape) +	(color) +	(material) +	NOUN

Examples:

> several high-strength black steel beams
> (a) long rectangular grey metal sheet
> numerous flashing multicolored lights
> several small black and white dogs

Word Order for Adverbs That Modify Adjectives

An adverb that modifies an adjective comes **before** the adjective.
Examples:

San Francisco is <u>extremely</u> beautiful.
This classroom is <u>unusually</u> small.
They have a <u>completely</u> remodeled kitchen.

Word Order for Direct and Indirect Objects of Verbs

Not many verbs in English take both a direct and an indirect object. However, the following two rules will help you master word order in sentences containing both objects.

1. **When a verb (V) has both a direct object (DO) and an indirect object (IO), the direct object must come first if the indirect object is preceded by *to* or *for*. If, however, the *to* or *for* is omitted, then the indirect object must come first.**

   Examples:

   <pre>   V   DO   IO</pre>
   The clerk <u>sold</u> <u>a book</u> <u>to me</u>.

   <pre>   V   IO   DO</pre>
   The clerk <u>sold</u> <u>me</u> <u>a book</u>.

   <pre>   V   DO   IO</pre>
   Matt <u>bought</u> <u>a present</u> <u>for me</u>.

   <pre>   V   IO   DO</pre>
   Matt <u>bought</u> <u>me</u> <u>a present</u>.

   Some common verbs that take an indirect object with *to* are *give, write, show, teach, sell, send, lend, bring, hand.*

   Some common verbs that take an indirect object with *for* are *buy, get, make, bake.*

2. **A small number of verbs must have the indirect object follow the direct object, and this indirect object must be preceded by *to* or *for*. Verbs in this group that take indirect objects with *for* include *answer, open, close*. Verbs in this group that take indirect objects with *to* include *announce, introduce, suggest, mention, describe.***

   <pre>   wo</pre>
   Incorrect: Richard [explained Mary the math problem].
   Correct: Richard explained <u>the math problem to Mary</u>.

   <pre>   wo</pre>
   Incorrect: Richard [answered Mary the question].
   Correct: Richard answered <u>the question for Mary</u>.

Word Order Guidelines for Placement of Adverbs

Generally, adverbs can be placed in several different positions in a sentence.

Initial position (at the beginning of the sentence)
Example: <u>Yesterday</u> I sailed for four hours.

Midposition (before the verb or in the middle of the verb phrase)
Examples: I <u>especially</u> like Boston.
                          I do not <u>really</u> like peanut butter ice cream.

End position (at the end of the sentence)
Example: I expect my friend to arrive <u>tomorrow</u>.

However, not all adverbs can be placed in all three positions. What follows are some general guidelines for adverb placement according to the function of the adverb.

1. Adverbs of place usually take the end position.

Correct: John is sitting <u>outside</u>.
                                        wo
Incorrect: <u>Outside</u> John is sitting.

Other common adverbs of place include *inside, here, there.*

2. Adverbs of definite time usually take the beginning or end position.

Correct: I went to my aerobics class <u>yesterday.</u>
Correct: <u>Yesterday,</u> I went to my aerobics class.
                                        wo
Incorrect: I went <u>yesterday</u> to my aerobics class.

Other common adverbs of definite time include *today, tomorrow, now.*

3. Adverbs of indefinite time can take the initial, middle, or end position.

Correct: <u>Recently,</u> I have become interested in karate.
Correct: I have <u>recently</u> become interested in karate.
Correct: I have become interested in karate <u>recently</u>.

Another adverb of indefinite time is *lately,* although it is not usually used in midposition.

4. Adverbs used to evaluate usually take the end position.

Correct: Bill did that cleaning job <u>well</u>.
                                        wo
Incorrect: Bill did <u>well</u> that cleaning job.

Other common adverbs used to evaluate include *badly, poorly.*

5. **Adverbs of manner** usually take the middle or end position but can take the initial position.

Correct: Luis <u>quietly</u> opened the door to the baby's room.
Correct: Luis opened the door to the baby's room <u>quietly</u>.
Correct: <u>Quietly,</u> Luis opened the door to the baby's room.

Other common adverbs of manner include *quickly, carelessly, softly.*

6. **Adverbs of frequency** follow very specific rules regarding their position in the sentence.

(Common adverbs of frequency include *always, frequently, occasionally, seldom, continually, hardly ever, often, sometimes, never, ever, rarely, usually.*)

a. **With the verb** *to be*—**usually after the verb**
Correct: John is <u>never</u> at home when I call him.
Correct: Vincent is <u>continually</u> busy.

b. **With the verb** *to be* + *not*—**after** *not*
Correct: Brian is not <u>always</u> nice to his little sister.
Correct: It is not <u>usually</u> so hot here during the summer.

> **Note:**   The adverbs *usually* and *often* can also be placed before <u>not</u> as in *It is usually not so hot here during the summer.*

c. **With other verbs—before the verb**
Correct: Lois <u>always</u> skates on the boardwalk.
Correct: I <u>never</u> ride my bicycle to class.

d. **In a verb phrase—after the first auxiliary verb**
Correct: Tim is <u>always</u> running out of money when we go out to eat.
Correct: I have <u>never</u> seen a comet.

e. **In a verb phrase with not—after not**
Correct: Maria does not <u>always</u> type her papers.
Correct: Mark does not <u>usually</u> have time to read the newspaper.

> **Note:**   The adverbs *usually* and *often* can also be placed before the first auxiliary verb as in *Maria <u>usually</u> does not type her papers* or *Maria <u>often</u> does not type her papers.*

Word Order Guidelines for Placement of Adverbials

When several adverbials (phrases and/or clauses that function like adverbs) occur at the end of a sentence in English, word-order problems often occur. Although the order of these adverbials in relation to each other sometimes varies, you will find the following guidelines helpful. These guidelines are based on the different types of adverbials listed below.

Adverbials of time:	at six o'clock, this morning, in the evening
Adverbials of frequency:	every morning, every Tuesday
Adverbials of position:	in the cafeteria, at home, in the classroom
Adverbials of direction:	to the cafeteria, from the lab
Adverbials of purpose:	(in order) to lose weight, so that I could stay in shape
Adverbials of reason:	because it is hot, because it was interesting

1. Adverbials of time and frequency generally come after adverbials of position and direction.

   Examples:

   > She walks <u>to campus every day at noon</u>.
   > She studies <u>at home every evening</u>.

2. Adverbials of time and frequency are generally interchangeable with each other in their position in a sentence.

   Examples:

   > She walks to campus <u>every day at noon</u>.
   > She walks to campus <u>at noon every day</u>.

3. Adverbials of purpose and reason generally come after all other adverbials.

   Examples:

   > Mark works out in the gym every night <u>to keep in shape</u>.
   > We left the party before 9 PM <u>because we had another commitment</u>.

Improve Your Writing Style

Use Adverb Placement to Achieve a More Formal Writing Style

As explained in the word-order guidelines above, adverbs in English can often be placed in a number of different positions within a sentence. These positions include initial position, final position, or midposition. To achieve a more formal writing style, place your adverbs midposition—that is, within the verb phrase either before the main verb (if there is only a main verb) or after the first auxiliary verb (if there is a verb phrase). See the examples below.

<u>Then</u> a solution can be found.
A solution can <u>then</u> be found. (more formal word order)

Since I have been here, my English skills have improved <u>gradually</u>.

IMPROVE YOUR WRITING STYLE, cont.

Since I have been here, my English skills have <u>gradually</u> improved. (more formal word order)

<u>Slowly,</u> the mixture is heated to the boiling point.
The mixture is <u>slowly</u> heated to the boiling point. (more formal word order)

<u>Sometimes</u> I work on weekends.
I work on weekends <u>sometimes</u>.
I <u>sometimes</u> work on weekends. (more formal word order)

PART III

EXERCISES FOR PRACTICE

EXERCISE 1 (Do this exercise on your own. Then check your answers with a classmate.)

Directions: **Some of the following sentences have incorrect or awkward word order. If a sentence is incorrect, rewrite the sentence correctly below the original. If a sentence is correct, write *correct* below it.**

1. I do not really know what is this issue all about.

   _____

2. I have been already advanced to candidacy for my Ph.D.

   _____

3. The only concern I have is how much will it cost the students to pay the rent.

   _____

4. I ran to the grocery store this morning because I needed some milk for my cereal.

   _____

5. A potential candidate must consider what his chances for winning the election are.

   _____

6. Tomas is planning to have for Luis a surprise birthday party.

   _____

7. I have not gotten my term paper back even though I handed in it a week ago.

   _____

8. I am going to buy my father a silk beautiful green tie for his birthday.

   _____

9. Bill often goes swimming to get regular exercise in the evening.

_____

10. The professor comes every day to class on time.

_____

EXERCISE 2 (Do this exercise on your own. Then check your answers with a classmate.)

Directions: **To practice correct word order for indirect questions, complete the following sentences using an indirect question.**

Example: I wonder where _the chemistry building is._

1. The professor said he doesn't know when _____.

2. Your term paper does not cover how _____.

3. I am sorry but I did not understand what _____.

4. Could you please tell me where _____.

5. It is not clear whether _____.

EXERCISE 3 (Do this exercise with a classmate.)

Directions: **The following paragraph has several errors in word order. First, read the paragraph, underlining any word-order problems. Then write the correct word order above each part you have underlined. The first error has been corrected for you.**

Although you can learn vocabulary in your English class and from your textbooks, you may never have considered the many other handy reference tools that you can use to build up your vocabulary. Have you ever thought, for instance, what a great teacher the supermarket can be? If you think about it, everything has either a label or a sign, making it easy for you to connect <u>with the product the words</u>, such as the words _choco-_ *the words with the product* _late chips_ on the label with a window on the package that lets you see the chips, or a picture of diced tomatoes on a can. Besides, if you are not still sure about what is a product, you can ask in the store another customer to help you, and you will be practicing your spoken English besides. Have you ever thought, too, what a great resource the Yellow Pages of the telephone directory can be? If you look at the advertisements, a wealth of words you can learn all organized in specialized categories. Just consider, for example, what you can learn under _Pizzas._ You can find ads for the different styles of pizzas and also learn just how many different kids of crusts are there. Many pizza places have in their ads helpful pictures, and you can also learn some interesting mottoes, such as "Fastest wheels west of the Rockies!" or "Only Chicago-style pizza in Montana!" Even if you are not living in an English-speaking country, many major libraries have telephone directories available so that you can sit down and look at the Yellow Pages for, say, Chicago or New York. Instead of throwing away those catalogs that come to your mailbox, have you thought ever what an excellent resource they can be for words? Because the buyer has to order sight unseen, the catalogs have excellent pictures with detailed descriptions of the products. In a large mail-order catalog, for example, you could learn what is a frost-free refrigerator or what are the names of different golf clubs. In a catalog for clothes, you could learn names exotic for colors and see the color itself illustrated. So, the next time you complain about not knowing enough vocabulary, get out of the house and go to the supermarket, or if you insist on staying home, pick up your telephone directory or the latest catalog that in the mail came and get busy!

PART IV
WRITING TOPICS

Select one or more of the following topics for writing and follow the steps in Appendix A.

Topic A: Write about a custom from your culture or from the United States that you either like or dislike. First, describe the custom. Then explain why you either like or dislike it.

Topic B: Write about a problem that you are facing personally or that you have recently faced. Explain what the problem is, including its possible causes and/or effects. Then suggest possible solutions to the problem (or if you have already solved it, explain how you did so).

Topic C: Think about the friendships that you have or have had. What qualities are important to you in a close friend and why?

PART V

CNN VIDEO ACTIVITY AND WRITING TOPIC

Shopping Malls—A Thing of the Past?

Useful Vocabulary: extinction   threat   consumer   retail   wholesale

Before You Watch

This video segment gives a brief history of shopping malls in the United States and their role in the lives of people.

- What are some pros and cons of shopping at malls?
- What other stores that are not in malls do you shop at and why?

While You Watch

- Write down the date when the first mall opened.
- Note ways in which malls are changing to ensure that shoppers will continue coming to them.

Various factors threaten the viability of shopping malls today.

After You Watch

I. **Write a personal reaction.**

Write a personal reaction of three to five sentences to what you saw in the video. What interested you most? What features or stores would attract you to go to a mall?

II. **Share your reactions.**

Answer the following questions either orally or in writing. Compare your answers with those of a classmate.

1. What are the advantages and disadvantages of malls that have "fifty-eight places to look for clothes and thirty-one shoe stores" like the mall in the video?

2. What factors are causing consumers to shop less at shopping malls?

3. What effects do large chains and superstores have on smaller individual shops?

WRITING TOPIC

Near the end of this video, the narrator emphasizes that certain things do not change, such as the law of supply and demand. However, stores must constantly change to continue to attract customers. What are some ways in which stores where you shop have changed over the past five or ten years? Are these changes for the better or for the worse?

Goals

- To learn the importance of mastering connecting words in writing
- To review four problems ESL writers commonly encounter with connecting words
- To learn to form and use connecting words correctly
- To develop confidence in using connecting words through practice with exercises and writing assignments

Connecting Words

A student at the City College of San Francisco helps a classmate during a study group session. Photo courtesy of Office of Public Information.

Think about and discuss the following question:
How could joining a study group
help you improve your
writing skills?

PART I

WHAT YOU NEED TO KNOW ABOUT ERRORS WITH CONNECTING WORDS

In Part I, you will learn

- The definition of an error with a connecting word
- The importance of using connecting words correctly in writing
- Suggestions for mastering connecting words in writing

Definition of the Error (conn*)

An error with a connecting word **(conn)** is a global error in which the connection between words, clauses, sentences, or paragraphs is either unclear or illogical because of a missing, incorrect, or misplaced connecting word or phrase. The sentence *I studied the material for five hours, I then took a break* has a connector error: a comma cannot connect two independent clauses. (This error is also called a comma splice.) The sentence should read: *I studied the material for five hours; I then took a break* or *I studied the material for five hours, and I then took a break*.

A connector is a word, or sometimes a phrase, used to link paragraphs, sentences, clauses, or words. To understand connecting words and phrases, you need to understand the types of connectors and their functions.

TYPES OF CONNECTORS AND THEIR FUNCTIONS

Coordinating conjunctions connect words, phrases, or independent clauses.
Examples:

The students bought juice, soft drinks, <u>and</u> cookies for the party.
The dog ran out of the house <u>and</u> started chasing the car.
Tonight we can go to a movie <u>or</u> to a disco.
Pedro wanted to study engineering, <u>but</u> his father convinced
him to study medicine. (Note that the two clauses have equal emphasis.)

Note: An **independent clause** can stand alone as a sentence because its meaning is complete.

Example: Last year my university had an enrollment of 15,000.

---

*conn = grading symbol for an error with a connecting word.

TYPES OF CONNECTORS AND THEIR FUNCTIONS, cont.

Correlative conjunctions connect similar grammatical structures.

Examples:

> You will have to <u>either</u> get a job <u>or</u> cut down on your expenses to stay in school.
> Thuy <u>not only</u> has two classes today <u>but</u> she <u>also</u> has a term paper due.

Transitional words and phrases link sentences and link paragraphs.

Example: I dislike working at night; <u>however,</u> I cannot find a day job.
(Some texts refer to these connecting words as conjunctive adverbs.)

Subordinating conjunctions connect a dependent (or subordinate) clause with an independent clause.

Example: <u>When</u> we have finished the chapter, we will have a test. (Note that the two clauses have unequal emphasis. The dependent clause is subordinate and thus has less emphasis.)

Note: Subordinating conjunctions are treated separately in Unit 5, "Relative, Adverbial, and Noun Clauses."

Importance of Using Connecting Words Correctly in Writing

Errors with connecting words are global (more serious) errors and, as such, affect the meaning of whole sentences. Connecting words are especially important because writers use them to link items together, such as two sentences, or to lead the reader to a new point *(for example)* or to show order of importance *(most importantly)*.

By providing smooth links between ideas, connecting words help make writing clear and easy for the reader to follow, but they are only one tool writers use to connect their ideas coherently. See Section 3, Part D, "Improving Flow of Ideas," for additional information on coherence.

Suggestions for Mastering Connecting Words in Writing

- Be certain of the meaning of the connector you want to use. (The chart in this unit, arranged by meaning, serves as a reference you can consult to make sure that you are using the appropriate connector.)

- Become aware of how connectors have been used and what their meaning is in the material that you read so that you can improve your ability to use connectors correctly.

- Remember that when using connecting words, you may have choices. For example, you may wish to use the coordinating conjunction *but* or the transitional word *however* to show a contrast when connecting two independent clauses.

Test Your Understanding of Connectors

Write answers to the following questions. Share your answers with another student.

1. What is the difference between a coordinating conjunction and a correlative conjunction?

2. What are some of the functions that connecting words perform in a piece of writing; that is, how do they help the reader move through a piece of text?

Grammar Journal Entry 9: Connectors

Write a short entry in your grammar journal in response to the following.

1. What was the best dream or worst nightmare that you have ever had?

2. What are five connecting words you frequently use? Use each one in a sentence.

PART II

COMMON PROBLEMS, SELF-HELP STRATEGIES, AND GRAMMAR GUIDELINES

In Part II, you will study

- Four problems ESL writers commonly encounter with connecting words
- Self-help strategies for controlling connecting words in your writing
- Grammar guidelines for connecting words

This section presents four problems that ESL writers commonly encounter with connecting words. First, take the pretest to see what you already know about connecting words. In checking your answers, note that the pretest questions cover the same types of errors in the same order as the problems in this section. Then carefully study each problem and the examples that illustrate it, giving particular attention to those problems that correspond to the pretest questions you had difficulty with. Using the boxes to the left of each problem, check [✓] *yes, no,* or *don't know* to indicate to yourself which problems you should focus the most attention on in this unit and also when you are using connecting words in English. Remember that becoming aware of the types of errors you most often make with connecting words will increase your chances of avoiding these errors in your writing.

Pretest: What Do You Already Know About Connecting Words?

Test your ability to recognize errors with connecting words by finding and correcting the one error with a connecting word in each of the following sentences.

Answers on p. 293

1. Natasha hoped to find an acting job in Hollywood, she had little talent.
2. Global warming poses a threat to our environment; for example, we are trying to solve the problem.
3. Even though we should be saving money, but we are always going shopping.
4. There are three obstacles to losing weight, however, they can be overcome with a strong commitment to having a healthier, better-looking body.

Four Problems ESL Writers Commonly Encounter with Connecting Words

yes   no   don't know   **PROBLEM 1**

☐   ☐   ☐   A connecting word is missing where it is needed.

conn

Incorrect: I did not study; I got an A on the test.
(These two clauses are grammatically correct, but without a connector, the reader cannot see how the ideas are connected.)

conn

Incorrect: I did not study, I got an A on the test.
(Two independent clauses cannot be connected with a comma.)

Correct: I did not study, <u>but</u> I got an A on the test.

Correct: I did not study; <u>however,</u> I got an A on the test.

Correct: <u>Although</u> I did not study, I got a A on the test. (An adverbial clause like this one here may also be used. To study these clauses, see Unit 5, "Relative, Adverbial, and Noun Clauses.")

conn

Incorrect: I frequently read magazines, go to the movies in my leisure time.

Correct: I frequently read magazines <u>and</u> go to the movies in my spare time.

yes	no	don't know	**PROBLEM 2**
☐	☐	☐	A connecting word with the wrong meaning has been used to join two independent clauses.

conn

Incorrect: I was very nervous about writing an essay in just one hour; <u>moreover</u>, I conquered my fears and finished the essay.

Correct: I was very nervous about writing an essay in just one hour; <u>however</u>, I conquered my fears and finished the essay.

(*Moreover* adds information, as in the sentence *I am very tired right now; <u>moreover</u>, I am hungry. However* sets up a contrast.)

Self-Help Strategy: Make sure the connecting word you have chosen gives the correct meaning to the sentence. Refer to Meanings of Commonly Used Connecting Words in this unit for a list of connecting words and their meanings.

yes	no	don't know	**PROBLEM 3**
☐	☐	☐	An adverbial clause is connected to an independent clause with a subordinating conjunction *and* a coordinating conjunction.

conn

Incorrect: <u>Even though</u> my mother is trying to learn English, <u>but</u> she finds studying it difficult.

Correct: <u>Even though</u> my mother is trying to learn English, she finds studying it difficult.

Note: An alternative way of phrasing this sentence would be: My mother is trying to learn English, <u>but</u> she finds studying it difficult.

Self-Help Strategy: Remember that a subordinating connector connects a dependent clause to an independent clause and a coordinating connector connects two independent clauses. In the preceding corrected sentences, note that you have the option of using either a subordinating or a coordinating connector, but not both.

yes	no	don't know	**PROBLEM 4**
☐	☐	☐	The wrong punctuation has been used with a connecting word.

conn

Incorrect: Arielle wanted to go home for vacation, however, she did not have the money.

Correct: Arielle wanted to go home for vacation; however, she did not have the money.

conn

Incorrect:	Vladimir craves sweets. For example he loves cake, cookies, and candy.
Correct:	Vladimir craves sweets. For example, he loves cake, cookies, and candy.

Self-Help Strategy: Make sure you know how to punctuate connecting words correctly. Refer to Rules for Punctuating Connecting Words in this unit for help with punctuation.

Grammar Guidelines for the Meaning and Punctuation of Connecting Words

To use connecting words correctly, you need to know not only their grammatical function but also their meaning. You also need to know how to punctuate connecting words correctly. In the following sections, you will learn the meaning of the most commonly used connecting words and also rules for punctuating sentences with connecting words.

Guide to Using Connecting Words: Meaning and Punctuation

Note: Subordinating Conjunctions are treated in Unit 5, "Relative, Adverbial, and Noun Clauses."

Meanings of Commonly Used Connecting Words

CONNECTING WORDS THAT ADD INFORMATION		
Coordinating Conjunctions	**Correlative Conjunctions**	**Transitional Words and Phrases**
and	not only . . . but also both . . . and	also besides moreover furthermore in addition additionally

Examples:

We have seen the movie *Gone with the Wind* twice, <u>and</u> we plan to see it again.

<u>Both</u> my brother <u>and</u> I know how to play tennis.

Ahmed speaks Arabic, French, and English; <u>in addition</u>, he can read German.

CONNECTING WORDS THAT GIVE AN EXAMPLE OR ILLUSTRATE A POINT

Coordinating Conjunctions	Correlative Conjunctions	Transitional Words and Phrases
		for example
		for instance
		to illustrate
		specifically
		in particular

Examples:

I like to travel; <u>specifically</u>, I visit countries where I can practice my Spanish.

<u>For example</u>, last summer I spent two weeks in Mexico.

CONNECTING WORDS THAT SHOW A CONTRAST

Coordinating Conjunctions	Correlative Conjunctions	Transitional Words and Phrases
but		however
		in contrast
		conversely
		on the contrary
		on the other hand
		otherwise
		still
		instead

Examples:

Bill received an A in his German class, <u>but</u> Antoinette got a B.

We were supposed to be in class at 8:00 AM sharp; <u>however</u>, Barry arrived at 8:10.

CONNECTING WORDS THAT SHOW A CONCESSION

Coordinating Conjunctions	Correlative Conjunctions	Transitional Words and Phrases
yet		nevertheless
		even so
		admittedly

Examples:

Albert knows that he should take vitamins, <u>yet</u> he refuses to buy them.

I need to wear reading glasses; <u>nevertheless</u>, I hate how I look in them.

CONNECTING WORDS THAT SHOW A SIMILARITY

Coordinating Conjunctions	Correlative Conjunctions	Transitional Words and Phrases
		likewise
		similarly
		in the same way

Example:

Algebra was hard for me in high school; <u>likewise</u>, I find calculus difficult in college.

CONNECTING WORDS THAT SHOW A RESULT

Coordinating Conjunctions	Correlative Conjunctions	Transitional Words and Phrases
so		accordingly
		as a result
		consequently
		as a consequence
		therefore
		thus

Examples:

Hiroshi finally got all his verb tenses right in an essay, <u>so</u> he is very happy.

Hiroshi got all his verb tenses right in an essay; <u>as a result</u>, he is happy.

CONNECTING WORDS THAT GIVE A REASON OR CAUSE

Coordinating Conjunctions	Correlative Conjunctions	Transitional Words and Phrases
for		

Example:

Mr. Cross received a plaque, <u>for</u> he was elected teacher of the year.

CONNECTING WORDS THAT ESTABLISH A TIME RELATIONSHIP OR ORDER

Coordinating Conjunctions	Correlative Conjunctions	Transitional Words and Phrases
		first
		second
		afterward
		finally
		in conclusion
		meanwhile
		previously
		next
		subsequently

Example:

Martin is now a student; <u>previously</u>, he was a sales representative for a pharmaceutical company.

CONNECTING WORDS THAT SHOW A CONDITION

Coordinating Conjunctions	Correlative Conjunctions	Transitional Words and Phrases
or	whether . . . or	

Examples:

I have to get dressed quickly, <u>or</u> I will be late for the movies.
(<u>Or else</u> can also be used.)
<u>Whether</u> she plans to accompany me <u>or</u> not, I still am going to the concert.

CONNECTING WORDS THAT EXPLAIN OR EMPHASIZE

Coordinating Conjunctions	Correlative Conjunctions	Transitional Words and Phrases
		in fact
		namely
		that is
		actually
		in other words

Examples:

The bookstore sells greeting cards; <u>in fact</u>, they have the best selection in town.
I have to study all weekend; <u>in other words</u>, I am behind in my homework.

CONNECTING WORDS THAT GIVE A CHOICE OR ALTERNATIVE

Coordinating Conjunctions	Correlative Conjunctions	Transitional Words and Phrases
or	either . . . or	

Examples:

We can go to the beach, <u>or</u> we can go to the mountains.
You can <u>either</u> ride the bus <u>or</u> take the subway to get to my apartment.

Rules for Punctuating Connecting Words

1. **Coordinating Conjunctions.** Put a comma before a coordinating conjunction unless the two sentences it connects are very short.

   Examples:

   > A new shopping center has opened five blocks from my apartment, <u>and</u> I have noticed that it is offering a special discount to senior citizens.
   >
   > The movie has started, <u>but</u> Jane has not arrived. (Note that the comma could be omitted.)

2. **Correlative Conjunctions.** Put a comma before the second correlative conjunction if it connects two clauses but not if it connects words or phrases.

   Examples:

   > Eric is <u>not only</u> an outstanding teacher, <u>but</u> he is <u>also</u> a gourmet cook.
   >
   > The French bakery downtown sells <u>not only</u> crusty bread <u>but also</u> flaky pastries.

3. **Transitional Words and Phrases.** Put a semicolon before and a comma after a transitional word or phrase if you want to use it to connect two independent clauses. Put a comma after a transitional word or phrase if you want to use it to introduce an independent clause. Put commas before and after a transitional word or phrase within a clause.

   Examples:

   > The weather forecast for today was for cooler temperatures with a possibility of rain; <u>however</u>, the sun is shining brightly. <u>Nevertheless</u>, I am going to take my umbrella to work. As an extra precaution, <u>moreover</u>, I am going to wear my raincoat.

Use Transitional Words and Phrases to Link Ideas

Writing without transitional words and phrases can make your writing choppy and make it hard for the reader to follow your ideas. With transitional words and phrases, you can move the reader smoothly from one idea to another. You can introduce an example, indicate the order of ideas, or tell the reader that you are about to show a contrast. For additional techniques you can use to link ideas, see Section 3, Part D.

IMPROVE YOUR WRITING STYLE, cont.

In the paragraph below, notice how the writer (an Asian American herself) uses transitional words and phrases to keep the flow of ideas smooth.

<u>First of all</u>, in terms of communication, Asian families need to strike a balance between assimilation and cultural segregation. This balance can affect our lives socially and economically. As Asian Americans, we need to master a second language other than our native language. <u>Yet</u>, we should still maintain the fluency of our own language and never negate our cultural identity. <u>For instance</u>, my father had a difficult time finding a job because he was unable to communicate in the workplace. <u>Finally</u>, after going to adult school for two years to study English, he found a job. <u>However</u>, my father maintains his first language (Korean) because he says that it forms a bond between our ancestors and us. My father is absolutely right. It is important for us Asian Americans to learn how to fit in; <u>nevertheless</u>, we still need to remember who we are.

PART III

EXERCISES FOR PRACTICE

EXERCISE 1 (Do this exercise on your own. Then check your answers with a classmate.)

Directions: Test your ability to use connecting words correctly by identifying and then correcting any errors with connecting words. If a sentence is correct, write (C). If it is incorrect, write (I). Then underline the error and write the correction above it.

so

Example: __*I*__   All humans know they have to eat, <u>for</u> they can live.

__C__   Sarah was angry at her brother; as a result, she couldn't think clearly.

___1. My sister is an accountant, she is very busy during tax time.

___2. The supermarket closes at 10 PM; however, it opens at 6 AM if you need milk for breakfast.

___3. He did not want to go to chemistry laboratory. He went anyway.

___4. Although a car is expensive to maintain, but I need one to commute to work.

___5. Not only did Ann dislike the color of my dress, she did not like its style.

___6. They could buy neither coffee or milk because the store was closed.

___7. Even though I dislike fish, I ate it at my friend's house to be polite.

___8. I went to the bank, I did not have any money.

EXERCISE 2 (Do this exercise on your own. Then check your answers with a classmate.)

Directions: **Write four sentences, using a connecting word with a different meaning in each sentence. Choose these connecting words from the list in Part I in this unit. Be sure that you also understand the grammatical function of the connector.**

Example: Canada's Northern Lights are fascinating; therefore, tourists come from all over the world to view them.

1. _____

_____

2. _____

_____

3. _____

_____

4. _____

_____

EXERCISE 3 (Do this exercise on your own. Then check your answers with a classmate.)

Directions: **In the following paragraph, fill in the blanks choosing the appropriate connecting word or words from the list below.**

for instance	therefore	however	moreover
another	second	in this way	

The most positive thing I have done since I started university is to get involved with cyberspace. First of all, I have learned to use the Internet as an adjunct to my classes. My Chemistry 2A professor, _____, has a Web site where he posts homework solutions, midterm examples, and lecture notes. Each day I visit the site to compare my class notes with his to make sure they are accurate. _____, for biology, I can do a step-by-step dissection of a frog, all online and interactive. However, teaching sites on the Web are not confined to the sciences, as I have heard about a "dynamite" Web site for Chinese 1, where it is possible to walk on the Great Wall. The _____ reason why learning to use cyberspace is so important is using e-mail. When I arrived at school, I eagerly set up my e-mail account and started contacting my friends on campus and back home. _____, I soon found that e-mail is more than simply entertainment, for I can use it to contact my professors. For example, my macroeconomics professor has open office hours from 7:00 to 9:00 PM. Thursdays on the net, where we can talk on line with her. Many professors also send out assignments via e-mail. In spite of these advan-

tages, it is important not to become an Internet freak. To avoid this problem, I am con-
fining my use of the Internet to academics during the week. On the weekends, I can
catch up with my friends via e-mail and surf the net for new and interesting sites.
_____, I will use the Internet positively.

EXERCISE 4 (Do this exercise with a classmate.)

Directions: Read the whole paragraph. Then underline each connecting word and discuss its
type and meaning with your classmates. If you are unsure, refer to Meanings of
Commonly Used Connecting Words. The first one has been done for you.

coordinating/reason or clause

Today's modern airport resembles a city in itself, <u>for</u> it has so many services to
offer travelers. First, like all cities, it offers food. If you want to purchase something to eat,
restaurants and snack bars abound, ranging from hotdog carts to sit-down restaurants.
However, if you just want a little quick energy, you can buy either your favorite candy bar
or a bag of chips from one of the many gift shops, which offer gifts, food, magazines,
newspapers, and drugstore items. Second, like any city, the modern airport has entertainment. Many airports now have a television area, but you could also read or perhaps
browse among the paperbacks in the airport's bookstores. Moreover, some airports now
have art exhibits on display. Of course, you can always entertain yourself just by
watching people. Third, if you were unable to get all your shopping or errands done,
modern airports have an array of shops and services, just like a mall in a city. For
example, you can go to the bank or florist, buy clothes, or pick up last-minute gifts. Last,
if you want to arrive looking neat and clean, in many airports you can go to a unisex
beauty salon. In modern airports, waiting for a flight no longer needs to be boring.

EXERCISE 5 (Do this exercise on your own. Then check your answers with a classmate.)

Directions: Choose a short article in a newspaper or a magazine. Read the article. Then underline the connecting words in two paragraphs and write down the function and
meaning of each connecting word. Check your work with a classmate.

PART IV

WRITING TOPICS

Select one or more of the following topics for writing and follow the steps in Appendix A.

Topic A: Pretend that someone is going to visit your country or your hometown. That person has asked you how to get from the nearest airport to your town. Write a step-by-step description of how to get there. (As an alternate topic, you can tell a student in your class how to get to your house, apartment, or room.)

Topic B: Although most people see a college education as a good investment in the future, not everyone sees a college education as useful. What are some of the major benefits of a college education? When would a college education not be necessary or even desirable?

Topic C: Think about the hobbies that people have. What is your favorite hobby and why is it important to you?

PART V

CNN VIDEO ACTIVITY AND WRITING TOPIC

Landfill Is Good Neighbor to Self-Sustaining Student Community

Useful Vocabulary: "Waste not, want not"   "Practice what you preach"   to be or to think "green"   sustainable living   compost   terrace

Before You Watch

This video segment examines a self-sustaining student community that has built a unique relationship with a neighboring landfill.

- Make a list of what you throw away for two days. Do you think there are ways you could minimize wastage?

- To what extent do you think the United States and/or your country are wasteful societies? Do you think people have been less wasteful in recent years than previously?

While You Watch

- Look for several different ways in which this community profits from living next to a landfill.

- Think about what questions you might like to ask the students living in this community.

Students live in harmony with the land in an experimental village in southern California.

After You Watch

I. Write a personal reaction.

Write a personal reaction of three to five sentences to what you saw in the video. What interested you most? Would you like to live in this community?

II. Share your reactions.

Answer the following questions either orally or in writing. Compare your answers with those of a classmate.

1. List three or four ways things are recycled or reused in this student community.

2. How do the students feel they are enhancing their lives by living in this community?

3. What would you like and dislike about living in this kind of a community?

WRITING TOPIC

Experiments in community living are common on university campuses. Some examples include international houses, cooperative living, and cross-cultural floors in dormitories. What are the pros and cons for students of living in these kinds of experimental communities?

Local Errors

This section contains six units, each one addressing a local error that ESL writers commonly have difficulty with. Each unit has an introduction to the error, examples of the kinds of problems writers frequently have with the error, self-help strategies and grammar guidelines, exercises for practice, writing topics, and a videotape activity with an additional writing topic.

Local errors are less serious errors because they usually do not significantly affect the reader's ability to comprehend what you have written. However, when local errors are frequent, they are distracting to the reader, often making it difficult to concentrate on the content of what you have written. In some cases, a local error, such as word choice, may be so frequent that it becomes serious and could be considered global rather than local. Because of the high demands for accuracy in academic and professional writing, we believe that if you are making these errors in your writing, you should work on them along with your global errors.

Goals

- To learn the importance of mastering subject-verb agreement in writing
- To review six problems ESL writers commonly encounter with subject-verb agreement
- To learn rules for correct subject-verb agreement
- To develop confidence in using correct subject-verb agreement through practice with exercises and writing assignments

Subject-Verb Agreement

A beautiful day in St. Louis allows this Washington University class to take place outdoors.
Photo courtesy of Photographic Services.

Think about and discuss the following question:
What are the advantages and disadvantages
of holding a writing class outside?

PART I

WHAT YOU NEED TO KNOW ABOUT SUBJECT-VERB AGREEMENT

In Part I, you will learn

- The definition of a subject-verb agreement error
- The importance of using correct subject-verb agreement in writing
- Suggestions for mastering subject-verb agreement in writing

Definition of the Error (sv*)

A subject-verb agreement error **(sv)** is one in which a verb does not show agreement in number (singular or plural) with its subject. For example, *he see* and *she have* illustrate errors in subject-verb agreement. *He see* should be *he <u>sees</u>* (third person singular) while *she have* should be *she <u>has</u>* (third person singular).

Importance of Mastering Subject-Verb Agreement in Writing

Subject-verb agreement errors are local (less serious) errors. Although a reader can still understand the meaning of a text even if it contains errors in subject-verb agreement, these errors will be highly noticeable and distracting. Subject-verb agreement errors will also make your piece of writing appear less professional (below the level of writing expected) because readers in the academic and professional worlds expect writers to be able to use correct subject-verb agreement.

Suggestions for Mastering Subject-Verb Agreement in Writing

- Be aware that the rules for subject-verb agreement are relatively easy to master. If you tend to make this kind of error, study the rules covered in this unit.
- Make a habit of checking your writing for agreement errors by looking carefully at each subject and verb to see if they agree. In particular, check the following:
    1. Check for correct agreement when using the simple present tense (e.g., *she reads, they read*).
    2. Check for correct agreement when several words appear between the subject and verb (e.g., *<u>The cabins</u> near the lake <u>are</u> the most expensive and the most popular*).

*__*sv__ = grading symbol for an error in subject-verb agreement.*

3. Check for correct agreement with forms of the verb *to have (has/have), to be (am/is/are; was/were),* and *to do (does, do).*

4. Check for correct agreement when two verbs with the same subject appear in the sentence (e.g., *Johnny <u>reads</u> the newspaper and <u>listens</u> to music when he is riding the bus to work*).

Test Your Understanding of Subject-Verb Agreement

Write answers to the following questions. Share your answers with another student.

1. What causes an error in subject-verb agreement?

2. What verb tense should you check carefully for correct subject-verb agreement?

Grammar Journal Entry 10: Subject-Verb Agreement

Respond to the following in your grammar journal.

1. Ask a classmate or friend what he or she likes to do when he or she has free time. In your journal, write about whether or not you and this individual share the same free-time interests.

2. Write two sample sentences in the present tense. One should be third-person singular (*he/she/it* or *a singular noun* as the subject), while the other should be third-person plural (*they* or *a plural noun* as the subject). After checking them for subject-verb agreement, use these sentences as models when you are writing.

PART II

COMMON PROBLEMS, SELF-HELP STRATEGIES, AND GRAMMAR GUIDELINES

In Part II, you will study

- Six problems ESL writers commonly encounter with subject-verb agreement
- Self-help strategies for controlling subject-verb agreement in your writing
- Grammar guidelines for correct subject-verb agreement

This section presents six problems that ESL writers commonly encounter with subject-verb agreement. First, take the pretest to see what you already know about subject-verb agreement. In checking your answers, note that the pretest questions cover the same types of errors in the same order as the problems in this section. Then carefully study each problem and the examples that illustrate it, giving particular attention to those problems that correspond to the pretest questions you had difficulty with. Using the boxes to the left of each problem, check [✓] *yes, no,* or *don't know* to indicate to yourself which problems you should focus the most attention on in this unit and also when you write in English. Remember that becoming aware of the type of errors you most often make with subject-verb agreement will increase your chances of avoiding these errors in your writing.

Pretest: What Do You Already Know About Subject-Verb Agreement?

Test your ability to recognize errors in subject-verb agreement by finding and correcting the one subject-verb agreement error in each of the following sentences.

Answers on p. 293

1. A good scientist observes closely and record data accurately.

2. An attorney from one of the most distinguished law firms have agreed to represent the suspect.

3. A supervisor who listen to others and whose style is collaborative is often the most effective.

4. Taking regular breaks often help a person work more efficiently.

5. There is six articles that I need to review this week in preparation for my presentation.

6. One of the two cars consume significantly more gas than the other.

Six Problems ESL Writers Commonly Encounter with Subject-Verb Agreement

yes   no   don't know   PROBLEM 1

☐   ☐   ☐   The final *-s* or *-es* has been left off a verb in the third person singular in the present tense.

sv

Incorrect: Each spring the doctor <u>tell</u> my father to take a vacation.
Correct: Each spring the doctor <u>tells</u> my father to take a vacation.

yes   no   don't know   **PROBLEM 2**

☐   ☐   ☐   The subject and verb do not agree when words come between them.

sv

Incorrect: Two members of the exploration party <u>has</u> been commended for bravery.

Correct: Two members of the exploration party <u>have</u> been commended for bravery.

sv

Incorrect: My manager, like many other managers, <u>want</u> to offer a flex-time work schedule as a new option for employees.

Correct: My manager, like many other managers, <u>wants</u> to offer a flex-time schedule as a new option for employees.

Note: In the example sentences above, the true subjects are *members* and *manager* (not *exploration party* or *other managers*). The verb in each case must agree with these true subjects.

Self-Help Strategy: Remember that words that appear between the subject and the verb do not affect agreement.

yes   no   don't know   **PROBLEM 3**

☐   ☐   ☐   The verb in a relative clause (sometimes called an adjective clause) does not agree with the noun that the clause modifies.

sv

Incorrect: Every person should try to choose a place to live that <u>suit</u> his or her needs.

(relative clause)

Correct: Every person should choose a place to live that <u>suits</u> his or her needs.

sv

Incorrect: The president, who <u>serve</u> a four-year term, lives in the White House.

(relative clause)

Correct: The president, who <u>serves</u> a four-year term, lives in the White House.

Self-Help Strategy: Remember that the verb in a relative clause always agrees with the word that the relative pronoun *(that, which, who, whose, whom)* refers to. Note that in the first example sentence in Problem 3 above, the verb in the relative clause must agree with the noun *place.* In the second sentence, it must agree with the noun *president.*

yes   no   don't know   **PROBLEM 4**

☐   ☐   ☐   The subject and verb do not agree when a gerund, infinitive, or noun clause is the subject of the verb.

          gerund   *sv*

Incorrect: Being a workaholic <u>have</u> many disadvantages.
Correct: Being a workaholic <u>has</u> many disadvantages.

          infinitive   *sv*

Incorrect: To copy someone else's answers on tests <u>are</u> wrong.
Correct: To copy someone else's answers on tests <u>is</u> wrong.

             noun clause   *sv*

Incorrect: What we requested <u>are</u> more supplies for the workroom.
Correct: What we requested <u>is</u> more supplies for the workroom.

Self-Help Strategy: Remember that when a gerund, an infinitive, or a noun clause serves as the subject of a sentence, the verb connected with this subject will be in the singular form.

yes   no   don't know   **PROBLEM 5**

☐   ☐   ☐   The subject and verb do not agree when the clause or sentence begins with *there is/there are*, *there was/there were*, or *there has been/there have been*.

          sv

Incorrect: There <u>are</u> a new six-screen movie theater being built downtown.

Correct: There <u>is</u> a new six-screen movie theater being built downtown.
             (The true subject is *theater.*)

          sv

Incorrect: There <u>is</u> ten students in my discussion class.
Correct: There <u>are</u> ten students in my discussion class. (The true subject is *ten students.*)

yes   no   don't know   **PROBLEM 6**

☐   ☐   ☐   The subject and verb do not agree following the words *one of the.*

             sv

Incorrect: One of the students <u>play</u> the flute.
Correct: One of the students <u>plays</u> the flute.

Self-Help Strategy: Remember that the verb must agree with *one* (the true subject of the sentence) even though the phrase *one of the* is always followed by a plural noun.

Grammar Guidelines for Subject-Verb Agreement

1. **In the present tense, a third-person singular subject takes a verb that ends in -s or -es. The third-person singular includes the pronouns *he, she*, and *it*, as well as all other singular subjects, such as *the doctor, a dog*, and *an athlete*.**

	sv *sv*
Incorrect:	Marta <u>work</u> as a clerk at the grocery store. She <u>like</u> it.
Correct:	Marta <u>works</u> as a clerk at the grocery store. She <u>likes</u> it.

	sv
Incorrect:	My back sometimes <u>hurt</u> after I have done heavy lifting.
Correct:	My back sometimes <u>hurts</u> after I have done heavy lifting.

2. **All other pronouns (*I, you, we, they*) and plural subjects, such as *books* or *classes*, do not take a verb ending in -s.**

	sv *sv*
Incorrect:	Many students <u>chooses</u> sports to stay in shape. As a result, they also <u>has</u> more energy to study hard.
Correct:	Many students <u>choose</u> sports to stay in shape. As a result, they also <u>have</u> more energy to study hard.

	sv
Incorrect:	Her children <u>has</u> many different kinds of toys.
Correct:	Her children <u>have</u> many different kinds of toys.

3. **Compound subjects (two noun phrases joined by and) usually take a plural verb rather than a verb ending in -s.**

	sv
Incorrect:	John F. Kennedy and Franklin D. Roosevelt <u>has</u> both been presidents of the United States.
Correct:	John F. Kennedy and Franklin D. Roosevelt <u>have</u> both been presidents of the United States.

4. **Uncountable nouns take a singular verb.**

	sv
Incorrect:	The money <u>are</u> in the wallet.
Correct:	The money <u>is</u> in the wallet.

5. **A few nouns that end in *-s* are actually singular. Some of these include *sports, news,* and some fields of study (*physics, mathematics, economics*).**

Incorrect: Economics <u>are</u> a very interesting field of study.
Correct: Economics <u>is</u> a very interesting field of study.

Incorrect: The news <u>begin</u> at 6:00 PM.
Correct: The news <u>begins</u> at 6:00 PM.

6. **The commonly used noun *people* takes a plural verb.**

Incorrect: The people going on the trip <u>is</u> already here.
Correct: The people going on the trip <u>are</u> already here.

7. **Collective nouns (nouns that define groups of people or animals) can take either a singular or plural verb. When the singular verb is used, the focus is on the group as a whole. When the plural verb is used, the focus is on the individual members of the group.**

Correct: The faculty <u>prefers</u> the semester system. (The focus is on the faculty as a whole group.)
Correct: The faculty <u>prefer</u> the semester system. (The focus is on the individual members that make up the faculty.)

Correct: The audience clearly <u>loves</u> the show. (The focus is on the audience as a whole group.)
Correct: The audience clearly <u>love</u> the show. (The focus is on the individual members of the audience.)

8. **When a sentence or clause begins with *there*, the verb agrees with the true subject, which follows the verb.**

- *There is* is used before a singular or uncountable subject.

  Examples:
  There <u>is</u> a new book on the bestseller list.
  There <u>is</u> enough air in my tires.

- *There are* is used before a plural subject.

  Example: There <u>are</u> two new books on the best-seller list.

- When *there* is followed by a compound subject (two noun phrases joined by *and*), the verb agrees with the noun immediately following it.

  Examples:
  There <u>is</u> a new stereo and a new tape deck in her room.
  There <u>are</u> new twin beds and a CD player in her room.

9. **Although many errors in subject-verb agreement involve verbs in the present tense, the verb *to be* in the past tense and the verb *to have* in the present perfect must always agree in number with the subject of the verb, as shown in the examples below.**

                sv

Incorrect: Max <u>were</u> a student for four years.

Correct: Max <u>was</u> a student for four years.

                    sv

Incorrect: Tomas and Blanca <u>was</u> students for four years.

Correct: Tomas and Blanca <u>were</u> students for four years.

              sv

Incorrect: We <u>was</u> students for four years.

Correct: We <u>were</u> students for four years

                        sv

Incorrect: The new laboratory samples <u>has</u> arrived.

Correct: The new laboratory samples <u>have</u> arrived.

10. **Rules for subject-verb agreement with quantifying words and phrases vary depending on the quantifying word or phrase. Below are some common examples.**

- *all of the*

  All of the students <u>are</u> working on the project. (Use a plural verb when the noun following *all of the* is plural.)

  All of the money <u>has</u> been carefully invested. (Use a singular verb when the noun following *all of the* is uncountable.)

- *some*

  Some samples <u>have</u> arrived. (Use a plural verb with *some.*)

- *none*

  None of the samples <u>have</u> arrived. (Use a plural verb when the noun following *none of the* is plural.)

  None of the money <u>has</u> arrived. (Use a singular verb when the noun following *none of the* is uncountable.)

- *everyone*

  Everyone <u>wants</u> to go away during spring break. (Use a singular verb with *everyone.*)

- *the number of*

  The number of voters <u>has</u> increased. (Use a singular verb with *the number of.*)

- *a number of*

  A number of voters <u>have</u> sent in absentee ballots. (Use a plural verb with *a number of.*)

Improve Your Writing Style

Use Correct Subject-Verb Agreement with Correlative Conjunctions

1. both . . . and	(Use a plural verb when two subjects are connected in this way.)
	Both Engineering 3 and Engineering 4 <u>fulfill</u> the elective requirement.
2. either . . . or	(The verb should agree with the noun after *or*.)
	Either the textbook or the assigned journal articles <u>cover</u> this topic.
	Either the assigned journal articles or the textbook <u>covers</u> this topic.
	Note: The following is also acceptable but considered less formal:
	Either the assigned journal articles or the textbook <u>cover</u> this topic.
3. neither . . . nor	(The verb should agree with the noun after *nor*.)
	Neither Amy nor her parents <u>have</u> a car.
	Neither the students nor the teaching assistant <u>understands</u> the situation fully.
	Note: The following is also acceptable but considered less formal:
	Neither the students nor the teaching assistant <u>understand</u> the situation fully.

PART III

EXERCISES FOR PRACTICE

EXERCISE 1 (Do this exercise on your own. Then check your answers with a classmate.)

Directions: Using the material you have just studied in this unit as a guide, identify and correct any problems with subject-verb agreement in the following sentences. First, decide whether a sentence is correct (C) or incorrect (I). Then cross out and correct the incorrect verbs.

Example: ___*I*___ A student in the Netherlands usually <del>learn</del> *learns* to speak English, French, and German in school.

_____ 1. A good presenter is aware of his or her audience and use eye contact.

_____ 2. Physics is a popular major at my university.

_____ **3.** Matthew, who is in second grade, already know how to read and write.

_____ **4.** One of the students in the class was selected to participate in the essay contest.

_____ **5.** Having good computer skills are required for many jobs today.

_____ **6.** The number of cars on surrounding freeways have increased.

_____ **7.** Brainstorming help a writer to gather ideas and avoid writer's block.

_____ **8.** There is several stages in the writing process, including prewriting, writing a draft, and revising.

_____ **9.** Because of the drought, there are not enough water for all the farmers who need it.

_____**10.** All of the conference attendees receive complimentary parking passes.

EXERCISE 2 (Do this exercise on your own. Then check your answers with a classmate.)

Directions: **Fill in each blank space with the correct form of the verb in parentheses. The paragraph comes from a student essay on the effects of technology and is written in the present. The first one has been done for you.**

Moreover, there is another way that people __*are*__ (be) affected by our high-tech society. Human contact _____ (be) missing from our electronic wonderland. People who _____ (enjoy) our high-tech equipment _____ (run into) this trap without knowing it. Computers, networks, and television _____ (tend) to isolate us from one another. We _____ (send) messages through the Internet rather than _____ (meet) each other over coffee. When we _____ (be) watching TV, we often _____ (ask) people around us to be quiet until the program we _____ (be) enjoying is over, even if someone _____ (have) something important to say. Also, an individual who _____ (play) video games or _____ (sit) at a computer would probably prefer to continue playing rather than to go out with friends. He or she might end up spending less and less time communicating with others because the games _____ (be) just too attractive to stop playing. These high-tech machines _____ (make) us feel less interested in the people around us. Thus, important aspects of human interaction _____ (be) de-emphasized because of our modern technology.

EXERCISE 3 (Do this exercise with a classmate.)

Directions: The following paragraph contains errors in subject-verb agreement. Cross out each incorrect verb and write the correct form above it. The first one has been done for you.

April 15 is a well-known date in the United States. Every year on this day, everyone who ~~work~~ *works* must file his or her income-tax forms with both the federal and state governments. Filing these forms are no easy task. First, a person needs to decide which forms to file. For federal income taxes, there is a long form for people who wishes to itemize their deductions. This form have at least five supplementary parts, called "schedules," and a person must decide which of these, if any, to file as well. Then there is a short form for people who plans to take the "standard" deduction, one that have been precalculated and is the same for everyone. The state income-tax forms are separate forms, and these must also be filed. In California, there is at least four supplementary schedules that a person may need to fill out. Once a person know which ones to file, completing all of these forms are not easy either, and many people hires an accountant to help them. Regardless of whether a taxpayer choose to complete the forms on his or her own or to seek assistance, the forms must be postmarked before midnight on April 15. This day is one of the busiest for the U.S. Postal Service since many taxpayers find themselves finishing the whole process at the last minute.

EXERCISE 4: (Do this exercise with a classmate.)

Directions: Take a newspaper or magazine and find several headlines that are in the present tense. Underline the verbs and notice whether or not they are singular or plural. Then read your headlines aloud to a classmate. (Note that some words, such as articles, are often omitted in headlines).

Example headline: It <u>Takes</u> Good Genes to Live to be 100, Researchers <u>Confirm</u>
(The verbs are underlined. *Takes* is singular because it agrees with the pronoun *it*. *Confirm* is plural because it agrees with the plural noun *researchers*.)

PART IV

WRITING TOPICS

Select one or more of the following topics for writing and follow the steps in Appendix A.

Topic A: Think of a person that you admire or greatly respect. This could be a relative, a friend, or a well-known person. Explain what this individual's qualities are and why you respect him or her.

Topic B: Interview someone about his or her job. This could be a classmate or friend who has done a part-time job or internship, or it could be a person who has had a permanent job for some time. Then write up a summary of what the person's job entails. What are his or her responsibilities? What does he or she like and dislike about the job? Comment on whether or not this job would be of interest to you.

Topic C: Think about the relationship people have with pets either in the United States or in your country of origin. What can pets contribute to people's lives?

PART V

CNN VIDEO ACTIVITY AND WRITING TOPIC

Washington, DC: Monuments and Memorials

Useful Vocabulary: monument memorial mall commemorate bureaucracy

Before You Watch

This video segment describes some famous monuments and memorials in Washington, DC that highlight various aspects of the history of the United States. Discuss the following questions with your classmates.

Monuments and memorials help visitors celebrate U.S. history.

- Write down three monuments or memorials you have visited in the United States or any other country. If you have not visited any, which ones have you heard about?

- What do monuments and memorials often commemorate?

While You Watch

- Write down three people or events that are remembered in the monuments and memorials you see in the video.

- Think about which monument or memorial you would be most interested in visiting.

After You Watch

I. **Write a personal reaction.**

Write a personal reaction of three to five sentences to what you saw in the video. What interested you most? Which of these places would you like to see and why? If you have already been to any of these monuments or memorials, what was your impression?

II. **Share your reactions.**

Answer the following questions either orally or in writing. Compare your answers with those of a classmate.

1. What kinds of famous people and historical events are the monuments and memorials in the video dedicated to?

2. List in order of preference three of the monuments and memorials you saw in the video and would like to visit.

3. If you could visit any monument or memorial in the world, which one would you choose and why?

WRITING TOPIC

The narrator of the video states, ". . . these monuments silently tell their visitors never to forget where the country came from. . . ." To what extent do you think memorials and monuments are an appropriate use of money and space?

Goals

- **To learn the importance of mastering articles in writing**
- **To review five problems ESL writers commonly encounter with articles**
- **To learn to use articles correctly**
- **To develop confidence in using articles through practice with exercises and writing assignments**

Articles

A student at Orange Coast College in Costa Mesa, California, meets with her professor in his office.
Photo by Hank Schellingerhout.

Think about and discuss the following question:
What are three good reasons for
attending your instructor's
office hours?

PART I

WHAT YOU NEED TO KNOW ABOUT ARTICLE ERRORS

In Part I, you will learn

- The definition of an article error
- The importance of using articles correctly in writing
- Suggestions for mastering article use in writing

Definition of the Error (art*)

An article error **(art)** is one in which the article has been used incorrectly. The articles, which belong to the group of modifiers called determiners, are *a(n)*, Ø (the zero article, meaning no article), and *the*. The articles *a* and Ø are indefinite articles, and *the* is a definite article. Before vowel sounds, *an* is used instead of *a* (*a* celebration, but *an* elephant, *an* honest day's work). (In this unit, *a* automatically includes *an*.)

Importance of Mastering Article Use in Writing

Errors in article use are local (less serious) errors and usually do not greatly affect how well the reader can understand what you have written. However, frequent article errors are distracting and can lead the reader to focus on article errors rather than on content. In spoken English, leaving out some articles may be tolerated; but in formal written English, article errors cannot be ignored.

Suggestions for Mastering Article Use in Writing

- Try to improve the percentage of articles you use correctly. Using a higher number of articles correctly will automatically make your writing easier to read. The rules governing **all** the uses of the article are complex; however, the rules given in this unit will help you use the article correctly in most cases. You can then look up additional rules as you need them in an advanced ESL grammar book.

- Be aware that if your native language does not contain articles, you must learn the rules for articles. However, even if your native language does use articles, you will need to become aware of any differences in their use in English.

- Memorize the use of the article with words or phrases that you often use. A particularly good strategy is to memorize phrases and terminology in your field of study, and classes you are taking, or in your profession.

*__art__ = grading symbol for an error with an article.

- Remember that listening will not help you very much in learning how to use articles because they are not stressed (said loudly and clearly) in spoken English. To learn how to use articles correctly, practice using them in writing and observe their use in your reading.

- Be careful when you read newspaper headlines because articles are often left out of them to save space as in, for example, "Amateur Astronomer Finds New Comet."

Test Your Understanding of Articles

Write answers to the following questions. Share your answers with another student.

1. List the articles and label each one as a definite or indefinite article. Which article has two forms and why?

2. Why is it important to improve the percentage of articles that you use correctly?

Grammar Journal Entry 11: Articles

Respond to the following in your grammar journal.

1. Have you experienced difficulty with using articles? If so, discuss two strategies that you could adopt to improve your ability to use articles correctly. If you have not had many problems with article use, explain why it is not a problem for you.

2. Write a list of five nouns you use often in your daily life, at school, or in your profession. Use each word in a sentence. Then check your sentences with a native speaker, a tutor, or your instructor to see if you have used the article correctly.

PART II

COMMON PROBLEMS, SELF-HELP STRATEGIES, AND GRAMMAR GUIDELINES

In Part II, you will study

- Five problems ESL writers commonly encounter with articles
- Self-help strategies for controlling article errors in your writing
- Grammar guidelines for articles

This section presents five problems that ESL writers commonly encounter with articles. First, take the pretest to see what you already know about using articles. In checking your answers, note that the pretest questions cover the same types of errors in the same order as the problems in this section. Then carefully study each problem and the examples that illustrate it, giving particular attention to those problems that correspond to the pretest questions you had difficulty with. Using the boxes to the left of each problem, check [✓] *yes, no,* or *don't know* to indicate to yourself which problems you should focus the most attention on in this unit and also when you are choosing articles in English. Remember that becoming aware of the type of article errors you most often make will increase your chances of avoiding these errors in your writing.*

Pretest: What Do You Already Know About Articles?

Test your ability to recognize errors with articles by finding and correcting the one article error in each of the following sentences.

Answers on p. 293

1. When a person buys a car, he or she usually has to make down payment.
2. My friend called the police because one of neighbors was having a loud party.
3. Students learn material more easily when they have a homework.
4. Many doctors in the United States no longer wear the uniform during office hours.
5. My cousin always makes sure she has the driver's license when she goes out.

Five Problems ESL Writers Commonly Encounter with Articles

yes   no   don't know   **PROBLEM 1**

☐   ☐   ☐   The zero article (Ø) has been used when *a* or *the* is needed.

                                                                    art
Incorrect: Yesterday, I finally went to pay my overdue fine at ∧ library.
Correct: Yesterday, I finally went to pay my overdue fine at <u>the</u> library.

                     art   *art*   *art*
Incorrect: She bought ∧ book and ∧ ballpoint pen as ∧ birthday gift.
Correct: She bought <u>a</u> book and <u>a</u> ballpoint pen as <u>a</u> birthday gift.

---

*   The material in this section is based in part on the binary system for teaching articles developed by Peter Master and reported in "Teaching the English Articles as a Binary System," *TESOL Quarterly,* vol. 24, no. 3, Autumn 1990.

yes   no   don't know   **PROBLEM 2**

☐   ☐   ☐   The article *the* has not been used after an *of* phrase showing quantity.

> **Note:**   Some *of* phrases are *one of the, most of the, some of the,* or *half of the.*

art

Incorrect: All of ͜ textbooks for this class have been sold.
Correct: All of <u>the</u> textbooks for this class have been sold.

Self-Help Strategy: Use *the* automatically after an *of* phrase showing quantity whether the noun is countable or uncountable.

yes   no   don't know   **PROBLEM 3**

☐   ☐   ☐   The article *a* has been used where Ø is needed.

art

Incorrect: A good friend gives <u>an</u> advice when asked.
Correct: A good friend gives <u>advice</u> when asked.

art

Incorrect: My uncle has <u>an</u> obvious reasons for his decision.
Correct: My uncle has <u>obvious reasons</u> for his decision.
Correct: My uncle has <u>an obvious reason</u> for his decision.

yes   no   don't know   **PROBLEM 4**

☐   ☐   ☐   The article *a* has been used for *the* or vice versa.

art

Incorrect: My cousin lived <u>the</u> productive life as a pharmacist.
Correct: My cousin lived <u>a</u> productive life as a pharmacist.

art

Incorrect: My lab partner has <u>a</u> books you wanted him to find.
Correct: My lab partner has <u>the</u> books you wanted him to find.

Self-Help Strategy: Remember that you must first determine whether the noun is countable or uncountable. Then, if you are classifying an uncountable noun, use *a*. If you are classifying an uncountable or plural noun, use Ø. To identify a noun, countable or uncountable, singular or plural, use *the*.

yes	no	don't know	**PROBLEM 5**
☐	☐	☐	The articles *a*, Ø, or *the* have been used instead of another determiner.

Note: Articles are part of the whole system of determiners, which includes possessive pronouns (for example: *my, your*), demonstrative adjectives (*this, these; that, those*), and quantifiers (for example: *some, any,* or *every*).

> *art*
Incorrect: Whenever I go to the library, I remember that I need <u>the</u> library card.
Correct: Whenever I go to the library, I remember that I need <u>my</u> library card. (*I need <u>a</u> library card* would also be correct but would not show possession.)

> *art*
Incorrect: Restaurant employees need to wash <u>the</u> hands frequently.
Correct: Restaurant employees need to wash <u>their</u> hands frequently.

> *art*
Incorrect: She wants <u>a</u> meat for dinner.
Correct: She wants <u>some</u> meat for dinner. (The emphasis is on the amount.)
Correct: She wants meat for dinner. (The emphasis is not on the amount but on what she wants to eat for dinner.)

Self-Help Strategy: Remember that articles classify or identify nouns; they do not show quantity or possession.

Grammar Guidelines for Using Articles

In this section, you will learn selected rules for using articles with common nouns. Every time you use a common noun or noun phrase (the noun plus its modifiers) in English, you must decide between *a*, Ø, or *the*. Articles are used to identify or not identify a noun as specified below.

Rules for Identifying Versus Not Identifying a Noun*

The article *the* identifies the noun.

Example: I ate <u>the apple in my lunch</u>. (*The apple* identifies which apple, the one in my lunch.)

The article *a* or the zero article (Ø) does not identify the noun but shows to what class or group the noun belongs.

Example: I eat <u>an apple</u> every day. (*an apple* = something that can be classified as an apple)†
Your pen needs <u>ink</u>. (*ink* = something that can be classified as ink)
I like <u>foreign films</u>. (*foreign films* = things that can be classified as foreign films)

1. **When you are not identifying a noun, use *a* or Ø.**

   Use *a* or Ø depending upon whether the noun is countable or uncountable. Countable nouns (like *book, test,* or *car*) can be counted and made plural, but uncountable nouns (like *writing, advice,* and *intelligence*) cannot be counted and do not have a plural form. Most ESL dictionaries indicate if a noun is countable or uncountable. Some nouns (like *paper* or *change*) can be either countable or uncountable depending on their meaning.

   a. **If the noun is a singular countable noun, use *a*.**

   Incorrect: Last week I bought chemistry textbook at Discount Books.
   Correct: Last week I bought <u>a</u> chemistry textbook at Discount Books. (The chemistry textbook is one of many chemistry texts the bookstore has; the writer has not identified a particular one.)
   Incorrect: When students are taking <u>the</u> composition class, they often complain about the time they must spend working on their essays.
   Correct: When students are taking <u>a</u> composition class, they often complain about the time they must spend working on their essays. (The writer has not identified a specific class but is talking about any composition class.)

   b. **If the noun is uncountable or if it is plural, use Ø.**

   Note: The determiner *some* can be used with uncountable and plural nouns but only when an amount can be indicated.

   Incorrect: Many people drink <u>the</u> bottled water as they prefer its taste.
   Incorrect: Many people drink <u>a</u> bottled water as they prefer its taste.
   Correct: Many people drink <u>bottled water</u> as they prefer its taste. (Water is uncountable and no special type of water has been indicated.)

---

*   Nouns that are not capitalized are known as common nouns. Nouns that are always capitalized are called proper nouns.
†   The wording "something that can be classified as . . ." comes from Peter Master's work on the binary schema of articles.

Incorrect:	<u>The</u> playing badminton is my favorite activity.
Correct:	<u>Playing badminton</u> is my favorite activity. (Gerunds and gerund phrases [the gerund with its object and modifiers] are uncountable See **2(b)** for modified gerunds.)

Incorrect:	Before I go to class, I had better buy <u>a</u> ruled notebook paper.
Correct:	Before I go to class, I had better buy <u>ruled notebook paper</u>. (Paper is uncountable and no amount is specified.)
Correct:	Before I go to class, I had better buy <u>some</u> ruled notebook paper. (Paper is uncountable and a nonspecific amount is indicated.)

Incorrect:	<u>The</u> soft-soled shoes are to be worn at all times in the gymnasium.
Correct:	<u>Soft-soled shoes</u> are to be worn at all times in the gymnasium. (The writer means soft-soled shoes of any kind.)

Incorrect:	<u>The</u> ballpoint pens are to be used during the final exam.
Correct:	<u>Ballpoint pens</u> are to be used during the final exam. (The writer has not identified any specific ballpoint pens.)

2. **When you are identifying a common noun, use *the*.**

   a. **After you have classified a noun with *a*, use *the* when you use the noun again.**

Incorrect:	I found <u>a</u> used car that I liked yesterday and bought it. I now have to buy insurance for <u>a</u> car.
Correct:	I found <u>a</u> used car that I liked yesterday and bought it. I now have to buy insurance for <u>the</u> car. (*The car* means specifically the car that has already been mentioned.)

   b. **When the following occur, use *the*. The noun can be singular or plural, countable or uncountable.**

   - The noun is identified by a ranking adjective that identifies it as one of a kind:

Correct:	<u>The best</u> ice cream is sold at that shop. (a superlative)
Correct:	In <u>the next</u> chapter, we will examine verb tense. (sequential)
Correct:	She is <u>the only</u> student with whom I will study. (unique)

   - The noun is identifiable to the reader and the writer through shared knowledge.

Correct:	<u>The sun</u> is going to rise at 5:43 AM tomorrow. (Both reader and writer know it is the sun we see from Earth.)
Correct:	My roommate left her backpack in <u>the computer room</u>. (Both reader and writer know which room it is.)
Correct:	Some of <u>the students</u> will need to take a makeup test. (Both reader and writer know who the students are.)

- The noun phrase is identified by the modification that follows it.

  Correct: Last week I finally read <u>the article about thunderstorms that Professor Johns recommended to us</u>. (The article has been identified as the one about thunderstorms and the one that was recommended.)

  Correct: Most of the <u>textbooks for this class</u> have been sold. (The textbooks have been identified as the ones for a certain class.)

  Correct: <u>The laughter of the children</u> made my grandfather happy. (The noun has been identified by an *of* phrase.)

  Correct: <u>The laughing of his grandchildren</u> made my grandfather happy. (Note that when a gerund or gerund phrase is modified, it is identified and thus uses *the*. The gerund phrase *playing badminton* was not identified in **1(b),** but if its direct object, *badminton*, became an *of* phrase modifying the gerund, the gerund would then be identified as in *the playing of badminton*.)

- The noun is part of an *of* phrase showing quantity.

  Correct: Raymond noticed that <u>half of the cake</u> had been eaten already.

  Correct: My supervisor said that <u>all of the fruit</u> in that shipment was spoiled.

  Correct: <u>Some of the monkeys</u> will be transferred to a bigger cage.

Rules for Using Articles with Proper Nouns

In academic and professional writing, you will often need to use the names of people, places, and things. When you are naming a particular person, place, or thing, you will use a proper noun, which is always capitalized. Because the rules for using articles with proper nouns have many exceptions, it is best to learn only a few general rules and to memorize article use for those proper nouns you frequently employ. You can also check article use for individual cases in an advanced ESL grammar book or an ESL dictionary for advanced language learners, or you can simply ask a native speaker what is correct.

For names of people, use the following guidelines:
- With singular names of people, Ø is usually used.

  Examples:
  > Have you read *A Tale of Two Cities* by <u>Charles Dickens</u>?
  > <u>Miriam</u> has just finished a French quiz.
  > <u>Dr. Hendrickson</u> will be a guest lecturer in my history class today.

- With plural family names, *the* is usually used.

  Example: Next week <u>the Campbells</u> will talk about their life as pioneers in Montana.

For names of places, use the following guidelines:
- States, cities, streets, and universities usually use Ø unless the name is introduced by a capitalized common noun (such as *City* or *University*) and *of*.

Examples:

> Last night, I telephoned my brother who attends <u>Stanford University</u> in <u>Palo Alto</u>, <u>California</u>.
> The bank is located on <u>State Street</u>.
> My sister works as a public defender for <u>The City of New York</u>.
> <u>The University of Arizona</u> is on the semester system.

- Oceans, rivers, mountain ranges, and public buildings usually use *the*.

Examples:

> <u>The Pacific Ocean</u> keeps San Francisco cool.
> <u>The Mississippi River</u> starts in Minnesota and ends in Louisiana.
> <u>The Rocky Mountains</u> have good snow for skiing.
> <u>The Metropolitan Museum of Art</u> is on Fifth Avenue.

- Singular names of countries usually use Ø.

Examples:

> In <u>Switzerland</u>, four languages are spoken.
> <u>Australia</u> has many unusual species of animals.

- Plural names of countries or names of countries that contain the words *united, union, kingdom,* or *republic* use *the*.

Examples:

> <u>The United States</u> is a country with wide expanses of land.
> <u>The Central African Republic</u> borders Zaire.
> <u>The Seychelles</u> are in the Indian Ocean.

Rules for Using Articles with Set Expressions

Certain set (or common) expressions use *the* or Ø. To make sure that you are using the correct article, look up the expression in an ESL dictionary or ask a native speaker what is correct. It is also a good idea to memorize set expressions that you use frequently.

The following brief list will help you become aware of article use in set expressions:

WITH THE <u>Ø</u> ARTICLE	WITH <u>THE</u>
by train, by plane, by car	on <u>the</u> other hand
to church, to school	in <u>the</u> morning
at seven o'clock	in <u>the</u> evening
in class	in <u>the</u> afternoon
at home, at school	to get <u>the</u> gist of
at night	to get <u>the</u> point
after breakfast, lunch, dinner	to play <u>the</u> part

Improve Your Writing Style

Know How to Vary Articles in Writing

In the following paragraph, pay attention to how the writer has varied the use of articles to talk about grizzly bears. Notice that the writer is talking about *all* grizzly bears as members of that class of animals known as grizzly bears.

The grizzly bear is a large animal that lives in North America. Grizzly bears are mammals, and it is not uncommon for them to be seen near garbage cans in national parks. Many people feel a grizzly bear is the most frightening of animals because of its size and ferocious look. The grizzly is a very dangerous animal and should never be given food because it has been known to kill humans.

In the following paragraph, notice how the writer has varied the use of articles to talk about computers in general.

Since the 1970s, the computer has gradually come into everyday use. At one time, computers were only used in business, but now they are used by everyone. In fact, the computer now is within the price range of almost everyone. If we were to compare inventions, the computer has become the car of the 1990s. [If the writer later says that he or she wants to buy a computer, he or she is talking about any computer, not computers in general.]

Note: The Ø article is used with an uncountable noun when talking about a class or when generalizing.

Examples:

Cadmium is a heavy metal.
It is very fashionable to drink mineral water.

Improve Your Writing Style

Know How to Be More Specific with Uncountable Nouns

Examples:

I want water. (no amount has been specified)
I want some water. (an unidentified amount of water)
I want a glass of water. (a specific amount)

She likes to give advice. (general)
She gave me a useful piece of advice. (more specific)
She gave me the best piece of advice that I have ever received. (more specific)

PART III

EXERCISES FOR PRACTICE

EXERCISE 1 (Do this exercise on your own. Then check your answers with a classmate.)

Directions: Test your ability to identify and correct article errors in the following sentences. First, decide if a sentence is correct (C) or if it contains any article errors (I). Then correct each article error. Some sentences may have more than one article error, and some errors can be corrected in more than one way.

Examples:

   _I_   Cheryl forgot to turn in *an* assignment for her math class.

   _C_   Will you stop at the grocery store on your way home?

_____ 1. At the end of each quarter, a final exams are held.

_____ 2. Most of students in Chemistry 1 have to study very hard.

_____ 3. She went to the bookstore and bought pencils, a textbook, and glue.

_____ 4. At the night, all patrons must wear the shirts and ties in this restaurant.

_____ 5. If I have problems with my car, I take bus to work.

_____ 6. Be sure that you study night before exam.

_____ 7. Instant noodles are quick and easy to prepare.

_____ 8. When there is full moon, I like to walk down the Beach Avenue.

_____ 9. In a dry state like California, the water is a precious commodity for agriculture.

_____ 10. Although I like to write down my thoughts, I never have enough time to write in the journal.

EXERCISE 2 (Do this exercise with a classmate.)

Directions: In the following paragraph, adapted from a student's writing, the articles have been used correctly. Examine the underlined nouns and noun phrases and explain why *a, Ø,* or *the* was used. The first one has been done for you.

                                                uncountable, not identified

When I was still very young, my parents taught me to love <u>learning</u>. Every evening after <u>dinner</u>, my father would teach me <u>simple math</u> and my mother would teach me how to write and read <u>Chinese characters</u>. At the age of five, I already knew a number of Chinese characters and was able to do addition, <u>subtraction</u>, and <u>simple multiplication</u>

<u>problems</u>. It was not that I was <u>a genius</u> or even a precocious child; it was <u>the simple fact</u> that my parents encouraged me to learn by praising me whenever I gave them <u>the correct answer</u> to their questions. Their praise made me feel that I was smart and could learn. What also helped me learn was that I had <u>few distractions</u>. I did not grow up with <u>a television</u>, a radio, or <u>video games</u> as children do now, for it was not common in <u>China</u> at that time to have a television or a radio at home. Therefore, our usual source of entertainment after dinner was <u>playing games</u>, <u>reading</u>, and learning. When I began school, I never had to depend on <u>the teacher</u> to motivate me to learn because I had already developed a love of learning. I also entered <u>school</u> with the attitude that I could learn because my parents' early teaching and <u>the learning</u> that had taken place in my house had helped me develop not only <u>confidence</u> in my abilities but also <u>a sense</u> that learning was enjoyable.

EXERCISE 3 (Do this exercise with a classmate.)

Directions: **The following paragraph, which was written by a student, has some articles left out. Test your mastery of articles by supplying the correct articles where needed. The first one has been done for you.**

My attitude toward English is negatively affecting my writing. I think the problem is that as ^a^ mathematics major, I love to spend my time doing as much math as possible. Often my math homework and my other classes, which also relate to my major, occupy most of my time. As a result, I devote rest of my time and energy, which is not much, to writing essays for my English class. However, I usually have trouble getting started. I waste my time eating, listening to music, or even looking in the mirror instead of trying to work on my paper. Furthermore, I always have negative feeling toward writing. Even before writing paper, I assume that my paper will not turn out well. Because of this negative attitude, my grade in English is suffering.

EXERCISE 4 (Do this exercise on your own. Then check your answers with a classmate.)

Directions: **Choose a short article in a newspaper or a magazine and read it. Then underline all the nouns or noun phrases in two paragraphs and explain why the author used *a, Ø,* or *the.***

PART IV

WRITING TOPICS

Select one or more of the following topics for writing and follow the steps in Appendix A.

Topic A: A friend has never seen where you live. Write a letter to a friend in which you describe your room or your apartment. If you live in a house, describe only your room. In your letter, be sure to tell your friend how comfortable you are living in this place or room.

Topic B: Do you think children should start formal learning at an early age or do you think that they should have more time to play?

Topic C: Whether they socialize at a preschool or in an informal setting, what kinds of skills do young children learn through interacting with one another? What skills, in your opinion, are most important for young children to learn?

PART V

CNN VIDEO ACTIVITY AND WRITING TOPIC

The African Rhino: An Endangered Species

Useful Vocabulary: endangered species   conservation   poacher   commodity   economic
resource   decade

Before You Watch

This video segment presents one approach to pre-
serving endangered species. Before learning about it,
answer the following questions.

- What causes an animal species to become endangered? What are some ways that are being tried to
  preserve species?
- List several species of plants or animals that you
  know are considered endangered.

While You Watch

- Determine what has caused the rhino to become
  endangered.
- Make a note of what happens to a dead rhino's horn.

Even the loss of one species "dimin-
ishes the entire world."

After You Watch

I. **Write a personal reaction.**

   Write a personal reaction of three to five sentences to what you saw in the video. What interested or surprised you most? Do you think it is important to preserve endangered species?
   Explain.

II. **Share your reactions.**

   Answer the following questions either orally or in writing. Compare your answers with those
   of a classmate.
   1. How many rhinos were killed in the last two decades and for what reason?
   2. How much does the value of a rhino horn change from the time it is taken from a dead rhino
      to the time it is sold for medicinal purposes in the market?
   3. What is the new approach to eliminating rhino poaching suggested in the video? What is
      your opinion of this approach?

WRITING TOPIC

Conserving endangered species can be very costly for governments. The approach presented in this
video involves the loss of some animals in order to preserve others and seeks to change the present
economic structure that encourages poachers. What, in your opinion, are the strengths and weaknesses of this approach? Do you have other suggestions for ways to preserve endangered species?

Goals

- To learn the importance of mastering the singular and plural of nouns in writing
- To review eight problems ESL writers commonly encounter with singulars and plurals of nouns
- To learn to form and use the singular and plural of nouns correctly
- To develop confidence in using the singular and plural of nouns through practice with exercises and writing assignments

Singular and Plural of Nouns

A San Francisco State University student takes advantage of good weather to work on her laptop computer outdoors. Photo courtesy of Office of Publications.

Think about and discuss the following question:
What are three benefits of using a
laptop computer for writing assignments?

PART I

WHAT YOU NEED TO KNOW ABOUT SINGULAR/PLURAL NOUN ERRORS

In Part I, you will learn

- The definition of a singular/plural noun error
- The importance of using the singular and plural of nouns correctly in writing
- Suggestions for mastering the singular and plural of nouns in writing

Definition of the Error (s/pl*)

A singular/plural noun error **(s/pl)** is one in which the singular form of a noun has been used instead of the plural or vice versa. For example, in the sentence *I have two sister*, there is a singular/plural noun error because *sister* should be *sisters*. Likewise, in the sentence *He gave me some informations*, there is a singular/plural noun error because *informations* should be *information.*

Importance of Mastering the Singular and Plural of Nouns in Writing

A singular/plural noun error is a local error and usually does not affect the meaning of a sentence, but frequent errors of this type can distract the reader's attention from the content of a piece of writing. In formal written English, readers expect to see correct use of the singular and plural of nouns.

Suggestions for Mastering the Singular and Plural of Nouns in Writing

- Know that by becoming aware of the rules for the singular and plural of nouns (which you will read about in this unit), you can reduce many of your singular/plural errors in writing.
- Look up a noun in an ESL dictionary if you are unsure whether it is countable or not. While writing, you may want to simply mark nouns that you need to check for singular/plural. In that way, you can revise for the singular or plural later and not disrupt your focus on content while you are searching for a noun in the dictionary.

*s/pl = grading symbol for an error with the singular or plural of a noun.

- Memorize the singular and plural forms of nouns that you use often in your classes or in your field of study. (As a first step, always put the ending *-s* on the *United States*.)

- Train yourself to use the singular and plural of nouns correctly in English if your native language does not have a plural marker. If your native language indicates singular and plural of nouns much as English does, focus on learning those nouns in English whose singular or plural is formed or used differently than in your own language.

- Listen closely to hear plurals in speaking. Because the plural *s* is often difficult to hear in spoken English, plural nouns may sometimes sound singular to you. (For example, when an instructor says, "I want you to read three chapters for tomorrow," the *s* may be difficult to hear as it is being said between two consonants.)

- Pay careful attention to singulars and plurals of nouns while you are reading.

Test Your Understanding of Singular/Plural Noun Errors

Write answers to the following questions. Share your answers with another student.

1. What is an error with the singular or plural of a noun?

2. What is a suggested strategy to use for checking the singular or plural of a noun while writing, and why would such a strategy be helpful for some ESL learners?

Grammar Journal Entry 12: Singular/Plural of Nouns

Respond to the following in your grammar journal.

1. Write three sentences in your native language, using at least one plural of a noun in each. Then write those same sentences in English and check the use of the plural in both your native language and English. Explain briefly how the use of the plural is similar or different.

2. Write a list of five nouns you use often in your daily life, at school, or in your profession. Then use each word in a sentence. Check your sentences with a native speaker, a tutor, or your instructor to see if you have formed the singular or the plural correctly.

PART II

COMMON PROBLEMS, SELF-HELP STRATEGIES, AND GRAMMAR GUIDELINES

In Part II, you will study

- Eight problems ESL writers commonly encounter with the singular and plural of nouns
- Self-help strategies for controlling the singular and plural of nouns in your writing
- Grammar guidelines for the singular and plural of nouns

This section presents eight problems that ESL writers commonly encounter with the singular and plural of nouns. First, take the pretest to see what you already know about the singular and plural of nouns. In checking your answers, note that the pretest questions cover the same types of errors in the same order as the problems in this section. Then carefully study each problem and the examples that illustrate it, giving particular attention to those problems that correspond to the pretest questions you had difficulty with. Using the boxes to the left of each problem, check [✓] *yes, no,* or *don't know* to indicate to yourself which problems you should focus the most attention on in this unit and also when you use the singular and plural of nouns in English. Remember that becoming aware of the types of errors you most often make with singular and plural of nouns will increase your chances of avoiding these errors in your writing.

Pretest: What Do You Already Know About the Singular and Plural of Nouns?

Test your ability to recognize errors with the singular and plural of nouns by finding and correcting the one singular/plural error in each of the following sentences.

Answers on p. 293

1. When I travel, I always take two suitcase.
2. My older sister is always willing to give me advices.
3. Perhaps you might like to read this two novels.
4. The little girl is selling red and yellows apples.
5. An old proverb says, "An eye for an eye and a tooths for a tooths."
6. On Valentine's Day, Andrea received one of the biggest box of chocolates I have ever seen.
7. Much of the works she did on that experiment had to be discarded.
8. When the meeting started, only two woman were in the audience.

Eight Problems ESL Writers Commonly Encounter with the Singular and Plural of Nouns

yes   no   don't know   **PROBLEM 1**

☐   ☐   ☐   A countable noun is singular when it should be plural.

s/pl   *s/pl*

Incorrect: The <u>student</u> in the class were asking <u>question</u>.
Correct: The <u>students</u> in the class were asking <u>questions</u>.

s/pl

Incorrect: I solved all but two <u>problem</u> on my calculus test.
Correct: I solved all but two <u>problems</u> on my calculus test.

yes   no   don't know   **PROBLEM 2**

☐   ☐   ☐   An uncountable noun has been made plural.

s/pl

Incorrect: You should seek <u>advices</u> when you are making an important decision.
Correct: You should seek <u>advice</u> when you are making an important decision.

s/pl   *s/pl*

Incorrect: Water consists of two parts <u>hydrogens</u> and one part <u>oxygens</u>.
Correct: Water consists of two parts <u>hydrogen</u> and one part <u>oxygen</u>.

Self-Help Strategy: Look at the noun and ask yourself whether it is countable or uncountable. If it is uncountable, do not add *-s* or *-es*.

yes   no   don't know   **PROBLEM 3**

☐   ☐   ☐   A noun and its demonstrative adjective do not agree.

s/pl

Incorrect: <u>These book</u> are for the other class, not yours.
Correct: <u>These books</u> are for the other class, not yours.
Correct: <u>This book</u> is for the other class, not yours.

Self-Help Strategy: Remember that, unlike adjectives, demonstrative adjectives agree in number with the noun they modify. If you are unsure, refer to the rules listed in this unit.

yes   no   don't know   **PROBLEM 4**

☐   ☐   ☐   A noun or an adjective modifying a noun has been made plural.

s/pl

Incorrect: The campus is made up of <u>reds bricks</u> buildings.
Correct: The campus is made up of <u>red brick</u> buildings.

s/pl

Incorrect: Next week we have to write a <u>five-hundreds</u>-word essay.
Correct: Next week we have to write a <u>five-hundred</u>-word essay.

Self-Help Strategy: If your native language makes adjectives plural to agree with the noun, be especially careful to avoid this error in English.

yes   no   don't know   **PROBLEM 5**

☐   ☐   ☐   An idiomatic expression has incorrectly been made singular or plural.

s/pl

Incorrect: To make a good decision, you need to weigh the <u>pro and con</u>.
Correct: To make a good decision, you need to weigh the <u>pros and cons</u>.

s/pl

Incorrect: Robert promised to keep <u>eyes out</u> for the blue shirt I want.
Correct: Robert promised to keep <u>an eye out</u> for the blue shirt I want.

Self-Help Strategy: Idiomatic expressions often have to be memorized. If you are unsure, look up the expression in a dictionary for nonnative English speakers. Such a dictionary often includes idiomatic expressions.

yes   no   don't know   **PROBLEM 6**

☐   ☐   ☐   A countable noun following an *of* phrase that shows quantity has not been made plural.

Note: Some *of* phrases are *one of the, most of the, any of the, half of the,* or *some of the.*

s/pl

Incorrect: One of the oldest <u>building</u> on campus is North Hall.
Correct: One of the oldest <u>buildings</u> on campus is North Hall.

yes   no   don't know   **PROBLEM 7**

☐   ☐   ☐   An uncountable noun following an *of* phrase has been made plural.

s/pl

Incorrect: Some of the <u>milks</u> has gone sour.
Correct: Some of the <u>milk</u> has gone sour. (Milk is not countable.)

yes   no   don't know   **PROBLEM 8**

☐   ☐   ☐   A countable noun that has an irregular plural has been incorrectly formed.

s/pl

Incorrect: Five <u>womans</u> signed up for the class in auto mechanics.
Correct: Five <u>women</u> signed up for the class in auto mechanics.

Self-Help Strategy: Be aware that some nouns in English have an irregular plural. Common examples are *tooth, teeth; fish, fish; thesis, theses.*

Grammar Guidelines for the Singular and Plural of Nouns

In this section, you will learn selected rules for forming the singular and plural of nouns correctly. A noun is used to name a person, place, or thing. Proper nouns are always capitalized and name a specific person, place, or thing (*John F. Kennedy, Boston, The Library of Congress*).

Rules for Forming the Singular and Plural of Nouns

1. **Nouns are either countable or uncountable (they are also called mass or noncountable nouns).**

   Examples of countable nouns: *table, building, road, carrot, horse*
   Examples of uncountable nouns: *air, jelly, foam, potassium*

2. **Countable nouns have singulars and plurals (*book, books*), and individual members of a group can be counted (*one book, two books, three books*). Countable nouns (like *textbook, test,* or *assignment*) can be made plural by adding -*s* or -*es*.**

3. Uncountable nouns have only one form *(money, air, happiness)* and cannot be counted. We cannot say *one money, one air,* or *one happiness.* Note that uncountable nouns take a singular verb *(The air is fresh).*

4. Uncountable nouns (like *vocabulary, homework,* and *stress*) do not take the plural.

5. Some nouns can be either countable or uncountable depending on their meaning.

    Examples:

    > Learning English is hard <u>work</u>.

    > The complete <u>works</u> of Dickens will be published in a new edition soon. (meaning all the different types of things he wrote)

    > Many painters like southern France because of its intense <u>light.</u> From that hill, the <u>lights</u> of the town are beautiful at night. (meaning all the different types of lights)

6. Some nouns have an irregular plural.

    Examples:

    > child, children
    > deer, deer

7. Adjectives can never be made plural in English. Nouns used as adjectives are also singular.

    Examples:

    > a <u>long</u> day, five <u>long</u> days
    > one <u>chocolate</u> bar, two <u>chocolate</u> bars

8. Demonstrative adjectives agree in number with the noun they modify. The demonstrative adjectives are *this, that* = singular; *these, those* = plural.

    Examples:

    > this room, these rooms
    > that castle, those castles

9. A countable noun after an *of* phrase that shows quantity is always plural. An uncountable noun after these phrases is always singular.

    Examples:

    > <u>Many of the workers</u> at that company would like higher pay.
    > <u>Two-thirds of the water</u> in that pond will be dried up by summer.

Improve Your Writing Style

Know When to Use Week(s), Year(s), and Month(s)

When *week*, *year*, or *month* is used as an adjective, it does not take an *-s*.

Examples:

Our school is on a ten-<u>week</u> quarter system.

When I was a four-<u>year</u>-old child, I was still living in Taiwan.

That problem is so simple that a two-<u>year</u>-old could figure it out.

(In the above example sentence, *old* is a noun denoting a person or thing of a certain age.)

My aunt will be taking a three-<u>month</u> vacation in Europe.

When *week*, *year*, or *month* is used as a noun, it takes an *-s*.

Examples:

Ferdinand traveled in Africa for four <u>weeks</u>.

Ten <u>months</u> ago, my uncle immigrated to the United States.

You must be at least sixty <u>years</u> old to take advantage of the senior discount. (*Years* is a noun and *sixty* and *old* are adjectives.)

PART III

EXERCISES FOR PRACTICE

EXERCISE 1 (Do this exercise on your own. Then check your answers with a classmate.)

Directions: **Using the material you have just studied as a guide, underline and then correct any errors with the singular or plural in the following sentences.**

> **Example:** Please don't forget to buy some <u>banana</u>^{s} on your way home.

1. When I read, I mark unfamiliar vocabularies, which I later look up in a dictionary.

2. This boys needs to sign up for the camping trip.

3. One of the best way to practice your English is to join a conversation club.

4. Many cultures teach respect for the elderlies.

5. I had three piece of candies and some cake at the party.

6. My writing needs improvements, so I am going to work with a tutor.

7. My friends are renting a hundreds-year-old house.

8. The professor is hiring students to analyze the datas she collected.

9. You need to follow the laboratory manual steps by steps to make your experiment come out right.

10. I had almost given up finding my watch when it suddenly caught my eyes from under a piece of paper.

11. My aunt has five childs: two sons and three daughter.

12. My roommate has excellent computers skills.

EXERCISE 2 (Do this exercise on your own. Then check your answers with a classmate.)

Directions: **In the following paragraph, which was written by a student, selected nouns and adjectives have been underlined. Decide whether you need to make the noun plural or leave the noun or adjective singular. Make any corrections by adding the appropriate ending or crossing out the word and rewriting it above. The first one has been done for you.**

During the fall quarter, I was overwhelmed with many <u>assignment</u>^{S}. The most unexpected one was writing. Even though I knew that education <u>class</u> required <u>writing</u>, the professors I had were especially fond of <u>essay</u> writing. Both of my education <u>class</u> required a total of eight <u>paper</u>, each of which were four to six <u>page</u> long; in addition, the final papers in both classes were twenty-page <u>research</u> papers. Furthermore, both of my biochemistry <u>class</u> required a total of eight lab write-ups and three essays. In sum, I had to write more than twenty papers last quarter, and <u>that</u> papers were a nightmare for me. Previously, I thought that only English classes would require a lot of writing which is not one of my favorite <u>activity</u>. Nevertheless, last semester was the only time during my four years in college that I had to write so much. Thus, I lost much of my fear of writing; however, I still hate <u>revision</u> because it is very time-consuming work.

EXERCISE 3 (Do this exercise with a classmate.)

Directions: **In the following paragraph, some errors with singulars and plurals occur. Do this exercise by following these steps:**

1. Underline each noun and any adjectives that modify the noun.
2. Using Part II as a guide, determine where errors with singulars or plurals occur in the paragraph.

3. If you are unsure whether a noun can take the plural, check a dictionary for nonnative English speakers to see if the noun is countable or uncountable.

4. Correct any singular/plural errors by writing the correct form above the noun or adjective. Make the verb agree with the corrected noun as necessary.

<u>Catalog shopping</u> has become very popular in the <u>United State</u>^s. According to a recent newspaper article, catalog sales have been growing at the rate of 15 percent annually, twice the growth rate of retail store sales. With the advents of 800 number, fax machines, and web sites, catalog shopping has indeed become fast and convenient. You can telephone in your order, speak to the sales representative at the other end, and usually find out if what you want is in stock, thus avoiding the tedious works of filling out an order form. Or, if you prefer a written record, you can use the order form provided in the catalog and fax it to the catalog company. These days, it is possible to buy everything from a simple white blouse to a whole set of garden furnitures without ever setting foot in a store. Most people also like the option of express mail that catalogs companies offer; customers can fax or telephone in an order one day and the item will arrive at their house in a day or two. People also find that if they purchase clothings from the same catalog companies, they can avoid much frustrations, for they can almost always gauge the right size. Also, catalogs help by showing a picture of the range of colors. However, what the catalogs do not mention is that while you can return your purchase, it is time-consuming to repack and send it. Thus, if you are satisfied, you have saved time. However, if you are disappointed, you will have to devote time to repackaging and returning the item. If you are too busy or lazy to do so and thus keep the unwanted item, you will lose money. A wonderful alternatives is the catalog store. You can see what you want in the catalog and then go to the catalog store and buy it. Then you have the best of both world.

EXERCISE 4 (Do this exercise on your own.)

Directions: Choose a short article in a newspaper or a magazine and read it. Then underline ten nouns in the article. Using the information you have learned in this unit, decide why the noun is singular or plural. If you are unsure why a noun is in the singular, check in an ESL dictionary to determine whether it is an uncountable noun and therefore cannot be made plural. Remember that set phrases are an exception to this rule.

PART IV

WRITING TOPICS

Select one or more of the following topics for writing and follow the steps in Appendix A.

Topic A: Discuss your favorite ways to relieve stress. Explain how they are beneficial to you.

Topic B: Using what you have learned from your reading or from watching television programs, answer the following question: If we humans do not conserve our natural resources, what will some of the effects be?

Topic C: Think about the various places that you study or work. Of these places, which one is your favorite? Describe this place and explain why you like to study or work there.

PART V

CNN VIDEO ACTIVITY AND WRITING TOPIC

The Ultimate in Shopping Convenience

Useful Vocabulary: window shopping   instant gratification   peruse   ultimate   outpace

Before You Watch

This video segment gives information and opinions on in-home shopping using catalogs, television shopping channels, and the Internet. Answer the following questions.

"Catalogs are still 'kings' of the home shopping market."

- What are some advantages and disadvantages of shopping from home?
- How do you usually shop?

While You Watch

- Compare your shopping experiences with those presented in the video.
- Find out which method of in-home shopping is the most popular.

After You Watch

I. **Write a personal reaction.**

   Write a personal reaction of three to five sentences to what you saw in the video. What interested or surprised you about in-home shopping? To what extent have you taken advantage of in-home shopping? If you have not, would you like to?

II. **Share your reactions.**

   Answer the following questions either orally or in writing. Compare your answers with those of a classmate.
   1. According to the video, what does the future hold for in-home shopping?
   2. In the last five years, how much has the growth in catalog shopping outpaced the growth in retail sales? What is your reaction to this information?
   3. What are some advantages and disadvantages of in-home shopping that were not mentioned in the video?

WRITING TOPIC

In addition to information about in-home shopping, this video also mentions some of the differences between shopping from home and going out to a store. Compare and contrast shopping from home with actually going to a place of business to make purchases.

Goals

- To learn the importance of mastering word choice in writing
- To review six problems ESL writers commonly encounter with word choice
- To learn to make accurate choices with words
- To develop confidence in word choice through practice with exercises and writing assignments

Word Choice

At Florida Community College–Jacksonville, an instructor asks students to "brainstorm" before beginning a writing assignment. Photo courtesy of Media Relations.

Think about and discuss the following question:

"Brainstorming" is an effective way of gathering ideas before you start writing. What techniques do you use to get ideas before you begin the writing process?

PART I

WHAT YOU NEED TO KNOW ABOUT ERRORS IN WORD CHOICE

In Part I, you will learn

- The definition of a word-choice error
- The importance of using words correctly in writing
- Suggestions for mastering word choice in writing

Definition of the Error (wc*)

A word-choice error **(wc)** is one in which the wrong word has been used in a sentence. For example, in the sentence *Even though she spoke very little English when she first arrived in the United States, my mother did not <u>abundant</u> her dream of being a bookkeeper,* the word *abundant* should be *abandon.*

Word-choice errors, although frequently local (less serious) and affecting only part of a sentence, can become global (more serious) when they affect a reader's ability to understand a significant portion of a text.

Importance of Mastering Word Choice in Writing

To convey exact meaning, the writer must master word choice. When a writer uses a word incorrectly, the reader must then either guess at the meaning or skip the word altogether. Thus, the reader, instead of the writer, is supplying meaning that may or may not be correct. Such work tires the reader and can cause him or her to lose interest in a piece of writing.

It is equally important that ESL writers expand their vocabulary so that they can choose effective words to convey exact meaning. See Section 3, Part B of this text for strategies to help you expand your vocabulary.

Suggestions for Mastering Word Choice in Writing

- Remember that word choice is governed not by rules but by usage. Because there are no rules for word choice, you will sometimes need to ask a native speaker if you have used a word correctly.

- Memorize how certain words are used, particularly words that you use frequently in your major fields of interest or on the job.

*****wc** = grading symbol for an error in word choice.

- Use an ESL dictionary that shows how a word is used in a sentence. When using a thesaurus, choose words carefully from it, making sure that each word you have selected fits the sentence you have written. It is particularly valuable to double-check the word in an ESL dictionary that illustrates the word in a sample sentence. Another useful reference tool is a lexicon in which words are organized by topics.
- Avoid, as much as possible, translating from your language into English since direct translation often results in word-choice problems.

Test Your Understanding of Word Choice

Write answers to the following questions. Share your answers with another student.

1. Why can word-choice errors become more serious (global) errors?
2. What are two strategies you can employ to avoid errors in word choice?

Grammar Journal Entry 13: Word Choice

Write a short entry in your grammar journal in response to the following questions.

1. What, in your opinion, are two good strategies for you to use to expand your vocabulary in English? For some ideas, you might want to look at Section 3, Part B, "Expanding Vocabulary."
2. Write a list of five words you have had difficulty with in the past but have now mastered. Then write a list of five words that you are currently having difficulty with. Look up each word in a dictionary that has example sentences. Write your own sample sentences and check them with your teacher or a writing tutor.

PART II

COMMON PROBLEMS AND SELF-HELP STRATEGIES

In Part II, you will study

- Six problems ESL writers commonly encounter with word choice
- Self-help strategies for controlling word-choice errors in your writing

This section presents six problems that ESL writers commonly encounter with word choice. First, take the pretest to see what you already know about word choice. In checking your answers, note that the pretest questions cover the same types of errors in the same order as the problems in this section. Then carefully study each problem and the examples that illustrate it, giving particular attention to those problems that correspond to the pretest questions you had difficulty with. Using the boxes to the left of each problem, check [✓] *yes, no,* or *don't know* to indicate to yourself which problems you should focus the most attention on in this unit and also when you are choosing the appropriate word in English. Remember that becoming aware of the types of errors you most often make with word choice will increase your chances of avoiding these errors in your writing.

Note: Prepositions are treated in Unit 15, "Prepositions," and conjunctions in Unit 9, "Connecting Words," as well as in Unit 6, "Relative, Adverbial, and Noun Clauses."

Pretest: What Do You Already Know About Word-Choice Errors?

Test your ability to recognize word-choice errors by finding and correcting the one word-choice error in each of the following sentences.

Answers on p. 294

1. Intuition fees will be increased 40 percent next year.
2. Because the driver was unconscious, the police could only spectaculate about what had caused the accident.
3. The rules expect that library books will be returned on time.
4. From my perceptive, a trip to Europe is very expensive.
5. Most teachers discuss about the importance of attending class.
6. His students all think Dr. Stern is an awesome teacher.

Six Problems ESL Writers Commonly Encounter with Word Choice

yes	no	don't know	**PROBLEM 1**
☐	☐	☐	A wrong word has been used in a sentence.

	wc
Incorrect:	The essay we just read is an <u>exception</u> from a longer work.
Correct:	The essay we just read is an <u>excerpt</u> from a longer work.

	wc
Incorrect:	My inability to communicate with others in English always <u>bounds</u> our friendship at a superficial level.
Correct:	My inability to communicate with others in English always <u>keeps</u> our friendship at a superficial level.

yes   no   don't know   **PROBLEM 2**

☐   ☐   ☐   A word has been used that does not exist in English.

wc

Incorrect: The article was fairly easy to read and <u>comprehenced</u>.
Correct: The article was fairly easy to read and <u>comprehend</u>.

wc

Incorrect: Being a student is <u>literarily</u> a full-time job.
Correct: Being a student is <u>literally</u> a full-time job.

Self-Help Strategy: Keep in mind that the spell-check on your computer can sometimes help, as it will indicate if a word is unknown. Some spell-checks also give suggested words that may help you find the correct word.

yes   no   don't know   **PROBLEM 3**

☐   ☐   ☐   A verb has been used that does not fit the subject and/or predicate.

Note: This serious error in word choice affects the subject and/or predicate of the sentence and affects meaning, making it a global error. This error is also treated in handbooks for native speakers. Such errors may sometimes be marked **predication** or **faulty predication.**

wc

Incorrect: Reading <u>collaborated</u> in opening Andrew's mind to a better understanding of the lives of the people around him. (Reading cannot collaborate.)
Correct: Reading <u>helped</u> Andrew better understand the lives of the people around him.

wc

Incorrect: Reiko's mother <u>suffered a struggle</u> to balance work and family. (A struggle cannot be suffered.)
Correct: Reiko's mother <u>suffered</u> while struggling to balance work and family.

Self-Help Strategy: To avoid predication errors, make sure that the subject or predicate and the verb fit together; that is, you need to verify that the verb you have chosen can do the action required by the subject or predicate. To correct a predication error, you need to change the verb, rewrite the subject or predicate, or rewrite the whole sentence.

yes   no   don't know   **PROBLEM 4**

☐   ☐   ☐   A word has been used that sounds somewhat like the target word but is not correct.

wc

Incorrect: Adults have been complaining about the younger generation for <u>decays</u>.
Correct: Adults have been complaining about the younger generation for <u>decades</u>.

wc

Incorrect: A serious student is not easily <u>allured</u> away from studying.
Correct: A serious student is not easily <u>lured</u> away from studying.

wc

Incorrect: Most first-year students eat their dinner in the dining <u>columns</u>.
Correct: Most first-year students eat their dinner in the dining <u>commons</u>.

Self-Help Strategy: Be aware that you might often confuse words that sound somewhat alike when you write them if you have learned English primarily through listening to it. The more you read, the less likely you will be to encounter this problem because you will be seeing the word used in written form in proper context.

yes   no   don't know   **PROBLEM 5**

☐   ☐   ☐   Two closely related expressions have been confused.

wc

Incorrect: She did not <u>just as exactly</u> know <u>how</u> to reach the airport.

wc

Incorrect: She did not know <u>exactly as how</u> to reach the airport.
Correct: She did not know <u>just how</u> to reach the airport.
Correct: She did not know <u>exactly how</u> to reach the airport.

wc

Incorrect: Jack is <u>seeking for</u> the answer on the Internet.
Correct: Jack is <u>looking for</u> the answer on the Internet.
Correct: Jack is <u>seeking</u> the answer on the Internet.

yes   no   don't know   **PROBLEM 6**

☐   ☐   ☐   An informal word or expression has been used in formal writing.

wc

Incorrect: My brother is a person with a lot of <u>smarts</u>.
Correct: My brother is an <u>intelligent person</u>.

Incorrect: Many people feel that the test for a driving license is a <u>tough</u> exam.
Correct: Many people feel that the test for a driving license is a <u>difficult</u> exam.

Self-Help Strategy: Be aware that in speaking, we frequently use informal words that are not acceptable in formal writing.

Improve Your Writing Style

Know When to Use One-Word Verbs

In written academic English, the writer needs to maintain a formal tone. One way to achieve such formality is to replace a two- or three-word verb (called a phrasal verb) with a one-word verb.

Examples:

> This paper will <u>talk about</u> the effects of isolation on the social behavior of rats.
>
> This paper will <u>discuss</u> the effects of isolation on the social behavior of rats.
>
> A second group of researchers will <u>look into</u> methods to recycle batteries.
>
> A second group of researchers will <u>investigate</u> methods to recycle batteries.

Good writers strive for the appropriate level of formality to suit their audience and purpose. For example, academic papers and professional reports are generally formal and memos tend to be relatively informal.

Improve Your Writing Style

Use More Precise Verbs to Make Your Writing Specific

To make your writing more specific, use a specific verb in place of a more general verb. In the examples below, the verb goes from general to very specific.

Examples:

> The captain <u>threw away</u> nonessential items in order to lighten the ship's load.
>
> The captain <u>tossed</u> nonessential items in order to lighten the ship's load.

IMPROVE YOUR WRITING STYLE, cont.

The captain <u>discarded</u> nonessential items in order to lighten the ship's load.

The captain <u>jettisoned</u> nonessential items in order to lighten the ship's load.

The server <u>is talking</u> about the fish special.

The server <u>is promoting</u> the fish special.

The server <u>is touting</u> the fish special.

The little girl was carrying her balloon down the street when it <u>broke</u>.

The little girl was carrying her balloon down the street when it <u>popped</u>.

Although in English an exact verb can be found to describe every action, it takes time and exposure to the language to acquire these skills. For suggestions on strategies for expanding your vocabulary, see Section 3, Part B.

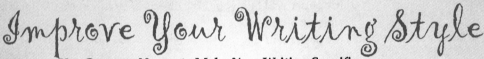

Improve Your Writing Style

Use Concrete Nouns to Make Your Writing Specific

To make your writing more specific, use a concrete noun in place of a more general noun.

Examples:

The psychologist advertised in the newspaper to find <u>people</u> to participate in his research study. (general)

The psychologist advertised in the newspaper to find <u>individuals</u> to participate in his research study. (more specific)

The psychologist advertised in the newspaper to find <u>subjects</u> to participate in his research study. (more specific)

PART III

EXERCISES FOR PRACTICE

EXERCISE 1 (Do this exercise on your own. Then check your answers with a classmate.)

Directions: Each of the following sentences has a word-choice error. Test your ability to identify incorrect words by underlining each error and then correcting it. The first one has been done for you.

uncomfortable

1. Because she did not know anyone there, Leah felt very <u>discomfortable</u> at the party.

2. Arturo called to say he would be late; in the meanwhile, I read a book.

3. My parents, who immigrated from China two years ago, are inliterated in English.

4. I once was in a math class where everyone was motivated to conquer the best test score.

5. When Samir cannot answer in class, he does not feel cool.

6. Jennifer's bad grade on her final exam in French unabled her from passing the course.

7. I became so courteous that I decided to investigate the noise.

8. Students are also putting their part to keep the school clean by not littering.

9. During the first few months of school, I was speakless both in class and at lunchtime because of my inability to speak English.

10. After she had been studying English for six weeks, Madeleine expected to know everything, but in replacement she found she had just begun.

EXERCISE 2 (Do this exercise with a classmate.)

Directions: This paragraph, which was written by a student, has been edited so that the only errors are in word choice. Read the whole paragraph. Then cross out each word you think has been used incorrectly. With your partner, decide on the correct word. If you are unsure, check the word in an ESL dictionary that shows usage. The first one has been done for you.

When I was a senior in high school, I dreamed about being a college student and often
be like
wondered what college would ~~appear~~. I also wondered about how much difference there would be between college and high school, particularly in class size. I assisted to a big-city high school, which was crowded; each class had an enrollment of 40 students. Therefore, when I sent in my application for college, I hoped that classes in col-

lege would be small. However, here at college, especially in chemistry and economics classes, the class halls are overcrowded. For instance, my chemistry class has more than 300 students in it and some of them cannot get a seat when they come late. Some students stand in the back, and others sit in the alleys. Unfortunately, when a class is very crowded, I cannot focus on what the teacher is emphasizing on. Therefore, I do not feel satisfied with what I am learning. Unfortunately, my wish that classes would be small in college has not been realized.

EXERCISE 3 (Do this exercise on your own. Then check your answers with a classmate.)

Directions: The following sentences all have phrasal verbs (two- or three-word verbs), which have been underlined. Replace each verb with a more formal, one-word verb from the list given. Be sure to use the appropriate tense of the verb. The first one has been done for you.

investigate   summarize   increase   mature   collapse

collapsed
1. During the baseball game, the rain-damaged roof of the stadium <u>fell in</u>, injuring several spectators.

2. When certain weather conditions occur, smog <u>builds up</u> in the Los Angeles area.

3. The ugly little Airedale puppy <u>has grown up</u> into a prize-winning champion.

4. When the rain stops, the police are going <u>to look into</u> the crime and take fingerprints.

5. At the next class meeting, the cancer specialist <u>will briefly tell about</u> his research on preventing melanoma.

EXERCISE 4 (Do this exercise on your own. Then share your answers with a classmate. If you are unsure of your answers, check them with your instructor.)

Directions: Read a short article in a newspaper or a magazine and underline any words that are new to you. Then check the meaning of each new word in a dictionary, preferably an ESL dictionary with sample sentences. After determining the meaning of the word, write a sentence in which you use it.

PART IV

WRITING TOPICS

Select one or more of the following topics for writing and follow the steps in Appendix A.

Topic A: Think of some strategies that you would like to try to improve your English skills. Then write about the two or three you think would most help you, indicating to the reader how and why you think they will work for you.

Topic B: Interview at least two people to find out about some interesting places they like to visit either in your city or near your city. Write a report on what you found out, including what the places are, what people can do or see there, and why the people you interviewed like these places. Conclude by saying whether or not you, personally, would like to visit these places as well.

Topic C: Many people find pleasure spending time in the outdoors. To what extent do you, personally, like to spend time in the outdoors? What kinds of places do you like to visit? If you do not like the outdoors, explain what kinds of places you like to go to in your free time and why.

PART IV

CNN VIDEO ACTIVITY AND WRITING TOPIC

School Uniforms: A Change for the Better?

Useful Vocabulary: controversial   individuality   policy   impact   gang   visible

Before You Watch

Requiring public school students to wear uniforms is a controversial subject which is addressed in this video. Discuss the following questions with your classmates.

- Have you ever attended a school where uniforms were required? If so, how did you feel about it? If not, how would you feel about wearing a uniform to school?

- What are some advantages and disadvantages of school uniforms?

While You Watch

- Look for different attitudes students have toward wearing uniforms.

Requiring public school students to wear uniforms stirs up a controversy.

- List some of the views of teachers and administrators about having students wear uniforms.

After You Watch

I. **Write a personal reaction.**

Write a personal reaction of three to five sentences to what you saw in the video. What interested you most? Why do you think students often reject the idea of uniforms?

II. **Share your reactions.**

Answer the following questions either orally or in writing. Compare your answers with those of a classmate.

1. List reasons students gave for liking uniforms.

2. What are the results of the school uniform policy at the school shown in the video?

3. Has information from the video changed your ideas about the advantages and disadvantages of school uniforms? In what way?

WRITING TOPIC

Think about any experiences you have had with uniform requirements (schools, certain professions such as nurses, religious orders, the military, and prisons). To what extent is it beneficial for certain groups of people to wear uniforms? How does it benefit or not benefit both the person wearing the uniform and those that interact with the person?

Word Forms

Goals

- **To learn the importance of mastering word forms in writing**
- **To review four problems ESL writers commonly encounter with word forms**
- **To learn about different parts of speech (nouns, verbs, adjectives, and adverbs) and their most common forms**
- **To develop confidence in using word forms correctly through practice with exercises and writing assignments**

A group of friends at Glendale Community College in California get together to study.
Photo courtesy of Glendale Community College.

Think about and discuss the following question:
What are the advantages and
disadvantages of studying
with friends?

PART I

WHAT YOU NEED TO KNOW ABOUT WORD-FORM ERRORS

In Part I, you will learn

- The definition of a word-form error
- The importance of using word forms correctly in writing
- Suggestions for mastering word forms in writing

Definition of the Error (wf*)

A word-form error **(wf)** is one in which the incorrect part of speech has been used. For example, in the sentence *I had a happiness day,* the adjective *happy* should be used instead of the noun *happiness.* Note that the parts of speech we will address in this unit are nouns, verbs, adjectives, adverbs, and present and past participles used as adjectives.

A word in English can have several different forms, depending on whether the word functions as a noun, verb, adjective, or adverb. Examine the following forms of the word *success.* Notice how each form has a different grammatical function.

- His <u>success</u> surprised everyone. (noun)
- She has been <u>successful</u> in persuading others. (adjective)
- I certainly hope she <u>succeeds</u>! (verb)
- The athlete could hardly believe that she had finished the race <u>successfully</u>. (adverb)

Errors with present and past participles that are used as adjectives are also covered in this unit. For example, the sentence *I am <u>interesting</u> in molecular genetics* is incorrect because the past participle *interested* should be used rather than the present participle *interesting.*

Note that word-<u>choice</u> errors (Unit 13) are errors in which an incorrect word has been chosen. Word-<u>form</u> errors (this unit), on the other hand, are those in which the word chosen is correct, but the grammatical form of the word (noun, verb, adjective, or adverb) is incorrect.

Importance of Mastering Word Forms in Writing

Academic and professional writers are expected to use word forms correctly. Although word-form errors are classified as local (less serious) errors because they affect individual clauses rather than larger parts of a text, they are highly notice-

*****wf** = grading symbol for an error in word form.

able to the reader because they affect content words (nouns, verbs, adjectives, and adverbs)—words that carry the most meaning in a sentence. Thus, ESL writers need to be aware that numerous word-form errors will cause a piece of writing to appear flawed to the reader.

Suggestions for Mastering Word Forms in Writing

- When you are unsure whether you are using the correct form of a word, look up the word in a dictionary to check its different forms. Most dictionaries, ESL or non-ESL, indicate the part of speech (noun, verb, adjective, adverb) next to the word.

- Become aware of common word endings (suffixes) that identify words as nouns, verbs, adjectives, or adverbs. For example, -*ness* and -*tion* are common noun endings; -*ous* and -*ful* are common adjective endings; -*en* and -*ify* are common verb endings; and -*ly* is a common adverb ending. A list of the most common word endings is included in this unit.

- Be aware of word formation when you read in English. For example, look carefully at several sentences in one of your textbooks, a newspaper, or a magazine. Analyze these sentences, making sure you can identify nouns, verbs, adjectives, and adverbs in each sentence. If you are having difficulty distinguishing these parts of speech, you may need to ask your instructor or a tutor for assistance.

Test Your Understanding of Word Forms

Write answers to the following questions. Share your answers with another student.

1. Choose two suffixes that you know of. Give two examples of words that take each suffix.

2. How can a dictionary help you with accurate word formation?

Grammar Journal Entry 14: Word Forms

Write a short entry in your grammar journal in response to the following questions.

1. What is your definition of success and/or a successful person?

2. Choose two words that you use frequently, such as *friend, education, environment,* or any other word you wish. Then list all of the different forms of these two words that you can think of. Label the different forms as nouns, adjectives, verbs, or adverbs.

COMMON PROBLEMS, SELF-HELP STRATEGIES, AND GRAMMAR GUIDELINES

In Part II, you will study

• Four problems ESL writers commonly encounter with word forms

• Grammar guidelines for word forms

• Self-help strategies for controlling word forms in your writing

This section presents four problems that ESL writers commonly encounter with word forms. First, take the pretest to see what you already know about word forms. In checking your answers, note that the pretest questions cover the same types of errors in the same order as the problems in this section. Then carefully study each problem and the examples that illustrate it, giving particular attention to those problems that correspond to the pretest questions you had difficulty with. Using the boxes to the left of each problem, check [✓] *yes, no,* or *don't know* to indicate to yourself which problems you should focus the most attention on in this unit and also when you write in English. Remember that becoming aware of the types of errors you most often make with word forms will increase your chances of avoiding these errors in your writing.

Pretest: What Do You Already Know About Word Forms?

Test your ability to recognize word-form errors by finding and correcting the one word-form error in each of the following sentences.

Answers on p. 294

1. Communicate via e-mail has become common around the world.

2. Employees must submit weekly progress reports in a timeful manner.

3. Eating a TV dinner is sometimes convenient than cooking a meal.

4. As a possible career goal, I am interesting in computer science.

Four Problems ESL Writers Commonly Encounter with Word Forms

yes   no   don't know   **PROBLEM 1**

☐   ☐   ☐   The choice of a word is correct, but the wrong part of speech has been used.

                  wf

Incorrect: She was <u>easy</u> persuaded to change her vote.
Correct: She was <u>easily</u> persuaded to change her vote.
         (An adverb instead of an adjective is needed to modify the verb *persuaded*.)

                  wf

Incorrect: The students will clearly feel the <u>lost</u> of Mr. Jensen, who will no longer be teaching here.
Correct: The students will clearly feel the <u>loss</u> of Mr. Jensen, who will no longer be teaching here.
         (A noun instead of an adjective is needed as the direct object of the verb *feel*.)

                  wf

Incorrect: Her attitude is a <u>reflect</u> of the views of society.
Correct: Her attitude is a <u>reflection</u> of the views of society.
         (A noun instead of a verb is needed in this position.)

yes   no   don't know   **PROBLEM 2**

☐   ☐   ☐   A suffix has been used incorrectly.

                                  wf

Incorrect: I am applying to the Department of Management and <u>Financement</u>.
Correct: I am applying to the Department of Management and <u>Finance</u>.

         wf

Incorrect: I studied <u>hardly</u> before I took the TOEFL exam.
Correct: I studied <u>hard</u> before I took the TOEFL exam.

Self-Help Strategy: Study the list of common word suffixes in this unit to become familiar with noun, verb, adjective, and adverb suffixes. However, keep in mind that there are no rules that will tell you whether a word requires a specific suffix to mark it as a certain part of speech. For example, the noun form of the verb *manage* in the first example sentence under Problem 2 requires the *-ment* ending, while the verb *finance* does not require an ending to form the noun *finance*. To verify word forms that you are unsure of, check your dictionary.

    Remember that while most adverbs have an *-ly* ending, three common adverbs, *hard*, *last*, and *fast*, do not have this *-ly* ending.

yes   no   don't know   PROBLEM 3

☐   ☐   ☐   The incorrect adjective or adverb form has been used in a comparison.

                                        wf

Incorrect: That was the <u>worse</u> movie I have seen in a long time.

Correct: That was the <u>worst</u> movie I have seen in a long time.

                                             wf

Incorrect: This semester, Faizah has been <u>more busier</u> than usual.

Correct: This semester, Faizah has been <u>busier</u> than usual.

                                  wf

Incorrect: Mario is working <u>hard</u> this year than last year.

Correct: Mario is working <u>harder</u> this year than last year.

yes   no   don't know   PROBLEM 4

☐   ☐   ☐   The incorrect present or past participle form has been used as an adjective.

                                       wf

Incorrect: The essay was <u>interested</u>.

Correct: The essay was <u>interesting</u>.

                            wf

Incorrect: The <u>interesting</u> members of the audience stayed after the lecture to ask further questions.

Correct: The <u>interested</u> members of the audience stayed after the lecture to ask further questions.

Grammar Guidelines for Word Forms

Common Word Suffixes

The list on the next two pages will help you recognize common noun, verb, adjective, and adverb suffixes. Study this list. For each suffix, add at least one additional word that has the same suffix.

Noun Suffixes

-ment	argument	establishment	_____
-ness	sadness	messiness	_____
-tion	application	indication	_____
-sion	expression	admission	_____
-ity	legibility	impossibility	_____
-ence	difference	excellence	_____
-ance	importance	distance	_____
-ure	departure	closure	_____
-er	teacher	speaker	_____
-ism	socialism	sexism	_____
-ist	specialist	typist	_____
-ship	scholarship	friendship	_____

Verb Suffixes

-ate	mediate	delegate	_____
-en	lengthen	brighten	_____
-ify	solidify	intensify	_____
-ize	finalize	customize	_____

Adjective Suffixes

-ous	dangerous	famous	_____
-ful	colorful	useful	_____
-less	colorless	useless	_____
-ive	expressive	competitive	_____
-able	agreeable	understandable	_____
-ent	different	excellent	_____
-ant	important	hesitant	_____

Adjective Suffixes, cont.

-ic	characteristic	electric	_____
-al	emotional	musical	_____
-some	worrisome	bothersome	_____
-ate	considerate	subordinate	_____
-y	dressy	noisy	_____
-ly	friendly	lonely	_____
-like	childlike	lifelike	_____
-an	American	Italian	_____
-ese	Japanese	Maltese	_____
-ing	interesting	challenging	_____
-ed	interested	challenged	_____

Adverb Suffix

-ly	usually	legibly	_____

Rules for Comparative and Superlative Forms of Adjectives

1. **One-syllable adjectives and adverbs: add [*-er + than*] for the comparative and [*the + -est*] for the superlative.**

   Examples:

   Some students think that short-answer tests are <u>harder than</u> multiple-choice tests. (comparative)
   Some students think that essay tests are <u>the hardest</u>. (superlative)
   My roommate usually stays up <u>later</u> than I do. (comparative)
   Monica stays up <u>the latest</u> of all my friends. (superlative)

2. **Most adjectives and adverbs of two or more syllables: use [*more ... than*] for the comparative and [*the most*] for the superlative.**

   Examples:

   The Mexican restaurant downtown is <u>more popular than</u> the Chinese restaurant.
   The Vietnamese restaurant is <u>the most popular</u>.

3. **Two-syllable words that end in -y:** Change the -y to -i. Then add [-er + than] for the comparative and [the + -est] for the superlative.

Examples:

>The red car is <u>sportier than</u> the blue car.
>The black convertible is <u>the sportiest</u> of all.

4. **The following words have irregular comparative and superlative forms.**

	Comparative	Superlative
good	*better than*	*the best*
bad	*worse than*	*the worst*
little	*less than*	*the least*
much/many	*more than*	*the most*

Examples:

>I like my chemistry class <u>better than</u> my math class.
>I like my history class <u>the best</u> of all.
>I am earning <u>less</u> money this year <u>than</u> last year.
>Of all my friends, Juan earns <u>the least</u> money.
>Jogging three times a week is <u>better</u> exercise <u>than</u> swimming once a week.
>The <u>best</u> exercise program is a daily workout.

Rules for Choosing the Appropriate Participle as an Adjective

1. **Use the past participle form of the verb when you are describing something or someone affected by someone or something else.**

Examples:

>The reader was <u>interested</u> in the essay.
>An <u>interested</u> reader can read for hours.
>(In both cases, the focus is on the reader's being interested in the essay.)

2. **Use the present participle form of the verb when you are describing something that affects someone or something else.**

Examples:

>The essay was <u>interesting</u>.
>An <u>interesting</u> essay holds the reader's attention.
>(In both cases, the focus is on the essay's being interesting.)

Improve Your Writing Style

Be Aware That Many Words in English Have Multiple Forms, Each with a Different Use, for the Same Part of Speech

Be aware that many words in English have more than one form for the same part of speech. However, the different forms are used in different contexts. As you encounter these different forms and uses, you will need to memorize them, since their usage is not rule-based but instead is vocabulary-based. The more you read and listen to English, the sooner you will become acquainted with these different forms. Below you will find selected examples. Review them in order to become more aware of this fact about English.

1. **friend** (noun)   **friendship** (noun)

    My <u>friend</u> helped me move to a new apartment.

    My <u>friendship</u> with Mr. Jones led me to go into the engineering field.

2. **comparable** (adjective)   **comparative** (adjective)

    This hotel is <u>comparable</u> to the one we stayed at last year.

    Kevin's research is a <u>comparative</u> study of health services in rural and urban areas.

3. **various** (adjective)   **variable** (adjective)   **varied** (adjective)

    Her job requires her to travel to <u>various</u> countries each year.

    The weather on the west coast of the United States is <u>variable</u> in the spring.

    The climate of the United States is <u>varied</u>, with some parts having a Mediterranean climate and others having a hot and humid climate.

4. **characteristic** (noun)   **character** (noun)

    Conscientiousness is one of John's <u>characteristics</u>.

    John's current behavior seems to contradict his <u>character</u>.

PART III

EXERCISES FOR PRACTICE

EXERCISE 1 (Do this exercise on your own. Then check your answers with a classmate.)

Directions: Check your knowledge of word formation and suffixes by filling in the blanks with the indicated forms of the following words commonly used by academic and professional writers.

Noun	Verb	Adjective	Adverb
1. characteristic	characterize	characteristic	characteristically
2. approximation			
3. production			
4. origin			
5. emphasis			
6. significance			
7. theory			

EXERCISE 2 (Do this exercise on your own. Then check your answers with a classmate.)

Directions: Examine the following sentences. First, decide if a sentence is correct (C) or if it contains any word-form errors (I). Then correct the incorrect word forms.

encouragement
Example: __I__   The young child did not receive much <u>encourage</u> to speak her native language.

_____ 1. Writing under the pressure of time gives us several beneficial including the ability to think fast and to organize fast.

_____ 2. The article very precisively and effectively explains the advantages and disadvantages of taking a class via the Internet.

_____ 3. Many immigrants become maturity by dealing with adult problems at an early age.

_____ 4. My supervisor quickly approval of my request for a two-week leave from work.

_____ 5. Gregorio came to the United States to pursuit his Ph.D.

_____ 6. In order to succeed, one must be able to make sacrifices.

_____ 7. My suggest is aimed at easing the problem.

_____ 8. If I keep writing in this fashion, my writing skills might even become worst, for I might get used to making those mistakes.

_____ **9.** When my roommate cooks, I have to clean up the messiness he makes.

_____**10.** Being able to interact with a variety of people makes my job thorough enjoyable.

EXERCISE 3 (Do this exercise on your own. Then check your answers with a classmate.)

Directions:　Check your ability to use present and past participles as adjectives by filling in the blanks with the correct form of the verb indicated.

>　**Examples:**
>
>　　　　　Writing in English is quite _challenging_ (challenge) to me.
>　　　　　I am _confused_ (confuse) about what the lecturer meant by some of his statements.

1. My professor's absence was _____ (surprise) to all of us in the class.

2. The room, with its chipping paint, leaking roof, and lack of light, was _____ (depress).

3. Mario is _____ (interest) in the topic of the lecture because it is related to his research.

4. Natalie was _____ (puzzle) by the grade she received on her midterm.

5. Your ability to type quickly and accurately is _____ (amaze).

6. The amount of money raised by the walkathon was _____ (astonish).

7. Jack was completely _____ (surprise) by the party his friends gave for him.

8. This book is one of the most _____ (entertain) books that I have ever read.

EXERCISE 4 (Do this exercise on your own. Then compare your answers with those of a classmate.)

Directions:　Practice making comparisons by writing sentences following the example given below.

>　　**Example:**　Compare two academic courses you have taken or are familiar with.
>　　　　　　　_The new course on cultural anthropology is more popular than the old course._

1. Compare two different makes of cars.

2. Compare the weather this month versus last month.

3. Compare two cities you have lived in or visited.

4. Compare the price of food in your country of origin versus that of another country.

5. Compare an aspect of life in the United States with your expectation of it before you came here.

EXERCISE 5 (Do this exercise with a classmate.)

Directions: The following paragraph, written by a student about the benefits of being bilingual, contains errors in word form. Each word-form error is underlined. Write the correct form of the word above it. The first one has been done for you.

My bilingualism may benefit me in terms of job opportunities. First of all, more and
immigrants
more <u>immigrates</u> arrive in the United States every year. To help these newcomers or to do

business with them, bilingual and multilingual employees are needed. For example,

banks, law firms, and insurance agencies often need employees who can <u>communicative</u>

with both non-English speakers and English-speaking clients. Therefore, because I speak

Spanish <u>good</u>, I might find many job opportunities in places where there are a lot of

Spanish speakers, such as Los Angeles, New York, Chicago, and Miami. Secondly, if I can

<u>achievement</u> my goal of having my own <u>dentist</u> clinic, Spanish-speaking clients may be a

good source for my <u>earns</u>. Many Spanish speakers <u>tendency</u> to feel more <u>comfort</u> with

Spanish-speaking doctors and dentists. Even Mexicans and Mexican Americans who

speak English very well often still <u>preference</u> to go to a Spanish-speaking dentist instead

of an English-speaking dentist. So, overall, I may benefit <u>economical</u> from my <u>knowledge-</u>

<u>ment</u> of two languages.

EXERCISE 6 (Do this exercise on your own. Then check your answers with a classmate.)

Directions: The following paragraph, written by a student, contains errors in word form. Underline each word-form error and write the correct form of the word above it. The first one has been done for you.

directly
Being multilingual enables me to communicate <u>direct</u> with many people. Even

though I mostly use English in my everyday life, especially at the university, I still use

Cantonese to communicate with my relatives. My grandmother, for example, who just

recently came to the United States from Vietnam and is now living with my family,

cannot understand English. The only language she speaks fluent is Cantonese. There-

fore, knowing how to speak Cantonese allows me to communicate easy with her. By

talking with her, I have learned some of my family's historical. She told me that she and

my grandfather were originally from China and she explanation what her life was like

there. She has also told me interest stories about China that I never would have heard if

I did not speak Cantonese. Moreover, being able to speak Cantonese or Vietnamese in Asian restaurants has also been benefit to me. The restaurant employees recognize that they and I are from similar backgrounds because we speak the same language. They, therefore, give more attentive to me than to customers who do not speak the language. Thus, being able to speak these languages opens the door for me to communication closely with many different people.

EXERCISE 7 (Do this exercise on your own. Then check your answers with a classmate.)

Directions: Read a short article from a newspaper or a magazine. Then underline all of the words with noun, verb, adjective, or adverb suffixes in two paragraphs of the article. Identify the part of speech (noun, verb, adjective, or adverb) of each word you have underlined.

PART IV

WRITING TOPICS

Select one or more of the following topics for writing and follow the steps in Appendix A.

Topic A: Choose a book that you enjoyed reading. Briefly explain what the book was about. Then explain what you particularly liked about it or how it influenced you in some way.

Topic B: Think about your birth order among your brothers and sisters. Are you the youngest, the oldest, or somewhere in the middle? First explain where you are in the order of birth of the siblings in your family. Then explain how you think this birth order has affected you as a person. If you are an only child, meaning you do not have any brothers or sisters, explain how this situation has affected you.

Topic C: Think about the favorite teachers you have had. What qualities must a teacher have to be effective?

PART V

CNN VIDEO ACTIVITY AND WRITING TOPIC

What's in a Nutshell?

Useful Vocabulary: by-product   activated-carbon filter   ground cover   landfill   stone-washed jeans   in a nutshell

Before You Watch

This video segment illustrates some creative solutions to a waste problem generated by technology.

- Are nuts an important part of the food of your culture? If so, what kinds are popular?
- Can you think of any agricultural products that generate waste?

While You Watch

- Listen for and write down various uses of pecan shells.
- Find out what advantage a pecan-shell activated carbon filter has over other, similar filters.

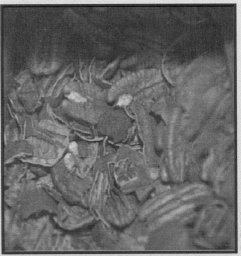

This processing plant in New Mexico generates not only pecans but also 40,000 pounds of pecan-shell waste per day.

After You Watch

I. **Write a personal reaction.**

   Write a personal reaction of three to five sentences to what you saw in the video. What interested you most? Do you feel that being concerned about the disposal of the large quantity of pecan shells is justified?

II. **Share your reactions.**

   Answer the following questions either orally or in writing. Compare your answers with those of a classmate.

   1. How important is it to find uses for pecan shells or other industrial waste?
   2. What other forms of using industrial or agricultural by-products are you aware of?
   3. How are such diverse things as blue jeans and pecan shells related in this video?

WRITING TOPIC

This video segment focuses on how a large company can reuse agricultural waste for people's benefit. On a lesser scale, to what extent do you feel it is important for individuals to participate in recycling? If you think it is important, what kinds of recycling do you think are most important?

Goals

- To learn the importance of mastering prepositions in writing
- To review three problems ESL writers commonly encounter when using prepositions
- To learn effective strategies for improving preposition use
- To develop confidence in using prepositions through practice with exercises and writing assignments

Prepositions

Students in a writing class at La Guardia Community College in New York spend part of their class time in the computer lab. Photo courtesy of Office of Communications.

Think about and discuss the following question:

What kinds of skills could you learn
and practice during a writing class
held in a computer lab?

PART I

WHAT YOU NEED TO KNOW ABOUT ERRORS WITH PREPOSITIONS

In Part I, you will study

- The definition of an error with a preposition
- The importance of using prepositions correctly in writing
- Suggestions for mastering prepositions in writing

Definition of the Error (prep*)

An error with a preposition **(prep)** occurs when a preposition has been incorrectly used. Prepositions can be used in a phrase (*during* the daytime), as a particle with a two- or three-word verb (*turn in, check up on*), or after a noun or an adjective (*to be happy about*).

Importance of Mastering Prepositions in Writing

Knowing how to use prepositions correctly is very important in formal writing. Although an error with a preposition is a local (less serious) error and thus affects only part of a sentence, many errors with prepositions in a piece of writing make it difficult for the reader to concentrate on the content while he or she is trying to supply the correct preposition.

In academic and professional writing, the reader expects to see correct use of prepositions. Correct preposition use depends more on memorization and usage than on rules. It is therefore difficult to master, but each small improvement in preposition use makes a text easier to read.

Suggestions for Mastering Prepositions

- Remember that there are few rules for prepositions because preposition use is learned chiefly through listening and reading.

  Memorize two- and three-word verbs (phrasal verbs) so that you can use them correctly and automatically. Use an ESL dictionary to look up two- and three-word verbs that you are unsure of.

- Improve your control of prepositions by paying attention to them when you read and listening for them when people speak.

- Ask a native speaker for help when you are unsure about a preposition.

*****prep** = grading symbol for a preposition error.

Test Your Understanding of Prepositions

Write answers to the following questions. Share your answers with another student.

1. What is an error with a preposition?

2. Why is it necessary to learn preposition use through usage and memorization?

Grammar Journal Entry 15: Prepositions

Write a short entry in your grammar journal in response to the following questions.

1. What are three things that you usually do in the morning, at noon, and at night? List what these activities are and at what time you do them. Then write a paragraph about whether or not you would like to change any of these activities to another time.

2. Look in a magazine or a newspaper for an article that interests you. Then underline five two- or three-word verbs that you find. Use each of those verbs in a sentence.

PART II

COMMON PROBLEMS, SELF-HELP STRATEGIES, AND GRAMMAR GUIDELINES

In Part II, you will study

- Common problems ESL writers encounter with prepositions
- Self-help strategies for controlling prepositions in your writing
- Grammar guidelines for using prepositions effectively

This section presents three problems that ESL writers commonly encounter with prepositions. First, take the pretest to see what you already know about prepositions. In checking your answers, note that the pretest questions cover the same types of errors in the same order as the problems in this section. Then carefully study each problem and the examples that illustrate it, giving particular attention to those problems that correspond to the pretest questions you had difficulty with. Using the boxes to the left of each problem, check [✓] *yes, no,* or *don't know* to indicate to yourself which problems you should focus the most attention on in this unit and also when you use prepositions in English. Remember that becoming aware of the types of errors you most often make with prepositions will increase your chances of avoiding these errors in your writing.

Pretest: What Do You Already Know About Prepositions?

Test your ability to recognize errors with prepositions by finding and correcting the one error with a preposition in each of the following sentences.

Answers on p. 294

1. Erik is taking summer school classes in Harvard University.

2. The dentist said there are three reasons of my having cavities: too much candy, too little flossing, and a too-soft toothbrush.

3. Jack is seeking for information about pythons on the Internet.

Three Problems ESL Writers Commonly Encounter with Prepositions

yes   no   don't know   **PROBLEM 1**

☐   ☐   ☐   A wrong preposition has been used in a prepositional phrase or in an idiomatic expression using a preposition.

                              prep

Incorrect: My brother lives <u>in</u> Anderson Street.
Correct: My brother lives <u>on</u> Anderson Street.

                                                               prep

Incorrect: My math teacher always praised me when I gave the correct answers <u>of</u> the home-work questions.
Correct: My math teacher always praised me when I gave the correct answers <u>to</u> the home-work questions.

                                        prep

Incorrect: Jaime gets frustrated if he makes the same error time <u>by</u> time.
Correct: Jaime gets frustrated if he makes the same error time <u>after</u> time.

                              prep

Incorrect: Marjan will often meet us for coffee <u>in</u> the night.
Correct: Marjan will often meet us for coffee <u>at</u> night (or <u>in</u> the evening).

Self-Help Strategy: Be aware that because the rules for preposition use are very limited, you may frequently have to ask a native speaker for help. However, since some rules do exist, it is a good idea not only to learn the rules below but also to read about preposition use in a comprehensive ESL grammar text.

yes   no   don't know   **PROBLEM 2**

☐   ☐   ☐   An incorrect preposition has been used following an adjective or a
                                noun.

                            prep

Incorrect: I sometimes feel <u>uncomfortable in</u> speaking up in class.

Correct: I sometimes feel <u>uncomfortable about</u> speaking up in class.

Correct: I sometimes feel <u>uncomfortable speaking up</u> in class. (no preposition needed)

                            prep

Incorrect: My mother worked, so the <u>responsibility of</u> the housework was mine.

Correct: My mother worked, so the <u>responsibility for</u> the housework was mine.

Self-Help Strategy: Remember that you can solve many of these problems
by looking up the adjective or noun in an ESL dictionary to see which preposi-
tion(s) it can take.

Example: I am <u>happy about</u> getting a part-time job. (In this sentence, the
preposition *about* is used with the adjective *happy*. An ESL dictionary will indicate that *about* can be used with *happy*.)

yes   no   don't know   **PROBLEM 3**

☐   ☐   ☐   A verb + preposition problem has occurred.

    a. The preposition that goes with a given verb is missing.

                                      prep

Incorrect: I will have to study more tonight <u>to compensate</u> the time I lost yesterday.

Correct: I will have to study more tonight <u>to compensate for</u> the time I lost
yesterday.

                                      prep

Incorrect: The two teams will <u>compete</u> each other next week.

Correct: The two teams will <u>compete with</u> each other next week.

          Note: *Compete against* is also correct.

    b. A preposition is used when it is not needed after a given verb.

                                      prep

Incorrect: In my paper, I <u>emphasized about</u> the need for smaller classes for
undergraduates.

Correct: In my paper, I <u>emphasized</u> the need for smaller classes for undergraduates.

prep
Incorrect: The reporter got her information by <u>interviewing with</u> three people.
Correct: The reporter got her information by <u>interviewing</u> three people.

c. The wrong preposition has been used after a given verb.

prep
Incorrect: The professor often <u>refers on</u> the textbook.
Correct: The professor often <u>refers to</u> the textbook.

prep
Incorrect: In the spring, Mike often <u>suffers of</u> allergies.
Correct: In the spring, Mike often <u>suffers from</u> allergies.

d. A preposition that is part of a phrasal verb (two-word or three-word verb) is incorrect or missing.

prep
Incorrect: He just <u>hung off</u> the phone.
Correct: He just <u>hung up</u> the phone.

prep
Incorrect: We will have to <u>call over</u> the birthday party.
Correct: We will have to <u>call off</u> the birthday party.

prep
Incorrect   I am going to have to work hard to <u>catch up</u> the work that I have missed.
Correct: I am going to have to work hard to <u>catch up on</u> the work that I have missed.

Grammar Guidelines for Preposition Use

In this section, you will learn selected rules for using prepositions. Learning these rules and following these guidelines will help you use prepositions correctly.

Prepositions of Time, Place, or Position

You will find the following charts helpful for using prepositions that indicate time, place, or position.

PREPOSITIONS OF TIME

Preposition	Time	Example
in	month, year	in February, in 1999
on	day of the week, date	on Monday, on June 1
in	time of day	in the morning, in the afternoon, in the evening (but **at** night)
at	specific time of day	at 8:00 AM, at 3:30 PM sharp

PREPOSITIONS OF PLACE

Preposition	Place	Example
in	city, country	in Dallas, in Canada
on	street	on First Street
at	address	at 1119 Harvard Drive
in	inside of a place	in the language lab, in the library
at	a specific place	at school, at home, at the airport, at the store, at the movies

PREPOSITIONS OF POSITION

Preposition	Position	Example
on	on top of	on the desk, on the bed
in	inside	in my room, in my desk, in the car

Using Prepositions with Verbs (Phrasal Verbs)

A phrasal verb is a verb + a preposition (sometimes called a **particle** when part of a phrasal verb). Together, the verb and its preposition or prepositions create the meaning of the verb. Although phrasal verbs are used more frequently in speaking than in writing, they are also used in written English.

These two-and three-word verbs sometimes, but not always, have a more formal one-word synonym that can be used in written English. For example, in the sentence *We had to call off the party, call off* has the same meaning as *cancel*. In the sentence *Could you turn down the volume, turn down* has the same meaning as *decrease*. These verbs and their synonyms are further treated in Unit 13, "Word Choice."

Phrasal verbs are highly complex in that a preposition can completely change the meaning of the verb. Read the following examples and note how the meaning changes:

> Please <u>turn on</u> the light. (meaning = start the operation of)
> Please <u>turn in</u> the assignment on Friday. (meaning = submit)
> I usually <u>turn over</u> a lot when I sleep. (meaning = roll from one side to the other)

Another complexity is that some phrasal verbs have more than one meaning depending on the context.

> Please <u>turn down</u> the volume. (meaning = decrease)
> I hope you will not <u>turn down</u> the job even though the pay is not what you had hoped for. (meaning = refuse)
> Five thousand people <u>turned out</u> to hear the concert. (meaning = came)
> Please <u>turn out</u> the light. (meaning = extinguish)

The best way to learn these two- and three-word verbs is to listen for them in conversations and to look for them in written material. They are also listed in ESL dictionaries.

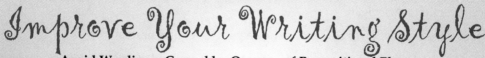

Improve Your Writing Style

Avoid Wordiness Caused by Overuse of Prepositional Phrases

Overuse of prepositional phrases can make a piece of writing very wordy as well as difficult to read. Some suggested ways to edit out wordiness with prepositional phrases are as follows:

You can turn the prepositional phrase into a verb.
Examples:

> What are the effects <u>of large chains and superstores on smaller, family-owned businesses</u>?
> How <u>do large chains and superstores affect smaller, family-owned businesses</u>?

IMPROVE YOUR WRITING STYLE, cont.

You can turn the prepositional phrase into a possessive.
Examples:

The illness <u>of her mother</u> left the family in turmoil.
<u>Her mother's illness</u> left the family in turmoil.

You can turn the prepositional phrase into an adjective.
Examples:

A country needs a president <u>with intelligence</u> and with good people skills.
A country needs an <u>intelligent</u> president with good people skills.

That school district requires students to wear shirts or blouses <u>with navy and white stripes</u>.
That school district requires students to wear <u>navy and white striped</u> shirts or blouses .

PART III

EXERCISES FOR PRACTICE

EXERCISE 1 (Do this exercise on your own. Then check your answers with a classmate.)

Directions: Each of the following sentences has a preposition error. Test your ability to identify incorrect prepositions by underlining each error and then correcting it. The first one has been done for you.

1. They had to be nice <u>with</u> their neighbors. *to*

2. My brother is a student in Harvard University, and I am a student in the music department at the University of Michigan.

3. The revised schedule gives students a choice with dates and times.

4. All the graduate classes in the education department are held at the early afternoon and evening.

5. It is easy to clean the kitchen when all you do is load the dishes to the dishwasher.

6. My lab partner lives in 1003 Rosemont Avenue.

7. Living in an apartment is difficult if you are not happy of your roommates.

8. If you are hunting for your car keys, I saw them lying in the table.

9. If my trip goes as planned, I will see you at Monday.

10. My uncle, who owns a successful business, has had a big influence in me.

EXERCISE 2 (Do this exercise on your own. Then check your answers with a classmate.)

Directions: **Check your knowledge of prepositions that accompany verbs, nouns, and adjectives by filling in each blank with the correct preposition.**

> **Example:**   My brother is upset because he has been accused __of__ lying.

1. My neighbors make so much noise that I have trouble concentrating _____ my work.

2. I dreamed _____ you last night.

3. I don't know if I can ever forgive you _____ lying to me.

4. Are you interested _____ going camping with us next weekend?

5. My advisor insisted _____ my submitting a research proposal by January.

6. I will have to think _____ what you have said before I give you an answer.

7. I am hopeful that I will succeed _____ finishing my B.S. by next year.

8. My parents do not object _____ my borrowing their car on weekends.

9. We want to take advantage _____ the nice weather and go on a picnic.

10. My brother's carelessness about food storage resulted _____ his getting food poisoning.

EXERCISE 3 (Do this exercise on your own. Then check your answers with a classmate.)

Directions: **Check your knowledge of prepositions in two- and three-word verbs by filling in each blank with the correct preposition or prepositions.**

> **Example:**   When her fever got worse, she was sorry she had put __off__ going to the doctor.

1. The school has not yet found _____ who gave that generous gift of $500.

2. If you have not finished your homework before class, you had better come up _____ a good excuse for the teacher.

3. He was so angry about being overcharged that he tore _____ the bill.

4. If you are not going to use that equipment, please get rid _____ it.

5. My brother is very gregarious; he likes to interact _____ people.

EXERCISE 4 (Do this exercise with a classmate.)

Directions: The writer of this paragraph has made some errors in preposition use which have been underlined. Correct these errors by writing in the correct preposition, adding a preposition, or taking out a preposition. The first one has been done for you.

Racism exists in every culture and country; however, combating racism is not completely hopeless <u>to</u> *for* a minority in U.S. society. Each member of a minority group must be aware <u>towards</u> any racism <u>in</u> school and <u>at</u> the work place. Being oversensitive to racism like an ostrich who buries his head <u>on</u> the ground is not advisable <u>to</u> a minority. However, a moderate awareness <u>toward</u> the existence of racism allows the minority to recognize <u>of</u> and emphasize <u>on</u> who they are, what they stand for, and what they are fighting for. Thus, instead of feeling inferior and not letting <u>go</u> ∧ the pain, minorities can navigate those obstacles and seek <u>for</u> more influence and a voice in today's highly diverse U.S. society.

PART IV

WRITING TOPICS

> Select one or more of the following topics for writing and follow the steps in Appendix A.

Topic A: Advise someone on how to be a successful student. What should a student do to be successful? If you are working, you may want to give advice on how to be successful in your line of work.

Topic B: Compare and contrast the person you are today with the person you were two or more years ago. What are the major changes in yourself and what has stayed the same?

Topic C: Think about your favorite restaurants. Choose one of them and describe what it is like in terms of food, atmosphere, service, and any other factors you would like to focus on. Then say why you would recommend this restaurant to your friends.

PART V

CNN VIDEO ACTIVITY AND WRITING TOPIC

Sushi: A New Japanese Export

Useful Vocabulary: sushi taste test condiments wasabi freshness test

Before You Watch

This video segment introduces viewers to sushi, a Japanese food now popular in the United States.

* What foods from your culture of origin do you think people from other cultures would find strange or difficult to eat?
* What foods from another culture do you particularly enjoy?

While You Watch

* Listen for and write down the main ingredients of sushi.
* Listen for important precautions in the preparation of sushi.

The art of sushi pleases the eye.

After You Watch

I. **Write a personal reaction.**

Write a personal reaction of three to five sentences to what you saw in the video. What interested you most? Have you ever tried sushi? Would you like to?

II. **Share your reactions.**

Answer the following questions either orally or in writing. Compare your answers with those of a classmate.

1. What do you think about eating raw fish?
2. Has watching this video enticed you to try sushi? If so, which kind?
3. Are there sushi restaurants in your area? What other ethnic food is popular where you live?

WRITING TOPIC

Describe a food unique to or special in your culture. (If you are Japanese, choose a food other than sushi.) Include ingredients, method of preparation, and how and when it is usually eaten. Would you like to see this food introduced around the world?

Beyond Grammar:
Other Ways to Make Writing Clear

This section contains five parts: Avoiding Unclear and Non-idiomatic Sentences and Phrases, Expanding Vocabulary, Achieving Academic Writing Style, Improving Flow of Ideas, and Revising for Clarity. Each part focuses on an aspect of writing that goes beyond grammatical errors but is necessary for clear writing.

We believe that the material in this section will help you, as an ESL writer, see that writing clearly is a combination of both clear sentences and an effective writing style.

AVOIDING NONIDIOMATIC AND UNCLEAR SENTENCES AND PHRASES

Errors with unclear and nonidiomatic sentences and phrases are not specifically grammatical but rather reflect the writer's inability to express a particular idea or concept clearly or idiomatically in English. This sort of difficulty is part of learning a new language; such errors are minimized through exposure to the language over a period of time.

Sentences marked nonidiomatic or unclear indicate to the ESL writer that he or she is not expressing himself or herself idiomatically (as a native speaker would) or clearly in English. Writers who must write at a high level of proficiency will need to write clearly and idiomatically.

Nonidiomatic Writing

In nonidiomatic writing **(nonidiom*),** the message of a phrase or sentence is clear, but a native speaker would not phrase the idea that way. For example, in the sentence *When I write under pressure, I feel that* <u>*I lack of knowledge of expressing myself with sophisticated English words,*</u> the underlined part is not written in idiomatic English. A native speaker might phrase the sentence in this way: *When I write under pressure I feel that* <u>*I cannot use sophisticated English words to express myself*</u> or <u>*I lack the knowledge to express myself in sophisticated English*</u>.

"Nonidiomatic" differs from "unclear" in that the reader can usually grasp the meaning in a nonidiomatic phrase or sentence but not in an unclear phrase or sentence. Nonidiomatic errors are usually local (less serious); however, if too much of a piece of writing is nonidiomatic, the error can become global (more serious).

Errors with idiomatic expressions differ from nonidiomatic writing. Idiomatic expressions are set words or phrases that are commonly used and that can be found in a dictionary of idioms or a text that focuses on idioms. Various errors can occur with idiomatic expressions. For example, in the sentence *I would rather use a computer than write by a hand, by a hand* should be *by hand,* an article error. In the sentence *I make the same mistakes in English times after times, times after times* should be *time after time,* a singular-plural error.

Importance of Mastering Idiomatic English in Writing

When reading nonidiomatic phrases or sentences, the native speaker's reaction often is: "I can understand what the writer is saying, but it sounds awkward to me." ESL writers need not only to master idiomatic English so that their writing

***nonidiom** = grading symbol for nonidiomatic writing.

does not sound foreign to a native speaker, but they also need to keep in mind that the closer their writing is to idiomatic English, the easier it will be for the reader to understand.

Suggestions for Mastering Idiomatic English

Improving your mastery of idiomatic English is a difficult task because idiomatic English is not based on rules; rather, it is based on usage. Therefore, the degree to which you master idiomatic English depends to a great extent on your commitment to using English and your desire to write like a native speaker.

Although mastering idiomatic English may seem like an enormous task, you can make this task much easier by attempting it in small chunks. For example, you could first focus on using more idiomatic English in your major or your field of interest, the field in which you are most likely to be doing the majority of your writing.

Five concrete suggestions for improving your command of idiomatic writing are as follows:

1. Read in English as much as possible.
2. Listen attentively to the way English is used.
3. Think in English as much as possible, rather than translating from your native language.
4. Realize that learning a language involves more than studying rules. The more you interact with native speakers, the more you will acquire idiomatic usage in English—that is, using the language the way native speakers do.
5. Ask a native speaker how he or she would say a phrase or sentence if a phrase or a sentence has been marked nonidiomatic in a paper you have written. Rewrite that sentence or phrase and memorize it for later use. Writing or saying it three times in a row will help you learn it.

EXERCISE 1 (Do this exercise on your own. Then check your answers with a classmate.)

Directions: **Test your ability to recognize idiomatic English. In the following sets of sentences, the writer is attempting to say the same thing in sentence A and sentence B, but one of the sentences is nonidiomatic. Read each set of sentences and then decide whether the underlined part is idiomatic or not; mark the sentence with an *I* for idiomatic or an *NI* for nonidiomatic.**

_____**1A.** Because the next history test is worth 100 points, I will have to study <u>to my fullest</u>.

_____ **B.** Because the history test is worth 100 points, I will have to study <u>very hard</u>.

_____**2A.** <u>The students in the residence halls</u> waved and smiled at me as I jogged by.

_____ **B.** <u>The residential students</u> waved and smiled at me as I jogged by.

_____**3A.** I like to study on the first floor of the library because of the <u>vast bloodline</u> of people I can see entering the library.

_____ **B.** I like to study on the first floor of the library because of the <u>variety</u> of people I can see entering the library.

_____**4A.** Writing compositions for my French class is <u>difficult for me</u>.

_____ **B.** Writing compositions for my French class is <u>causing me struggles</u>.

_____ **C.** Writing compositions for my French class is <u>a struggle for me</u>.

EXERCISE 2 (Do this exercise on your own. Then check your answers with a classmate.)

Directions: **Test your ability to recognize nonidiomatic English by underlining the non-idiomatic parts of these sentences and then rewriting them in idiomatic English.**

Based on my experience

Example: <u>As my feeling</u> during the last year, the biggest challenge for a new university student is gaining enough confidence to participate fully in class discussions.

1. My mother did not let us go to the mall alone when we were small ages.

2. By talking to native speakers, I can have a little bit of knowledge about American customs.

3. According to an essay in *Time* for May 20th issue, job openings for college graduates dropped 10 percent during the last year.

4. That red blouse doesn't suit of those purple jeans.

5. My aunt, who lives in Los Angeles, takes the bus everywhere because she is afraid to drive freeway.

6. Now that my English has improved, I can make communication with my friends.

7. After talking with my teacher, I am more understanding of the lecture.

8. It was blowing very hard and then the wind died down in a sudden.

Unclear Writing

In an unclear **(unclear*)** sentence, the reader cannot understand the message the writer wants to convey. The error is global (more serious) because it affects more than a clause and may affect whole parts of a text.

An unclear message may or may not be related to problems with grammar in a sentence. For example, unclear sentences like *Pressure is one of equipment to bring up our skill by ourself* or *I can experienced the truth of studying by a coffee* are grammatically incorrect <u>and</u> have an unclear message. On the other hand, unclear sentences like *Waiting for these negatives to grow is not a particular way* or *I felt sick that I missed some tasteful water* are correct grammatically but their message is unclear. In

***unclear** = grading symbol for unclear sentences.

an unclear sentence, the whole sentence or just part of the sentence may be unclear.

Unclear sentences differ from sentences with sentence-structure errors or non-idiomatic sentences because the meaning in sentences with these errors is usually understandable to the reader, whereas the message of an unclear sentence is not.

Importance of Mastering Sentence Clarity in Writing

In academic and professional writing, the reader should not have to guess at meaning. However, in an unclear sentence, the reader must try to guess what the writer is saying—in the absence of the writer. This error is particularly serious as it interferes with the reader's ability to understand the content of a piece of writing. In other words, the meaning of the text is at least partially lost.

Notice how the unclear sentences in the following passage take away from its effectiveness because a whole piece of meaning is lost to the reader.

> An example of how decorations can identify us is a stuffed toy stuck on the car's windshield. These toys bring our car to people's attention, and therefore people in other cars [can know what our *unclear* message is], even at a very fast speed. [These toys mostly show that person really the car and animals.] *unclear*

Suggestions for Mastering Sentence Clarity

Often, writers who can write quite easily and correctly about their personal experiences find themselves writing unclear sentences when, in academic or professional writing, they begin writing on more abstract topics. A good strategy for becoming familiar with the language you will need to use and with the kinds of writing you will have to do in either academic or professional writing is to read examples of this kind of writing in textbooks, journals, newspapers, or magazines.

Remember that you, as a writer, have the responsibility for conveying your ideas clearly to the reader. The following are five strategies that will help you write clear sentences:

1. Avoid translating from your native language. Try to think and write in English as much as possible.

2. Tell a classmate or your teacher an idea you are trying to express in writing. Then write it the way you said it. Do not worry that your English is "too simple." Being clear is more important than sounding sophisticated.

3. Use words that you know rather than "big words" whose meanings you are unsure of. You can then refine your language in later drafts of a paper. You will also find that as you gain more confidence in your writing skills, you will improve your command of vocabulary.

4. Take a sentence that has been marked unclear on your paper and try to rewrite it yourself. Rethink the idea you want to express, determine what you really want to say, and then restate the sentence.

5. Do not be afraid to write some short, simple sentences to clarify your meaning to yourself when you are writing a draft and are in the process of formulating your ideas. Then, in later drafts, you can combine some of these ideas into more complex sentences.

EXERCISE 3 (Do this exercise with a classmate.)

Directions: **This paragraph, which was written by a student, has been edited so that the only errors in grammar are unclear sentences. Read the paragraph out loud to each other and listen for unclear sentences. Put any unclear sentences or parts of sentences you hear between brackets. Then read the paragraph silently to check it again for unclear sentences. Try to rewrite the unclear sentences to make them clear. Be prepared to discuss how easy or difficult it is to revise the unclear sentences of another writer.**

There are many differences between third-world and industrialized nations. One important difference is in the types of worries individuals have in their daily lives. All humans have worries, but one hard tension for some people may differ hardness other people. In many parts of the world, people never think about buying new clothes or the latest model TV set or car. All that they think about is how they can get a food from hunger. People have a great terror and this thing has a lot of tension. In contrast, people who live in wealthy nations usually never think about food except where or when they are going to eat, but they have different problems in their lives, such as too much work, family problems, and stress. In both types of countries, rich or poor, people are never free from worry.

PART B

EXPANDING VOCABULARY

As an English language learner, no matter what your proficiency level, you probably have a great desire to expand your vocabulary—that is, to be able not only to comprehend but also to use a broad range of vocabulary words. You no doubt realize that the broader your vocabulary, the more precise and accurate you can be in your writing. Also, if you have a broad vocabulary, you have options to choose among different words with similar meanings and you can make your writing more colorful, vivid, and effective overall.

Just as a native speaker acquires vocabulary in his or her first language, the process of acquiring new vocabulary for a second-language learner is a gradual one that occurs naturally over a period of time through exposure to the language—through reading, listening to the language, and interacting with others who speak it. However, a second-language learner can speed up the process of vocabulary acquisition. This section suggests several strategies that will help you take a more active role in expanding your English vocabulary.

Strategies for Expanding Your Vocabulary

1. **Read in English as much as possible.**

   One of the best ways to acquire new vocabulary is through reading. When you are reading, aim for overall meaning. Guess the meanings of words from context whenever possible, but look up key words (those that are central to the meaning of the text) in a dictionary when necessary.

   You will acquire some words "passively"—that is, without effort while you are reading. To acquire vocabulary more actively while reading, try some of the suggestions listed under the second strategy below.

2. **Use strategies that will help make the vocabulary-expansion process faster and more active.**

   Some language learners find it helpful to make up vocabulary cards and review them regularly. Others find it useful to keep a vocabulary notebook, which they can carry around with them. Others prefer to use a highlighter pen when they are reading to highlight words they are unsure of and then go back and look up or review the highlighted words.

3. **Put yourself in an English-speaking environment as much as possible.**

   Try to be an active listener. Listen for new words or phrases. If you cannot catch them the first time you hear them, perhaps you will be able to do so the second or third time. When you hear new words you do not understand, do not be afraid to ask the person speaking what the words mean—for example, by saying, *"What did you mean by . . . . ?"* or *"I'm not sure I understand what . . . means."* If you do not want to ask the person you are speaking with at the time you hear a new word, you can wait to ask someone else later.

If you do not have the chance to interact with people as much as you would like to, keep in mind that the radio and television are also good resources for you. Many radio and TV stations, such as National Public Radio (NPR) and Cable News Network (CNN), offer informational and feature programs that you might be interested in and which would serve as a source of new vocabulary in English.

4. **When you learn a new word, focus on more than just the meaning.**

When you learn a new word, you will have a better chance of remembering it and making it a part of your active vocabulary if you learn more than just its meaning. You should also learn how to pronounce the word. Then focus on how to use the word in context—that is, in a phrase or a sentence. Make it a point to write each new word in a phrase or a sentence to help you remember the correct context in which it is used.

5. **Decide which words you need to know and focus on learning those.**

As you come across new vocabulary words, you should keep in mind that there are many words that you do not need to learn because you will probably not need to use them. You will also find that there are words you only need to understand when you hear or read them. However, there are other words that you need to be able to understand *and use*. These words are the ones on which you should focus the most attention. Generally, such words are those that are used frequently in your field of study or work. You can discover what these words are by noticing which words appear frequently in your textbooks, in the classroom, in articles you read, and in discussions with your colleagues and professors.

6. **Become familiar with the meanings of common prefixes, suffixes, and roots of words.**

Knowing the meaning of common prefixes, suffixes, and roots of words will help you guess the meaning of words of which they are a part. For example, if you know that the meaning of the prefix *anti* is *against* and that the meaning of the prefix *post* is *after,* you will more easily be able to guess the meaning of words such as *antisocial, antibiotic, postwar,* or *postgraduate* if these words are new to you. If you know that the root *dict* means *say,* you will more easily be able to guess that the words *predict, diction, dictionary, dictation,* and *valedictorian* have something to do with *saying* or *words.* Similarly, if you know the root *hydro* means *water,* you will know that the words *hydrology* and *hydraulic* have something to do with water.

Knowing suffixes will help you identify the part of speech (noun, verb, adjective, adverb) of a word. For example, the suffix *-ment* as in *requirement* or *agree-*

ment identifies a word as a noun. The suffix *-en*, on the other hand, as in *widen* or *straighten*, identifies a word as a verb and also has the meaning of *to make*, as in *to make wide* or *to make straight*. The suffix *-ee*, as in *employee* or *payee*, identifies a word as a noun and also has the meaning of *a person who is doing or has "received" a certain action.* For example, an *employee* is a person who *is employed* and a *payee* is a person who *has been* or *will be paid.* For more information on common suffixes, see Unit 14, "Word Forms," in this textbook. If you want more information on common prefixes and word roots, you can look for this information in ESL vocabulary textbooks or ask your instructor to recommend some useful resources.

7. **Relax and take your time.**

   Try to relax and realize that expanding your vocabulary *will* take time. However, commit yourself to working actively to expand it by using some of the strategies above. Most important, whenever possible, try to use the new words that you have learned in your own speaking and writing in order to move them from your passive vocabulary—words that you have heard and are familiar with—to your active vocabulary—words that you can confidently use in your speaking and writing.

Exercises for Practice

EXERCISE 1 (Do this exercise on your own. Then share your results with a classmate.)

Directions: Interview at least two native speakers of English. Ask them how they think they learn new words and expand their vocabulary. Then interview at least two non-native speakers of English and ask them how they learn new words and what strategies they find useful for expanding their vocabulary. Finally, write up a list of all the ways that people you have interviewed expand their vocabulary and discuss which ones you feel would be most useful and appropriate for you, as an ESL writer, to use for expanding your own vocabulary.

EXERCISE 2 (Do this exercise on your own.)

Directions: Choose an article that interests you in a newspaper or magazine, or choose a section in a chapter from one of your textbooks. As you read the article or section, underline or highlight all the words that are new or unfamiliar to you. Decide which of the underlined words are important for you to know in order to understand the text and look those up in a dictionary. After you have read the article or section, make a list of the words you want to learn and incorporate into your active vocabulary. On your list, include each new word and its definition, along with a sentence that illustrates its use. If you are unsure of any of the words, ask a classmate, a tutor, or your instructor for help.

PART C

ACHIEVING ACADEMIC WRITING STYLE

As an academic or professional writer, you will want to adopt an academic writing style. Although many of the features of this style are covered in the units in this textbook, this section has been designed to highlight some important features of academic writing style, beyond grammar, that you will want to keep in mind in addition to improving the grammatical accuracy of your writing.

Academic writing in English is clear and concise. It is also direct, meaning that the writer gets to the main point as quickly as possible. Academic writing in English is sometimes referred to as "linear" in development, meaning that the writer makes a point and immediately supports that point with evidence and then moves on to the next point. This linear development in English is in contrast to writing styles in other languages in which the writer might, for example, go around the point but never address it directly or digress to another point before finishing the first point. Academic writing is also formal in its use of vocabulary and correct sentence structure, whereas spoken English is often more informal in these areas.

In addition to reviewing the characteristics listed in this section, keep in mind that one of the best ways to become familiar with academic and professional writing style is to read authentic samples of it and to use them as models for your own writing. These samples, such as articles and reports, will help you not only see the formal word choice and sentence structure mentioned above but also will help you become familiar with standard formats and common language used in many types of academic and professional writing, such as term papers, lab reports, journal articles, business letters, memos, grant proposals, and progress reports.

Below are several specific suggestions that, when incorporated into your writing, will help you achieve academic writing style.

Suggestions for Achieving Academic Writing Style

1. **Avoid informal or colloquial language.**

   Original: I need to spend some time sorting the <u>junk</u> in my office.
   Revision: I need to spend some time sorting the <u>material</u> in my office.

   Original: Analyzing the data has been <u>rough</u>.
   Revision: Analyzing the data has been <u>challenging</u> (or <u>difficult</u>).

2. **Use single-word verbs as much as possible rather than phrasal verbs (two- and three-word verbs), as single-word verbs are generally more formal and concise.**

   Original: First, heat the solution to the boiling point. <u>Keep on</u> boiling it for at least two minutes.

   Revision: First, heat the solution to the boiling point. <u>Continue</u> boiling it for at least two minutes.

   Original: The medicine will not <u>get rid of</u> the problem, but it will lessen the symptoms.

   Revision: The medicine will not <u>cure</u> (or <u>alleviate</u>) the problem, but it will lessen the symptoms.

   Note: For more information on using single-word verbs, see Unit 13, "Word Choice."

3. **Avoid contractions.**

   Original: Applicants who <u>don't</u> have strong computer skills <u>won't</u> be as competitive as those who do.

   Revision: Applicants who <u>do not</u> have strong computer skills <u>will not</u> be as competitive as those who do.

4. **Avoid addressing the reader directly as "you."**

   Note: In process analysis, the use of "you" *is* often acceptable.

   Original: If you receive less than 550 on the TOEFL examination, <u>you</u> may not be able to enter some U.S. universities.

   Revision: <u>Applicants who receive less than 550 on the TOEFL examination</u> may not be able to enter some U.S. universities.

   Original: First, <u>you heat</u> the solution. Then <u>you let</u> it boil for five minutes.

   Revision: First, <u>heat</u> the solution. Then <u>let</u> it boil for five minutes.

5. **Avoid asking the reader direct questions.**

   Note: Direct questions are common in textbooks and are also often used as essay titles.

   Original: What are the reasons for homelessness?

   Revision: The reasons for homelessness include . . .

   Original: How were the data collected?

   Revision: The data were collected by . . .

6. **As much as possible, place adverbs midposition in a sentence (before the main verb or in a verb phrase after the first auxiliary verb) rather than initially or finally.**

   Original: I feel I will be able to expand my vocabulary <u>eventually</u>.
   Revision: I feel I will <u>eventually</u> be able to expand my vocabulary.

   Original: Mark uses the computer room <u>regularly</u>.
   Revision: Mark <u>regularly</u> uses the computer room.

7. **Use formal negative forms.**

   Original: Many programs <u>do not admit any</u> new students in spring semester.
   Revision: Many programs <u>admit no new students</u> in spring semester.

   Original: <u>Not very much</u> research has been done in this area.
   Revision: <u>Little research has been</u> done in this area.

8. **Avoid the use of *etc., and so on,* and *and so forth* because these terms are vague.**

   Original: In my free time, I enjoy sports, <u>etc</u>.
   Revision: In my free time, I enjoy sports <u>and other activities such as reading</u>.

   Note: The term *such as* in the revised sentence above tells the reader that not all examples have been given.

   Original: At the meeting, the new project, the old project, the new pay scale, <u>etc</u>. were discussed.
   Revision: At the meeting, the new project, the old project, the new pay scale, <u>and several other agenda items</u> were discussed.

9. **Try to vary the sentences in your writing by using simple, compound, and complex sentences.**

   Flooding has been a serious problem in the past few weeks. (simple sentence)

   Although flooding has been a serious problem recently, our area has not been affected so far. (complex sentence involving an adverbial clause)

   Flooding has been a serious problem in parts of northern California, causing mandatory evacuation of houses in some areas. (complex sentence involving a reduced relative clause)

   Ski resorts are affected in that they have suffered lack of business because of road closures. (complex sentence involving the connector "in that")

   A combination of the amount of rain and the warm weather melting the snow earlier than usual led to the flooding we have recently experienced. (compound subject)

Most of the reservoirs are almost full to capacity, yet farmers are still worried about a possible shortage of irrigation water. (compound sentence)

Note: For more information on complex sentences (sentences with dependent clauses), see Unit 6, "Relative, Adverbial, and Noun Clauses." For more information on compound sentences and ways to connect sentences, see Unit 9, "Connecting Words."

10. **Use passive voice when appropriate.**

Note: The passive voice is common in some types of academic writing, especially when the writer is describing methods and procedures. For more information on passive voice, see Unit 5, "Passive Voice."

Examples: The fruit was <u>harvested,</u> <u>cleaned,</u> and <u>dried.</u>
In the past five years, a number of studies <u>have been done</u> on this topic.

11. **Use words that indicate the strength of your claims.**

Examples:
The data <u>clearly show</u> that . . . (strong claim)
The data <u>indicate</u> that . . . (weaker claim)
The data <u>suggest</u> that . . . (weaker claim)

Examples:
A <u>dramatic</u> difference was observed. (a very big difference)
A <u>significant</u> difference was observed. (a clearly noticeable difference)
A <u>slight</u> difference was observed. (a minor difference)

Note: See the section Improve Your Writing Style in Unit 3, "Modals," for other ways to show the strength of a claim.

Exercises for Practice

EXERCISE 1 (Do this exercise on your own. Then share your answers with a classmate.)

Directions: **Practice some of the features of academic style discussed in this section by revising each of the following sentences to make its style more academic. The features that you should revise are underlined for you in each sentence.**

1. When <u>you</u> are applying for a job, <u>you</u> may want to use the services of the Career Placement Center on <u>your</u> campus.

2. There <u>has not been any</u> snow this year.

3. Although <u>they've</u> lived here for 10 years, my parents <u>haven't</u> had a chance to learn English well.

4. <u>Usually</u>, I communicate with my parents in our native language, Chinese.

5. I have a number of things I need to accomplish today: errands, <u>etc</u>.

6. <u>Why is this procedure helpful</u>? First, it is simple and inexpensive to perform.

EXERCISE 2 (Do this exercise with a classmate.)

Directions: **Using not only formal but also precise vocabulary is one of the most important aspects of academic writing style. Practice this important feature by choosing a more formal or precise word for each of the underlined words or phrases taken from student writing.**

Example: (Original)   I <u>couldn't figure out</u> which method to use.
(Revision)   I <u>could not determine</u> which method to use.

1. The job description <u>talks about</u> the requirements for potential candidates.

2. In my research, I will <u>look at</u> the effects of pesticides on soil.

3. <u>Now</u> I am finishing my senior year as a chemistry major at the University of Arizona.

4. I am <u>thinking about</u> applying for the position available at your company.

5. I am writing to inquire about <u>some more</u> details on the research I will be expected to do.

6. I am <u>really</u> interested in a flight attendant job with your company.

7. Today has been a <u>tough</u> day.

8. Through the use of animals in research, thousands of people can survive <u>bad</u> diseases.

9. To obtain some <u>good</u> information on visiting Lake Tahoe, a visitor can call (530) 544-5050.

PART D

IMPROVING FLOW OF IDEAS

As a writer, you will want your ideas to flow together as smoothly as possible. Writers achieve this smooth flow of ideas, sometimes called *coherence,* by using a variety of techniques that are outlined in this section. In addition to reviewing the material in this section, keep in mind that one of the best ways to become familiar with how writers achieve flow of ideas is to read authentic written material and notice what techniques the writers have used to make their ideas move in a smooth progression. Most importantly, keep in mind that writers achieve flow of ideas using **a variety** of techniques. Although the use of connecting words is an important part of flow of ideas, overall flow is more than just plugging in connecting words between your sentences.

Suggestions for Achieving Smooth Flow of Ideas in Writing

1. **Combine ideas using subordination and coordination. While you may have some simple sentences consisting of one independent clause, avoid strings of simple sentences.**

   Original: The houses are made of mud bricks. They vary in size. They contain no modern conveniences. A few have electricity.

   Revision: The houses, which vary in size, are made of mud bricks. Although they contain no modern conveniences, a few have electricity.

   Original: Robert Arneson was a famous professor and artist. He taught in the art department at UC Davis. He was a native Californian. He began his teaching job at UC Davis in 1962.

   Revision: Robert Arneson was a famous professor and artist who taught at UC Davis. A native Californian and contemporary artist, he began teaching here in 1962.

   Note: For more information on combining ideas using dependent clauses and connectors, see Unit 6, "Relative, Adverbial, and Noun Clauses," and Unit 9, "Connecting Words."

2. **Point back to old information using *this* or *these* plus a noun that refers to the old information (for example, *this feature, this process, these difficulties*).**

   Example: On the first day of class, students write a diagnostic essay. <u>This essay</u> is used to help determine the strengths and weaknesses of each student's writing.

   Example: Some callers experienced difficulties making telephone connections on Christmas Day. <u>These difficulties</u> were a result of the high demand for telephone calls on a major holiday.

3. **Point back to old information using pronouns (for example *he, she, it, they*) as reference words.**

   Example: The new factory produces a variety of audio and video equipment. According to production statistics, <u>its</u> output has increased significantly despite some initial problems.

   Example: The new residential subdivision features three different sizes and models of houses. <u>They</u> are all energy-efficient and reasonably priced.

4. **Use introductory prepositional phrases.**

> **Example:** As a graduate student in the sciences, I am deeply concerned about the small number of women compared to men in the math and science fields. <u>In my department,</u> there are only two female faculty members.
>
> I like to study in varying places, depending on the time of day. <u>During the daytime,</u> I like to study at home. <u>At night,</u> on the other hand, it is noisy at home and I prefer to study in the library.

5. **Repeat key words and ideas.**

> **Example:** <u>Caffeine</u> withdrawal can indeed cause headaches. Many <u>coffee</u> drinkers find that if they stop drinking <u>coffee</u> for one day, they get a headache. This result seems to occur whether or not the <u>coffee</u> drinker drinks a large or small amount of <u>coffee</u> every day.

6. **Use connecting words.**

> **Note:** Although you should not rely on connectors alone to achieve flow of ideas in your writing, connecting words are certainly one important aspect of flow of ideas in writing.
>
> **Example:** The effect of color on individuals' emotions has been studied by a number of researchers in various fields. Red is thought by some researchers to be a tense and stimulating color. Blue, <u>on the other hand,</u> is thought to be calm, cool, and soothing.

Exercises for Practice

EXERCISE 1 (Do this exercise on your own. Then check your answers with a classmate.)

Directions: **Read the following sample of student writing. Find and underline the techniques the writer uses to make the ideas flow smoothly.**

This quarter, I am taking four courses. Because I am doing my Ph.D. degree in the Epidemiology Graduate Group, it is necessary for me to take one required course, Principles of Epidemiology, and two prerequisite courses, Statistics and Short Calculus. The other important course is ESL. Since I am an international student in my first year, I will be spending a lot of time adjusting to the different teaching style here as well as working on improving my English. Also, I have gotten a job as a research assistant doing some laboratory work, which is scheduled on Wednesday and Friday afternoons. In short, I think this quarter will be very challenging for me, especially in terms of handling a busy time schedule.

EXERCISE 2 (Do this exercise on your own. Then check your answers with a classmate.)

Directions: **Read the following sample of student writing. Revise it in order to make the ideas flow more smoothly.**

I am taking an engineering course (Advanced Dynamics), an ESL course, a seminar, and research. Totally, it is 12 units. It is a light load for me. I only pay attention to dynamics and English. Because this is my first semester, what is the most important is to improve my English.

PART E

REVISING FOR CLARITY: GUIDELINES FOR THE ESL WRITER

In academic and professional writing, once the writer has written a first draft, revision begins. Although revising is hard work, it is rewarding in terms of producing clear, polished writing. ESL writers can and should revise. The ESL writer, even though he or she may initially be afraid of adding more grammatical errors to a piece of writing, needs to realize that a sentence can be reworked after it has been written and that more than grammatical errors should be addressed during revision. For ESL writers, and all writers, the end result of becoming a careful reviser is that they begin to see their writing as words in progress, not as words set in stone.

The following guidelines for revision are designed specifically for the ESL writer:

1. Make a commitment to revision. Realize that good writing is worked and reworked and that it is done to provide clarity, accuracy, and precision for the reader. Good writers know that it may take much rewriting to "get it right."

2. Do not try to revise a large piece of writing in one sitting. It takes mental energy to rewrite; trying to do too much at one time will result in uneven revision, with the writing getting noticeably less polished as you become tired.

3. Think of revising in terms of an abstract-to-concrete approach. Divide the revision into three parts: organization, development, and sentences. During revision for organization, make sure that what you have written has a beginning, middle, and an end. Also make sure that the whole piece of writing fits together—that meaning flows from one sentence to another and from one paragraph to another. For development, make sure that you have provided enough detail for the reader to "see" what you are writing about. In revising for clear

and correct sentences, prioritize your errors, working first on those that you, as an efficient self-editor, know need the most work. For example, you might first choose to edit for verb tenses and subject-verb agreement. Then you can go back and look carefully at another possible problem area, such as use of dependent clauses, or word choice.

4. Work with the whole manuscript and write on it with a pencil or pen. If you are using a computer, too much work with only the screen is not efficient. To see your text, you need, from time to time, to work with the entire text during revision, not only with what you see on one screen.

5. Once you have revised heavily, read your writing out loud to hear its rhythm. As practice, read formal prose out loud, on a regular basis, and you will begin to hear how the words fit together in a steady beat. Good writers recognize that spoken English uses different structures and, thus, has a different rhythm than that of formal written English.

6. Know that you can develop a self-monitor; that is, you will be able to consciously recognize and correct grammatical errors based on the rules that you have learned. Decide whether it is more efficient for you to monitor for your errors as you are composing your text or to compose your text and then go back and edit for your most serious and frequent errors.

7. Be patient. The rewards of a well-written, revised text are well worth the effort. Moreover, *all* good writers revise, even the most widely published authors.

EXERCISE 1 (Do this activity on your own. Then share your ideas with a classmate.)

Directions: **Think about and answer the following questions.**

How do you approach revising what you have written? Explain the steps you currently use. Would you like to incorporate some of the strategies from this set of guidelines? If so, which ones?

EXERCISE 2 (Do this activity on your own. Then share your ideas with a classmate.)

Directions: **Think about and answer the following questions.**

To what extent do you feel you have developed a self-monitor for finding and correcting grammatical errors? At this time, what errors do you look for and how successful are you at finding and correcting them? When during the writing process do you monitor for errors?

Steps to Writing and Revising Responses to Writing Topics

After you have chosen a writing topic, follow these steps. These steps have been designed to lead you through the process of writing an essay.

Step 1: Gathering Information

Once you have selected a topic, discuss it with a classmate or in a small group.

Step 2: Prewriting

Working by yourself, list some of the ideas you have discussed with a classmate or in a small group. List any other ideas that come to mind related to your topic.

Step 3: Writing Your First Draft

Use your list from prewriting to help you write your first draft. Focus on content.

Step 4: Sharing Your Draft

Working with a classmate, read each other's draft. Give feedback to each other using the format given below.

A. Reading for Content

    1. What do you like most about this paper?

    2. What would you still like to know more about?

    3. What suggestions for revision do you have for the writer?

B. Checking for Language Errors

    1. Do you notice any patterns of language errors in the response?

    2. Do you notice any errors of the type you have been studying in this unit (e.g., dependent-clause errors, verb-tense errors, or preposition errors)?

    3. Discuss with your classmate how to correct the above errors.

Step 5:   Revising Your Writing

Using your classmate's suggestions as well as your own ideas for revising, write your second draft. Focus on content and accuracy of language. As you examine each sentence, be especially aware of how well you have mastered the grammatical structure(s) you have studied in this text.

Step 6:   Proofreading Your Final Draft

Read your final draft once again, paying particular attention to the grammatical structure(s) you have studied in this text. Make any necessary changes.

Additional Exercises for Practice:
Editing for a Variety of Errors

EXERCISE 1 EDITING FOR ERRORS WITH VERB TENSE AND VERB FORM

Directions: The following paragraph, written by an exchange student from Korea who is studying in the United States, has errors in verb tense and verb form. Find and correct these errors.

Aside from study for a degree, I have learned and experience many things from being a student here. First, I had many opportunities to broaden my views. By encounter people of many different backgrounds, I learned about many different points of view. I also came to understand more about the issues facing people from different countries and how people from many different cultures thought. Second, I have learned much about American culture and people. In the United States, I have encounter many unfamiliar aspects of culture that I have never seen. Also, the way American people interact is different from what I was used to in my home country. I have try to understand these differences and in the future hope to be a sort of "bridge" that can connect Americans and Koreans. In terms of customs, one of the best ones that I learn is to smile at people. Finally, I improve my English greatly. I do not have any fear of speak English, and think in English feels very natural to me. Nowadays, I even dream in English. In my dreams, I spoke in English even to my family! In conclusion, the experience of being here was a great asset for me. When I will return home after a year here, I will be a person who is more open-minded and a person who is a better "citizen of the world."

EXERCISE 2 EDITING FOR ERRORS WITH ARTICLES AND SINGULAR/PLURAL OF NOUNS

Directions: The following passage was written by a student in an intensive English program in response to the writing topic that is included in the videotape activity on sushi. Find and correct the errors with articles and with the singular/plural of nouns.

Note: *Onigiri* and *sushi* are uncountable nouns.

Rice balls (called onigiri) are a type of Japanese food that is much older than the sushi. It is the most popular food to take along while traveling in the Japan. Rice balls are taken on picnics and trips, found at school and work, and put in box lunch. They are made from a cooked rice and shaped into a triangles or a ball. The three ingredient that are needed to make Japanese rice balls are cooked rice, salt, some type of filling that has strong flavor, and seaweeds. The filling is put in the center of ball of rice and then it is shaped by hand. Ball of rice is then wrapped in a seaweed.

In my opinion, onigiri could become as popular around the world as the sushi. It is a delicious yet easy-to-make food. A problem that has to be solved, however, is choice of filling. In Japan, the most popular filling are dried plums, barbecued salmons, and flaked, dried bonito. Recently, tuna and chicken with the mayonnaise have been used and the barbecued beef is becoming more and more popular. In Japan, every family has its own favorites. However, it is more difficult to know what kind of fillings would be appropriate for foreigner. The people I interviewed in California said that they would like some type of fish, cucumber, chicken, crab meats, or barbecued pork. To my surprise, all of them were very interested in the onigiri. I am sure that if we experiment with recipe to get the right taste, onigiri will become popular food around the world.

EXERCISE 3 EDITING FOR ERRORS WITH SENTENCE STRUCTURE AND CLAUSES

Directions: The following paragraph, written by an undergraduate student, contains errors in sentence structure and clauses. Find and correct these errors.

For immigrants to a different country, learning a new language is a problem that they will inevitably encounter. Most Taiwanese immigrants to the United States have a hard time learning English because of their background. In Taiwan, because English is rarely used, so most people have not had any contact with English before coming to the United States. Moreover, English totally different from Mandarin or Taiwanese in both grammar and pronunciation, so requires a lot of practice for an immigrant to be able to use English well and having the confidence to speak it. When immigrants arrive here, many of them have to learn English starting with the alphabet. Even though they may have had professional skills in their home country.

While it is difficult for immigrants to learn English, it also hard for them to find time to study the language. Immigrants usually start to work within a community uses the same language as they do because they need to work before they acquire good English skills. At work, they usually communicate with people only in their home language, and, unfortunately, even they want to take English classes, they often cannot find one that they are able to attend because of their busy schedules. By communicating in their home language at work and by not attending language classes, immigrants can spend the whole day without saying even one English sentence. This weekend I went home to San Francisco, I spoke no more than twenty complete sentences in English because I always communicate with my family and friends there in Mandarin. In some communities, a person can spend his or her entire life in this country without learning how to speak English. This situation is much more common the older the immigrants are and sometimes results in a feeling of isolation. Many immigrants feel have lost their social identities and become people without a voice in this "land of opportunity."

EXERCISE 4   EDITING FOR ERRORS WITH SUBJECT-VERB AGREEMENT AND PREPOSITIONS

Directions: The following passage, a biographical statement written by a student in civil engineering, has errors in subject-verb agreement and errors with prepositions. Find and correct these errors.

Kazuhiro Ito is a first-year graduate student working in a master's degree in civil engineering in the University of Michigan. He already have a B.S. degree in civil engineering, which he did in Hokkaido University in Japan. Before coming to Ann Arbor, he worked for Tokyo Engineering Corporation, Ltd., which plan, design, construct, and manage urban freeway systems at the Tokyo metropolitan area. While working there, he was engaged on planning new freeways. He have not determined his research topic yet, but he is very interested on studies related to reducing and eliminating transportation problems, such as traffic congestion and air pollution. He is also interested on driving, especially in freeways so that he can learn about multi-lane highways. He have a family, consisting in a wife and a daughter who are one year and three months old. Besides his academic interests, he likes reading, listening music and dancing.

EXERCISE 5 EDITING FOR ERRORS WITH MODALS AND CONDITIONAL SENTENCES

Directions: In this passage, taken from a longer paper, a student in an advanced ESL composition class is analyzing one of the advantages of going to school via computer instead of attending class in person. Find and correct errors with modals and conditional sentences.

If on-line universities became a reality, one positive effect would be that working adults who wanted to study English as a second language will be able to go to school at their convenience. Nowadays, many older people are eager to enrich their education by attending adult school. However, attending school on a daily basis would be very difficult for some because they have to work at night, the school is far away from their home, or because the classes are full. When I was a sophomore at Richmond High School, I earned some extra high school credits by attending Richmond Adult School. On the first day of class, the air was filled with excitement and the class was full. However, the very next week when I went to my English writing class, some students should have been missing because I overheard someone say, "Fong-Wai won't be here today because he's working at night. Mei-Ling's sick, so she is staying home."

If these students were there, my English instructor would not have been so frustrated. She would not have felt as if she were losing her audience. Moreover, the eager students from the first class had turned into exhausted human beings. Although I did not know their backgrounds at that time, some of the housewives can have three children to raise, or some businessmen could had just gotten off work. Today, if these same students were enroll in an on-line institution, they can just attend class by sitting in front of a computer at any time of day. They will not have to make a tremendous effort to get to class after a long and tiring day. While moving a mouse and looking at a computer screen, they could relax and feel the joy of education instead of the exhaustion of adding hours to their day. For older students, studying at their own pace and having control over their time should be one of the major benefits of an on-line institution. Their struggle between work, childrearing, and school will be alleviated, and they could get the education that they desire—but only if they have the willingness to sit down and pursue it via the computer screen.

EXERCISE 6 EDITING FOR ERRORS WITH WORD FORM AND THE PASSIVE VOICE
AND CHOOSING APPROPRIATE CONNECTORS

Directions: The following paragraph, written by a teacher whose first language is not English, is about two of the factors that make his job satisfying. It has errors with word form and the passive. Find and correct these errors. Then, test your ability to use connectors by choosing the appropriate connector to fill in each blank from the list of connectors given below.

Choose an appropriate connector to fill in the blanks from this list: *first of all, nonetheless, of course, thus, for example.*

The two factors which make my job as a high school teacher satisfying are developing a sense of trust with the students and seeing their progress. _____, it is necessary to develop a sense of trust between my students and myself. I have always felt that it is indispensable for the teacher to build a good relation with students, including developing one with their parents, too. A good relationship with the students makes the atmosphere in class one of learning and the students find themselves eagerly to learn. _____, last year a student of mine, Juan, told me that he was very unsure of his ability to do mathematics because he had transferred from a school that had a poor math department. To help him gain confidence, I worked with him during the lunch period and helped him catch up with the class. At the end of the semester, he was getting a B, and he said to me, "You trusted me and helped me learn to trust myself. Thank you."

The second factor that makes my job as a teacher satisfying is seeing the progress of my students. _____, it is part of my job to encouragement students to get good results on their examinations; yet, it gives me a sense of personal satisfaction when they are been accepted by the university of their choice or get a summer job based on some of the skills they have been teached. Their succeed encourages me to work harder so that their dreams, and those of their parents, will come true. While it is true that I am often evaluate by whether or not my students success, it is the personal investment in their future that makes me feel satisfy with my job. If I had to choice a career all over again, I would definitely choose teaching.

Answers to Pretest

Unit 1

1. Since I moved to my new house 15 days ago, I <u>have been</u> very busy.

2. Human beings make mistakes. Sometimes we <u>do</u> things we <u>regret</u>.

Unit 2

1. Mario <u>chose</u> to live in the dormitory rather than in an apartment.

2. The hikers <u>had walked</u> approximately ten miles when they decided to set up camp.

3. Sometimes I <u>am</u> totally <u>confused</u> about English grammar.

4. The company clearly <u>deserved</u> to obtain a large research grant to continue their innovative research.

5. An effective speaker tries <u>to look</u> directly at his or her audience.

6. A grant writer hopes to <u>present</u> a convincing argument that clearly shows the value of a piece of research.

7. After <u>finishing</u> work, Margarita likes to work out in the gym for at least an hour.

Unit 3

1. I have not seen my next door neighbor for a week. She <u>might</u> be out of town. or She <u>could</u> be out of town. or She <u>may</u> be out of town. or She <u>might have gone</u> out of town. or She <u>must</u> be out of town. or She <u>must have gone</u> out of town.

2. In order to be successful, a person must <u>have</u> the determination to achieve his or her goals.

3. I cannot find my favorite pen. I must <u>have left</u> it at home.

Unit 4

1. If the weather improves, I <u>will</u> play tennis after finishing my homework.

   If the weather <u>improved</u>, I would play tennis after finishing my homework.

2. The travel agent would never have <u>fixed</u> the problem if we had not brought it to her attention.

3. <u>If</u> some good movies are playing at the foreign film theater, I would like to see one.

4. If I <u>were</u> you, I would not believe what she says because she likes to gossip.

5. If the ATM had not been working, Sheila would have been without any money when she arrived in San Diego. Also, she <u>would have felt</u> very hungry after a few days of not eating very much.

Unit 5

1. Some math problems can be <u>solved</u> very easily.

2. The speaker's question <u>was</u> directed at the younger members of the audience.

3. Despite the efforts of the United Nations, peace still <u>does not exist</u> in the world.

4. Many animals are disappearing in the wild. Today, zoos play an increasingly important role in keeping endangered animals from becoming extinct. Furthermore, <u>people can visit zoos</u> to see and enjoy these animals.

Unit 6

Relative Clauses

1. The people <u>who</u> (or <u>that</u>) live in Florida are used to warm, sunny weather for much of the year.

2. In high school, the students <u>whose</u> cars were illegally parked would get a ticket.

   In high school, the students <u>who</u> parked their car illegally would get a ticket.

3. After college, David wants to find a job <u>in which</u> he will need to use mathematics.

4. One chemistry experiment in particular that I <u>did in Chemistry 2A</u> gave me the idea that I might want to major in chemistry in college.

Adverbial Clauses

1. Although Henry hates <u>grammar, he</u> studies it anyway.

2. We have purchased one of those pens <u>because</u> we like them.

3. <u>When Meena went to the doctor,</u> she got a prescription.

4. <u>Because</u> the rain has stopped, we can go on our picnic.

5. <u>When</u> I see shoes, I want to buy them.

6. While you were at the <u>movies, Alexander</u> called to ask about the homework.

7. Many travelers fly business <u>class because</u> they like the wider seats.

8. While he <u>is working</u> in Australia, we will visit him.

Noun Clauses

1. <u>That</u> she got a job so quickly is amazing.

2. We were worried <u>that you were lost</u>.

3. Christy needs to face up to <u>the fact that</u> she is not prepared for the exam.

4. The city council supports <u>the proposition that</u> as many bicycle paths as possible should be built in the city.

5. Barry needs to find out <u>whether</u> his supervisor wants him to proceed on the project.

6. Matthew promised that <u>he would go</u> to the potluck.

7. Marcel is not sure <u>what the assignment for tomorrow was</u>.

8. Her professor prefers that Marta <u>write</u> a thesis.

9. The students were <u>surprised that the exam</u> was going to be given on Monday.

Unit 7

1. In my opinion, speaking in English <u>is</u> easier than writing in English.

2. <u>It</u> is a very interesting point you have raised. or <u>That</u> is a very interesting point you have raised. or You have raised a very interesting point.

3. My summer internship, for example, <u>is</u> one way for me to obtain valuable work experience.

4. My parents are first-generation immigrants to the United States, and they communicate mostly <u>in their</u> native language.

5. I think that some people do not want to help others in an emergency <u>because</u> they do not want to interfere in other people's lives.

6. At present, I am <u>finishing</u> a project and also <u>starting</u> a new one. or At present, <u>I am finishing</u> a project, and <u>I am also starting</u> a new one.

7. If you are working as an attorney, the problem is not the quantity of work <u>itself. It</u> is the responsibility you feel for defending your clients' interests. or If you are working as an attorney, the problem is not the quantity of work but the responsibility you feel for defending your clients' interests.

Unit 8

1. I do not remember when <u>the job application is</u> due.
2. The meeting has been postponed because the chairperson is <u>getting over the flu</u>.
3. O'Hare airport in Chicago is <u>extremely busy</u>.
4. The <u>long-stemmed red roses</u> are the loveliest.
5. My department <u>awarded me</u> a certificate of commendation. or My department <u>awarded a certificate of commendation to me</u>.
6. The movies at the downtown six-screen cinema <u>always change</u> on Fridays.
7. We left the laboratory <u>at 7:00 PM</u> because we did not have time to finish the experiment.

Unit 9

1. Natasha hoped to find an acting job in Hollywood, <u>but</u> she had little talent.
   Natasha hoped to find an acting job in Hollywood; <u>unfortunately</u>, she had little talent.
   <u>Although she had little talent</u>, Natasha hoped to find an acting job in Hollywood.
2. Global warming poses a threat to our environment; <u>however</u>, we are trying to solve the problem.
3. Even though we should be saving <u>money, we</u> are always going shopping.
4. There are three obstacles to losing <u>weight; however</u>, they can be overcome with a strong commitment to having a healthier, better-looking body.

Unit 10

1. A good scientist observes closely and <u>records</u> data accurately.
2. An attorney from one of the most distinguished law firms <u>has</u> agreed to represent the suspect.
3. A supervisor who <u>listens</u> to others and whose style is collaborative is often the most effective.
4. Taking regular breaks often <u>helps</u> a person work more efficiently.
5. There <u>are</u> six articles that I need to review this week in preparation for my presentation.
6. One of the two cars <u>consumes</u> significantly more gas than the other.

Unit 11

1. When a person buys a car, he or she usually has to make <u>a</u> down payment.
2. My friend called the police because one of <u>the</u> neighbors was having <u>a</u> loud party.
3. Students learn material more easily when they <u>have homework</u>.
4. Many doctors in the United States no longer wear <u>a</u> uniform during office hours. or
   Many doctors in the United States no longer wear <u>uniforms</u> during office hours.
5. My cousin always makes sure she has <u>her</u> driver's license when she goes out.

Unit 12

1. When I travel, I always take two <u>suitcases</u>.
2. My older sister is always willing to give me <u>advice</u>.
3. Perhaps you might like to read <u>these</u> two novels.
4. The little girl is selling red and <u>yellow</u> apples.
5. An old proverb says, "An eye for an eye and a <u>tooth</u> for a <u>tooth</u>."
6. On Valentine's Day, Andrea received one of the biggest <u>boxes</u> of chocolates I have ever seen.
7. Much of the <u>work</u> she did on that experiment had to be discarded.
8. When the meeting started, only two <u>women</u> were in the audience.

Unit 13

1. <u>Tuition</u> fees will be increased 40 percent next year.

2. Because the driver was unconscious, the police could only <u>speculate</u> about what had caused the accident.

3. <u>It is expected</u> that library books will be returned on time.

   <u>According to the rules</u>, library books <u>must be returned</u> on time.

4. From my <u>perspective</u>, a trip to Europe is very expensive.

5. Most teachers <u>talk about</u> the importance of attending class.

   Most teachers <u>discuss</u> the importance of attending class.

6. His students all think Dr. Stern is an <u>excellent</u> teacher.

Unit 14

1. <u>Communicating</u> via e-mail has become common around the world. or E-mail <u>communication</u> has become common around the world. or <u>To communicate</u> via e-mail has become common around the world.

2. Employees must submit weekly progress reports in a <u>timely</u> manner.

3. Eating a TV dinner is sometimes <u>more convenient than</u> cooking a meal.

4. As a possible career goal, I am <u>interested</u> in computer science.

Unit 15

1. Erik is taking summer school classes <u>at</u> Harvard University.

2. The dentist said there are three reasons <u>for</u> my having cavities: too much candy, too little flossing, and a too-soft toothbrush.

3. Jack is <u>seeking</u> information about pythons on the Internet.

Glossary of Grammatical Terminology

Active voice   a sentence construction in which the verb is doing the action.

Albert *crossed* the room after he *finished* talking to his friend.

Adjective   a word that modifies (adds information to) a noun.

My parents gave me a *red sports* car for graduation.
The house is *dark;* they must not be at home.

Adjective clause   a dependent (or **subordinate**) clause, also called a **relative clause,** which is connected to a noun by a relative pronoun *(that, which, who, whom, whose, where, why,* or *when)* and provides specific information about the noun.

The cabin *in which we stayed last summer* was made of logs.
Abraham Lincoln, *who was president of the United States during the Civil War,* was nicknamed Honest Abe.

Adverb   a word that modifies (adds information to) a verb, an adjective, another adverb, or a whole sentence.

Maurice stepped *gingerly* over the homeless man sleeping on the grate.
Please put the box *there.*
Perhaps the test will be canceled *tomorrow.*
Until recently, one had to cross the bridge *very carefully.*

Adverbial clause   a dependent (or **subordinate**) clause that is connected to an independent clause by a subordinating conjunction such as *because, although,* or *while.*

While Gregorio was vacationing in Paris, his house in Chicago flooded.
Although farmers always hope for a good crop, sometimes the weather works against them.

Agent   the doer of the action in a passive sentence. It may be preceded by the preposition *by* or may simply be implied.

The woman who was trapped in the burning building was rescued *by a man* passing by.
The flyer advertising the concert was posted on every bulletin board. *(by someone,* but it is not important to know who)

Article	one of the determiners *a, an, the,* or the *zero article,* which classifies or identifies a noun.
	The trip was canceled because of (zero article) fog; *a* new trip will be announced.
Auxiliary verb	a helping verb (or verbs) that comes before the main verb in a verb phrase and serves as an indicator of tense, mood, or voice. Auxiliary verbs include *do, be, have,* and the modal auxiliaries (such as *can, would,* or *should*).
	Now that my car *has been* repaired, the clutch *does* not squeak.
Base form	the infinitive form of a verb without *to.*
	Please let me *help* you. The train will *leave* the station in five minutes.
Clause	a group of words that has at least a subject and a verb and is either independent (can stand alone) or dependent (cannot stand alone).
	After the class ended (dependent clause), everyone went out for coffee (independent clause).
Collective noun	a noun that refers to a group of people, animals, or things that is treated as one unit.
	The *team* won the tournament. In some developing countries, the *government* is inexperienced.
Comma splice	a comma that has been incorrectly used to connect two independent clauses.
	Incorrect: A big city offers cultural events, a small town is usually safer. Revised: A big city offers cultural events; a small town is usually safer. Revised: A big city offers cultural events, but a small town is usually safer.
Common noun	a noun that is not used to refer to a specific person, place, or thing.
	For *breakfast,* Nurten likes to drink *juice* and eat a *bowl* of *cereal.*
Comparative form	the form an adjective or adverb takes to show the similarity or difference between two things.
	This test is *easier* than I thought it would be. Working with a group is *more satisfying* than working alone. Yoshi writes *more legibly* than Akira.
Complement (subject)	a word or phrase that follows a linking verb, such as *be, feel, seem,* or *look,* and which completes the meaning of the subject either by renaming it or describing it. Nouns and adjectives used as subject complements are also called **predicate nouns** and **predicate adjectives.**
	Pine trees are *conifers.* Edna looks *pale.*

Compound sentence	a sentence that is made up of at least two independent clauses which are connected by a coordinating conjunction or a semicolon.

> Recycling helps us reuse plastic (independent clause), so it makes us feel that we are working to save the environment (independent clause).

Complex sentence	a sentence made up of at least one independent clause and one dependent clause that is connected to the independent clause with a subordinating conjunction.

> Fatima returned the dress to the store (independent clause) because it did not fit her properly (dependent clause).

Conjunction	a word used to show a relationship between words, phrases, and clauses. Conjunctions are divided into different types according to their function: coordinating, subordinating, and correlative conjunctions; and conjunctive adverbs.

> The teacher asked the students to listen carefully *and* take notes.
> *Because* it was raining so hard, we took the bus home.
> *Whether* it is cold *or* warm, we will still go swimming.
> The soup was cold; *furthermore,* it was tasteless.

Connecting words	a word or words that are used to connect words, phrases, clauses, sentences, and paragraphs. Connecting words include conjunctions and transitional words and phrases.

> My dress is wrinkled; *however,* I do not have time to iron it.
> My mother easily shows her anger. *For example,* she gets red and her voice rises.

Coordinating conjunction	a connecting word used to join two independent clauses, such as *for, and, but.*

> This supermarket has good prices, *but* that small store has better meat.

Correlative conjunction	two connecting words that are used together, such as *either . . . or, not only . . . but also,* or *both . . . and.*

> We have to *either* buy a new car *or* fix the old one.

Countable noun	a noun that can be counted and made plural.

> My *friend* Joanna has two *dogs* and a *cat.*

Dangling modifier	a word or group of words that does not modify the proper word in a sentence.

> Incorrect: *Unprepared and unaware,* the situation was confusing.
> Revised: Unprepared and unaware, Michelle found the situation confusing.

Definite article	the word *the,* which, when modifying a noun, indicates that the noun is being specifically identified.

> *The* keyboard needs repair.

Demonstrative adjective the words *this, that, these,* and *those* when they are placed before nouns.

> *This* process is called photosynthesis.

Demonstrative pronoun the words *this, that, these,* and *those* when used alone in a subject or object position in a sentence.

> I will look through these papers and you look through *those.*
> (*These* in *these papers* is a demonstrative adjective.)

Dependent clause a clause, sometimes called a **subordinate clause,** that cannot stand alone but must work together with an independent clause to complete its meaning and form a complete sentence.

> *Because the population of the town has grown,* a number of new houses are being built.

Determiner a noun marker that precedes the noun and includes the following types of words: articles *(a, an, the)*, demonstratives *(this, that, these, those)*, possessive adjectives and nouns *(her, my, Susan's)*, quantity words *(some, many, much)* and numerals *(one, two, fourteen)*.

> *My* opinion on *the* matter has not changed.

Direct object a noun, noun phrase, or pronoun that follows a verb and receives the action of the verb.

> John received *a promotion.*
> His employer offered John *a promotion.*

Faulty predication the subject and the predicate do not work together in a sentence.

> Incorrect: *The reason for my tardiness is because* my car would not start.
> Revised: The reason for my tardiness is that my car would not start.

> Incorrect: The *chair walked* across the room.
> Revised: The chair appeared to walk across the room.

Fragment a group of words that do not make up a complete sentence.

> Incorrect: Because the weather was beautiful over the weekend.
> Revised: Because the weather was beautiful over the weekend, we went hiking.

> Incorrect: Three people standing in the corner.
> Revised: I noticed three people standing in the corner.

Gerund a verb with an *-ing* ending that functions in a noun position in a sentence.

> *Running* is good exercise.
> I enjoy *running.*

Global error	one of the most serious errors in writing. Global errors generally affect more than one clause and are likely to affect the reader's ability to comprehend a text. Some examples include verb tense, verb form, and sentence structure errors.

Incorrect: *When we move to a new environment is sometimes scary.* (sentence structure error)

Revised: Moving to a new environment is sometimes scary.

Incorrect: Simon *studied* Spanish since he was in high school. (verb-tense error)

Revised: Simon has studied Spanish since he was in high school.

Idiomatic language	language written or spoken correctly and in such a way that sounds natural to a native speaker of English.

Incorrect: I have had many opportunities *to enlarge my sight.*

Revised: I have had many opportunities *to broaden my view.*

Indefinite article	the words *a* or *an,* which, when modifying a noun, indicate that the noun is not being specifically identified but rather that it belongs to a class or group.

(**Note:** Indefinite articles can be used only with countable nouns in English.)

Most students own and use *a* bicycle.
The columnist reviewed *an* interesting book yesterday.

Independent clause	a group of words that consists of at least a subject and a verb and which can stand alone as a sentence.

The population of the city has increased to 55,000 residents.

Indirect question	a question in the form of a dependent clause that is embedded in a statement.

I am not sure *where I left my keys.*

Indirect object	a noun, noun phrase, or a pronoun that follows a verb and that identifies *to whom* or *what* or *for whom* or *what* a transitive verb's action is performed.

I gave my keys to *John.*
I gave *John* my keys.

Infinitive	the form of a verb that consists of [*to* + base form].

The building is starting *to age.*

Irregular verb	a verb that does not form the past tense or past participle by adding *-ed.*

The choir *sang* all evening.
We have *thought* about your request and have *made* a decision.

Irregular plural	a noun which does not form the plural form by adding *-s* or *-es.*

The *children* saw several *fish* in the stream.
The *data* show an increase in demand for the new product.

Intransitive verb	a verb that cannot take a direct object. A rainbow suddenly *appeared*.
Local error	one of the less serious errors in writing. Local errors generally affect only one clause and, although they are distracting, do not usually impede the reader's ability to comprehend a text. Some examples are subject-verb agreement, article, and preposition errors. Incorrect: I live close to where I work, but my husband *commute* 40 miles. (subject-verb agreement error) Revised: I live close to where I work, but my husband *commutes* 40 miles. Incorrect: Do you have extra key for the lock? (article error) Revised: Do you have *an* extra key for the lock?
Main verb	a word that indicates the action or state of being in a sentence. The rain *started* at 2 PM. It has been *raining* since 2 PM. The train *was* late.
Modifier	a word that accompanies another part of speech and which describes the other part of speech in some way. For example, adjectives and determiners are modifiers of nouns; adverbs are modifiers of verbs, adjectives, and adverbs. We used *red* paint on the barn. The hikers walked *cautiously* along the steep trail.
Noun	a word that can be a subject or object in a sentence and which refers to a person, place, thing, or idea. *Friendship* is golden. *Mary* loves all of your *plants*.
Noun clause	a dependent (or subordinate) clause that takes a noun position in a sentence. *The fact that you exercise regularly* has contributed to your good health. I very much like *what you wrote*.
Noun phrase	a noun and any adjectives and/or determiners that modify it. *The white house* is for sale.
Parallel structure	the use of structures that are grammatically the same. My grandfather walks his dogs *in the morning* and *in the evening*. (prepositional phrases) All participants should bring *a tape recorder, a pencil, and a pad of paper*. (nouns)
Part of speech	describes how a word functions in a sentence, such as a noun, pronoun, adjective, verb, or adverb. Christopher (noun) ate (verb) slowly (adverb).

Passive voice	a sentence construction in which the subject of the verb is receiving the action. *The toxic chemicals were dumped* at a nearby waste site.
Past participle	formed by adding *-ed* to the base form of the verb except in the case of irregular verbs. Used as an adjective, in verb phrases, and as part of the passive voice. The *frightened* boy hid behind his mother. Many elementary schools have *switched* to a year-round calendar. The articles you requested have been *sent.*
Perfect infinitive	the past form of the infinitive, formed by using [to + have + past participle] for the active voice and [to + have + been + past participle] for the passive voice. She was supposed *to have completed* the project. The witness claimed *to have been forced* to give testimony.
Phrasal verb	[a verb + a preposition or prepositions], also known as a two-word or a three-word verb. The instructor is *passing out* the test. The injured athlete could not *keep up with* the other players.
Plural noun	the form of a noun that indicates more than one. We will need two more *weeks* of sunshine for the roses to bloom. Do you agree with the saying, "*Children* should be seen but not heard"?
Possessive noun or pronoun	a noun or pronoun that shows possession or ownership. *Tanya's* mother wants her to go to college. Ice cream is *his* favorite dessert. That car is *ours.*
Predicate	the part of the sentence that comes after the subject and says something about it. The student *felt relieved after he had taken the exam.*
Preposition	a word used to link nouns or pronouns grammatically to other words. The post office is located *next to* the bridge.
Prepositional phrase	a preposition plus its object and its modifiers. *In the next block,* you will find an auto repair shop.
Present participle	[the base form + *ing*] which functions as an adjective or as a main verb in a verb phrase. Alfred is *reading* a novel that he cannot bear to put down. The dog ran down the street *barking* at cars.

Pronoun	a word that takes the place of a noun or a noun phrase in a sentence. The noun that a pronoun refers to is called its antecedent.

We love *your* new car. *It* is quite sporty.

Pronoun reference and agreement	the way a pronoun refers to another noun, called its antecedent. A pronoun must agree with its antecedent in number, meaning that a singular antecedent should have a singular pronoun and a plural antecedent should have a plural pronoun. Also, a pronoun should always refer clearly to its specific antecedent.

Correct: The president's late arrival at the meeting was not *his* fault.
Correct: Employees should turn in *their* time sheets immediately if *they* want to be paid by the first of the month.

Incorrect: David told John that *he* had passed the exam.
Revised: David passed the exam and told John about having passed it.

Incorrect: My favorite high school teacher was a biologist, a fact that led me to major in *it*.
Correct: My favorite high school teacher was a biologist, a fact that led me to major in *the field of biology*.

Proper noun	a noun that refers to a specific person, place, religion, holiday, language, nationality, or time period. A proper noun always begins with a capital letter (upper case) in English.

Tanya lives in *Los Angeles, California*.
Yosemite is one of the most popular national parks in the *United States*.
To qualify for this job, applicants need to know a little *Spanish*.
Thanksgiving is in *November* in the *United States*.

Regular verb	a verb that forms the past tense and the past participle by adding *-ed*.

We frequently *walked* to work when we *lived* in the downtown area.
Maggie has *lived* in Miami for 10 years.

Relative pronoun	one of a group of words—including *who, whom, whose, which,* and *that*—which connect a relative (or adjective) clause to the item it modifies.

The actor *who* plays the lead role is very popular.
The man *whose* house I am renting is a lawyer.
The new method, *which* was developed in 1997, has greatly simplified my data collection process.

Relative clause	a dependent (or subordinate) clause, also called an **adjective clause,** that is connected to a noun by a relative pronoun *(that, which, who, whom, whose, where, when, why)* and provides specific information about the noun.

The movie *that opened yesterday* is worth seeing.
A person *who studies fossils* is known as a paleontologist.

Run-on sentence   a sentence-boundary problem in which two independent clauses are inappropriately run together with no punctuation.

Incorrect: *Traveling to Europe was a wonderful experience I met many people and visited interesting places.*

Revised: Traveling to Europe was a wonderful experience. I met many people and visited interesting places.

Revised: Traveling to Europe was a wonderful experience in that I met many people and visited interesting places.

Singular noun   a word that names one person, place, or thing and is countable.

A *calendar* is hanging on the *wall.*

Subjunctive form   a special form of a verb, which is infrequently used, that expresses a wish or something that is contrary to fact, or that occurs in a *that* clause expressing a command, a suggestion, a recommendation, or a piece of advice.

I wish I *were* younger.
If I *were* mayor, I would add more parks to the city.
The committee recommended that John *retake* his exams.

Subordinate clause   a clause, sometimes called a **dependent clause,** that cannot stand alone but must work together with an independent clause to complete its meaning and to form a complete sentence.

The book *that you lent me* is excellent.
While I was downtown, I went to the bank.

Subordinating conjunction   a connecting word—such as *before, although, because,* or *while*—that joins a dependent clause to an independent clause to create a complex sentence.

Before we went to the movies, we had dinner.
We could not return the books *because* the library was closed.

Superlative form   a form of comparison that refers to the maximum degree and that is usually indicated by the suffix *-est* or by the phrase *the most* before an adjective. Some superlative forms are irregular, such as *the best* and *the worst.*

The *easiest* problem on the exam was number four.
These shoes are *the most comfortable* ones I own.
This dinner is one of *the best* I have ever made.

Transitional word or phrase   a word or phrase that connects ideas and that adds to the smooth flow of ideas in a piece of writing.

First, we need to decide on a project. *Then* we should apply for a grant.
To summarize, this research has shown that the majority of people have reduced their yearly water use.
One cause of air pollution is the number of automobiles. *Another cause* is the burning of agricultural fields.

Transitive verb a verb that can take a direct object.

> JoAnn *visits* her parents once a month.
> We *ate* fish for dinner.

Unclear language a phrase or sentence which has been incorrectly worded in such a way that the reader cannot understand the message the writer wants to convey.

> Unlike Hong Kong, the streets here are busy yet quiet, and *only solitude cars are on their wheels.*

Uncountable noun a noun, also sometimes called a **mass noun,** that refers to a concrete thing that is not usually counted (such as *sand, air, rice,* or *information*), although plural forms of uncountable nouns may occur, as in *the white <u>sands</u> of the tropical island or <u>rices</u> that resist disease.*

> The new store carries sports *equipment.*
> *Traffic* has been heavy now that the city has grown so rapidly.

Verb a word or group of words in a sentence that expresses what action the subject does or receives, what the subject is, or what the subject's state of being is.

> The dog *is barking* loudly.
> This instrument *is* an electron microscope.
> The cat *is* scared.

Verb phrase a main verb preceded by one or more auxiliary verbs.

> We *should have spent* more time in Yosemite.
> Max *has been living* in New York for 10 years.

Verb-tense shift an inappropriate mixing of verb tenses in a sentence, paragraph, or larger piece of text.

> Incorrect: Over the holiday weekend, we traveled to our friend's cabin in the mountains. We enjoyed the outdoors and *do* some hiking and fishing.
> Revised: Over the holiday weekend, we traveled to our friend's cabin in the mountains. We enjoyed the outdoors and *did* some hiking and fishing.

Verbal a gerund or infinitive form of the verb that serves as a subject, object, or adjective complement in a sentence.

> *Reading* is one of Frank's favorite free-time activities.
> Frank enjoys *reading* mystery novels in his free time.
> I am pleased *to inform* you that you have been accepted for admission to our institution.

Zero article the use of no article *(a, an, the)* before either an uncountable noun or the plural of a noun to show that the noun belongs to a class or group.

> Unless I absolutely have to, I do not like to borrow *money.*
> My biology project is on *butterflies.*

Index